READERS' GUIDES TO ESSENTIAL CRITICISM

CONSULTANT EDITOR: NICOLAS TREDELL

CU00765346

Sara Lodge	Charlotte Brontë: *Jane Eyre*
Philippa Lyon	Twentieth-Century War Poetry
Merja Makinen	The Novels of Jeanette Winterson
Stephen Marino	Arthur Miller: *Death of a Salesman/The Crucible*
Matt McGuire	Contemporary Scottish Literature
Timothy Milnes	Wordsworth: *The Prelude*
Jago Morrison	The Fiction of Chinua Achebe
Merritt Moseley	The Fiction of Pat Barker
Pat Pinsent	Children's Literature
Carl Plasa	Toni Morrison: *Beloved*
Carl Plasa	Jean Rhys: *Wide Sargasso Sea*
Nicholas Potter	Shakespeare: *Antony and Cleopatra*
Nicholas Potter	Shakespeare: *Othello*
Nicholas Potter	Shakespeare's Late Plays: *Pericles/Cymbeline/The Winter's Tale/ The Tempest*
Steven Price	The Plays, Screenplays and Films of David Mamet
Berthold Schoene-Harwood	Mary Shelley: *Frankenstein*
Nicholas Seager	The Rise of the Novel
Nick Selby	T. S. Eliot: *The Waste Land*
Nick Selby	Herman Melville: *Moby Dick*
Nick Selby	The Poetry of Walt Whitman
David Smale	Salman Rushdie: *Midnight's Children/The Satanic Verses*
Enit Karafili Steiner	Jane Austen: *Northanger Abbey/Persuasion*
Patsy Stoneman	Emily Brontë: *Wuthering Heights*
Susie Thomas	Hanif Kureishi
Nicolas Tredell	Joseph Conrad: *Heart of Darkness*
Nicolas Tredell	Charles Dickens: *Great Expectations*
Nicolas Tredell	William Faulkner: *The Sound and the Fury/As I Lay Dying*
Nicolas Tredell	F. Scott Fitzgerald: *The Great Gatsby*
Nicolas Tredell	Shakespeare: *A Midsummer Night's Dream*
Nicolas Tredell	Shakespeare: *Macbeth*
Nicolas Tredell	Shakespeare: The Tragedies
Nicolas Tredell	The Fiction of Martin Amis
David Wheatley	Contemporary British Poetry
Martin Willis	Literature and Science
Matthew Woodcock	Shakespeare: *Henry V*
Gillian Woods	Shakespeare: *Romeo and Juliet*
Angela Wright	Gothic Fiction
Michael Whitworth	Virginia Woolf: *Mrs Dalloway*

Forthcoming

Britta Martens	The Poetry of Robert Browning
Robert Evans	Philip Larkin
Andrew Wylie and Catherine Rees	The Plays of Harold Pinter
Nick Bentley	Contemporary British Fiction

Readers' Guides to Essential Criticism
Series Standing Order ISBN 978–1–4039–0108–8
(*outside North America only*)

You can receive future titles in this series as they are published by placing a standing order. Please contact your bookseller or, in the case of difficulty, write to us at the address below with your name and address, the title of the series and the ISBN quoted above.

Customer Services Department, Macmillan Distribution Ltd, Houndmills, Basingstoke, Hampshire, RG21 6XS, UK

Children's Literature

PAT PINSENT

Consultant Editor: NICOLAS TREDELL

First published 2016 by
PALGRAVE

Palgrave in the UK is an imprint of Macmillan Publishers Limited, registered in England, company number 785998, of 4 Crinan Street, London, N1 9XW.

Palgrave Macmillan in the US is a division of St Martin's Press LLC, 175 Fifth Avenue, New York, NY 10010.

Palgrave is a global imprint of the above companies and is represented throughout the world.

Palgrave® and Macmillan® are registered trademarks in the United States, the United Kingdom, Europe and other countries.

ISBN 978–1–137–33546–3 hardback
ISBN 978–1–137–33545–6 paperback

This book is printed on paper suitable for recycling and made from fully managed and sustained forest sources. Logging, pulping and manufacturing processes are expected to conform to the environmental regulations of the country of origin.

A catalogue record for this book is available from the British Library.

A catalog record for this book is available from the Library of Congress.

Printed and bound by CPI Group (UK) Ltd, Croydon, CR0 4YY

CONTENTS

PART II
Genres

PART III
Theoretical Approaches

ACKNOWLEDGEMENTS

I would like to pay special tribute to the contribution of Clare Walsh, University of Bedfordshire, in the writing of this volume. In addition to her own chapter, the overall structure owes a great deal to her knowledge and insight. Darja Mazi-Leskovar's expertise in the area of translation has been invaluable. I should also like to thank Catherine Butler and Valerie Coghlan for their help in providing information in the areas of fantasy and Irish Children's Literature respectively, and Julie Mills of the Roehampton University Library for her assistance. My special thanks too to Rachel Bridgewater at Palgrave and Nicolas Tredell, Series Editor, for their advice and their tolerance of an unavoidable delay.

INTRODUCTION

The second half of the twentieth century witnessed considerable changes in how the academic establishment regarded the study of children's literature. From being an optional supplement on teacher training courses (on which, at the beginning of this period, students were not even awarded degrees), it had become, by the end of the century, a respectable academic discipline, attracting both undergraduates and a significant number of graduates studying for higher degrees. This process was inevitably accompanied by changes in the kinds of recommended critical and theoretical texts, shifting from handbooks on pedagogy to theoretical material comparable to that presented to students of adult literature. In the early part of the period, a dichotomy was sometimes claimed between 'book' people (literary scholars) and 'child' people (educationalists). However, since the 1980s, children's literature studies have been dominated by what might be termed 'theory' people. This book traces these developments and points readers towards some of the most significant critical writing, especially that which scrutinises children's texts from this period.

The range and audience for literary criticism

Changes in the academic status of children's literature study have inevitably been accompanied by changes in the audience addressed in critical texts. Probably most of the earliest such readers had enjoyed children's books when they were young and wanted to learn about their history. Many of them were parents wishing their own children to share their positive experiences; others were teachers keen to keep up with developments and to encourage their pupils to read both the classics of children's literature and more recent fiction. The objectives of this latter group included the fostering in young readers of values such as empathy and tolerance, as well as increasing their reading competence. While these readers of children's literature criticism certainly still exist, they are likely to have been outnumbered in recent years by students, some young but more of them 'mature', who are undertaking the serious study of children's books within an academic context.

This expanding group, however, is faced with a paradox – despite their interest in literature written for children, they are not themselves children: however sophisticated their approach to its study may be, in analysing any children's text they have to admit that they are not the readers primarily envisaged by its author. Thus their reading of criticism about children's literature is governed, whether consciously or not, by implicit concepts about the nature of childhood. Karín Lesnik-Oberstein goes so far as to claim that: 'Children's literature criticism is about saying: "I know what children like to read/are able to read/should read *because I know what children are like*"' (1994: 2, italics original).

This gap between adult readers of children's literature and its implied audience has preoccupied some writers and readers of literary criticism, especially since the publication of an influential book by Jacqueline Rose, *The Case of Peter Pan or The Impossibility of Children's Fiction* (1984). This challenges any facile assumptions about the role of adults involved in any way with children's books. Rose observes that:

■ Children's fiction sets up a world in which the adult comes first (author, maker, giver) and the child comes after (reader, product, receiver), but where neither of them enter the space in between. □

■ ... There is, in one sense, no body of literature which rests so openly on an acknowledged difference, a rupture almost, between writer and addressee. Children's fiction sets up the child as an outsider to its own process, and then aims, unashamedly, to take the child in. (1984: 1–2) □

Focusing mainly on Barrie's 'Peter Pan' story in its diverse manifestations, Rose, who perhaps unsurprisingly has produced no further critical texts about children's literature, challenges the facile way in which the concept of 'the child' often tends to be used, contending that children's literature cannot be regarded as an 'isolate':

■ The story of *Peter Pan* cannot be fitted into a framework which sees the child as a historical entity which literature reflects. It shows history as a divided entity which is given a false unity in the image of the child. (1984: 143) □

As David Rudd comments:

■ Although [Rose] wrote only one work in children's literature studies, it could be said to have revolutionized the discipline, disturbing a former cosiness about its object of study, the child. (2010: 238) □

Whether *post hoc* or *propter hoc*, there is no doubt that in the wake of Rose's book, and subsequently the work of Lesnik-Oberstein, children's literary criticism has evidenced a greater degree of awareness of literary theory than it had previously, to the extent that Perry Nodelman, reviewing five recent guides to children's literature studies,[1] surmises that recent trends in academic criticism tend to ignore 'the ways in which not only children, parents, teachers, librarians and children's book editors but also specialists in faculties of education and information science talk about children's literature' (2013: 153). There is an evident danger that the implied consumer of the literature concerned is forgotten:

> ■ a lack of interest in the connections between children's literature and children as well as between children's literature and childhood also expresses itself in terms of the kinds of texts these guides cover and, more importantly, the kinds of texts they tend not to cover. (2013: 156) □

Omissions highlighted by Nodelman include realistic fiction, poetry, non-fiction, drama, series books, Christian literature, picturebooks and, by and large, interpretations in other media. Nevertheless, almost in spite of himself it seems, Nodelman admits that:

> ■ the limited range of texts these guides focus on and the limited range of approaches they take to those texts do in fact represent the current tendencies in the fields of children's literature studies accurately enough to act as useful introductions to it. (2013: 161) □

Some attention has been given to this short article by Nodelman not only because of its relevance to the question of contemporary trends in criticism, but also because the current book, while addressing theoretical issues, is wider in its remit, devoting attention to those areas of both literature and criticism which concern teachers and librarians and also to the genres listed above as omitted from these recent guides.

In addition to developments in literary theory, the last half of the twentieth century witnessed many changes in society and in the world at large, together with an increase in multi-disciplinary approaches to literature, especially from psychology and sociology. Many recent critics of children's literature, while being aware both of the theoretical and socio-historical aspects noted above and of the contradictions inherent in their writing about a body of literature not addressed to themselves as adults, have contributed to the substantial body of writing which now exists. While their work commands due attention in its appropriate place below, several of them, because of their broader perspective, also demand mention here.

Particularly significant in this context among the substantial body of work by Peter Hunt are his two collections of influential critical writing by other authors (1990 and 1992) and his own exploration of the relationship between criticism and children's literature in the attempt to:

> ■ give the individual an understanding of ways of reading texts, so that she or he can then evaluate or use a text in whatever way seems most useful or valid. (1991: 4) □

In this process, Hunt gives attention to a large range of children's fiction and poetry, concluding that there is an argument for suggesting that the 'educational' value of a children's text be separated from any other judgement, in order for children's literature to be 'seen as of equal status with other literature' (1991: 199). Torn between the value judgements of its implied readers and those of its critics, children's books will probably never cease to arouse controversy for not fulfilling a role which may never have been the aim of those who write them.

Two Canadian writers, Perry Nodelman and Roderick McGillis, have produced texts uniting scholarship with a creative fusion between theory and practice. Nodelman's *The Pleasures of Children's Literature* (1992, 1996, 2003) bears evidence of its being intended as a course book for graduate and undergraduate students of children's literature. Thus readers' unquestioned assumptions about assessing the quality of texts and about childhood are constantly challenged, while (as might be anticipated from what he says about the critical neglect of some areas of children's literature) Nodelman does not overlook the genres of poetry and picturebooks. Roderick McGillis's *The Nimble Reader: Literary Theory and Children's Literature* (1996) demonstrates the relevance to children's fiction of a range of twentieth-century literary critical approaches – formalism, the new critics, psychoanalytic, archetypal, political, and so on – by applying them to popular classics such as E.B. White's *Charlotte's Web* (1952). His light touch, sometimes including parody, belies the serious scholarship underlying the endeavour.

Another contemporary critic, Maria Nikolajeva, reveals the benefit of her international perspective as she brings perspectives from world literature and criticism, particularly that deriving from Sweden, to bear on questions concerning research into children's literature. She claims that it was only towards the end of the twentieth century that children's literature was approached as literature, the pedagogical view having previously dominated in particular the histories of the subject. She contributes an informed awareness of intertextual aspects, highlighting the chronotope[2] as an indication of the sophistication of much current writing for children, and providing what she terms 'a semiotically inspired model' (1996: 10) to support her claim that 'children's literature, which emerged several thousand years later than mainstream literature, is now catching up with it' (1996: 10), particularly in the area of modernist and postmodernist developments. Nikolajeva has continued to be in the forefront in the incorporation of contemporary critical insights into readings of children's literature; her recent work links the developing field of cognitive criticism with narrative perspective (in (ed.) Butler and Reynolds 2014: 251–267).

Finally, a name which recurs in several of the chapters of the current book is that of Peter Hollindale, whose short but very influential articles, originally published in the journal *Signal,* have contributed new critical perspectives to the topic. In the present context, 'The Critic and the Child'[3] provides a very useful set of cautions to the intending critic of children's literature. Starting from John Rowe Townsend's 1971 lecture[4] which 'distinguished between general critical competences ... and those that place the children's literature critic in a special position', Hollindale remarks on the degree of self-awareness about personal involvement that it is incumbent on the children's literature critic to possess, ranging from an understanding of how childhood experiences can shape thinking, through caution in exercising disciplines in which the critic has no personal qualifications, consciousness of the influence of a personal ideology, and the avoidance of generalisations about 'the child' or 'all children', to the final question 'What purpose do I hope this publication will serve?' It is safe to say that few, if any, critics have managed to comply with all seventeen points in his 'additional (and fearsome) code of self-interrogation for practising critics' (Hollindale 2011: 17–20).

Structure of this book

The order in which the material in the current book is presented reflects an endeavour to follow a logical progression. The first section starts with a summary of the overall development of the field up to the latter part of the twentieth century, and continues with a survey of criticism to which, in one way or another, the child is central, an emphasis which leads logically to a scrutiny of work which focuses on narrative. The central section is devoted to some of the genres in which children's literature's contribution is most distinctive: fairytale, fantasy, picturebook, poetry and drama. In the third section, gender-related criticism, translation and increasing globalisation are discussed, while the book concludes with consideration of the future of both children's literature itself and of criticism related to it. Inevitably within the chapters there are many overlaps and interconnections, and wherever possible these are signalled.

The first chapter looks at the period from the end of the Second World War up to about 1990, during the early part of which there was a preponderance of somewhat subjective studies of stories which their authors ('book' people) had enjoyed in their own childhood, together with recommendations of certain texts for children often on somewhat moralistic grounds. Invaluable work was done by the historians, and gradually historical writing has become more specialised, focusing on certain sub-genres, notably the school story.

The focus of Chapter Two is the child reader, beginning with the development of reader-response theory and its subsequent application to young people. Attention is also given to writers who are concerned with the needs and the behaviour of young readers, in so far as these can be determined – whether theoretically or from observation of actual children, both individually and in surveys of larger groups.

Criticism which foregrounds the centrality of the relationship between authorial stance and the voice of the narrator is the topic of Chapter Three, together with the effect this has on how the implied child reader is positioned. It could be claimed that this asymmetry between adult writer and child reader goes to the heart of what makes the study of children's literature so fascinating.

Some of the earliest scholarly approaches to children's literature have emerged from work in the fields of child psychology and psychotherapy, and these are discussed in Chapter Four, focusing on theoretical work on fairytales. The influence of psychotherapy is not surprising given Freud's emphasis on the formative role of childhood in the development of the psyche. Similarly, the identification by formalist critics such as Vladimir Propp of recurring character types and motifs in fairytales seems to have lent itself to analysis using Jungian archetypal patterns. Such universalist readings of fairytales and fantasy texts for children have subsequently been challenged by historicist and materialist critics.

Fantasy has tended to occupy a prominent place in the criticism of children's literature, despite not infrequently being denigrated by people outside the discipline who have a limited understanding of it. In Chapter Five, criticism concerning its function and range is discussed, together with some attempts at classification.

Picturebooks, the topic of Chapter Six, have a special place in children's literature since they comprise the only genre which it has sometimes been claimed is unique to it. Critical approaches to these texts, together with investigations of children's reading of them, precede a consideration of comics and graphic novels.

It has often been claimed that poetry for children is marginalised in critical discussion, something which may result from the difficulty in defining it. In Chapter Seven, the question of definition is explored in terms of what both anthologists and historians of poetry for children have to say about their terms of reference; other topics considered are criticism related to oral verse and nonsense poetry and to the children's verse written by major poets. A short concluding section in the same chapter is devoted to the criticism of drama for children (as distinct from adaptations, the consideration of which occurs in the final chapter).

Chapter Eight, on criticism related to gender, begins with a scrutiny of the links with the concerns of second wave feminists to critique and deconstruct what were perceived to be potentially harmful representations of femininity in children's books. More recently there has been a shift from a primary focus on female representation towards constructions of masculinity and sexuality.

The international dimension of children's literature is central to Chapter Nine, much of which is contributed by the Slovenian scholar, Darja Mazi-Leskovar. A dominant theme concerns the problems involved in the process of translation, especially to and from English as a world language in which so many important children's texts were originally produced. Additionally, the relationship between literature and national identity has become a major focus for recent criticism.

Consequently, Chapter Ten examines the expanding field of multicultural and post-colonial approaches to the criticism of children's literature, both in relation to the rereading of established texts and to the increasing number of books produced by indigenous writers of the former colonies. The special situation of Irish children's literature is also given some attention. The gradual recognition of the need to critique fiction featuring other subjugated groups, notably disabled people, is also considered.

Chapter Eleven, by Clare Walsh, examines the debate concerning whether the recent phenomenon of crossover fiction is purely market-driven or whether adult readers are turning to children's fiction out of a nostalgia for plot-driven fiction.

Chapter Twelve looks at areas not considered earlier but likely to attract increasing critical attention: religion, eco-criticism and multimedia adaptation. In the Conclusion, brief reference is made to subjects likely to be to the forefront in the future, notably the phenomenon of children being their own writers and critics, and the interaction between children's literature and cognitive studies.

Perhaps because of the seminal role of Anglophone writers in the creation of children's literature, scholars from the English-speaking world have also been to the fore within literary criticism related to the literature. Other than in the chapter devoted to translation and the international scene, it has not been possible to give the important contribution of scholars from other parts of Europe the attention it deserves.

Just as children's literature itself is no longer disparaged as 'kiddie lit', whose only adult readers were thought to be teachers and parents of young children, literary criticism of contemporary work for children has come of age throughout the world. It is no longer marginalised as merely an optional addition to 'proper' literary criticism.

PART I

Readers

CHAPTER ONE

Beginnings

Introduction

It is unsurprising that children's literature study as an academic discipline was not taken seriously at university level until quite late in the twentieth century. The discipline of English literature itself had for many years been regarded as something that any educated person (man?) would pick up incidentally; traditionally only Greek and Latin were seen as subjects that demanded serious study. As a result, academic scholarship was fairly slow in interrogating even the classics of children's literature; there was a relatively small market for books which regarded children's literature as more than an adjunct to literature written for adults.

Children's literature really only began to be regarded as a 'respectable' academic discipline from the 1970s onwards. A natural consequence of the opportunity to take it as part of a degree course (even though this was often initially only available to students preparing for teaching) was the emergence of a demand for criticism which took this body of material as a central concern, rather than seeing it merely as an offshoot of general literature. Much of this criticism, again unsurprisingly, focused on the classroom, both in terms of assisting teachers in their choice and presentation of books, and in looking at the responses of their pupils to these books. Nevertheless, the currently impressive body of critical work had most of its origins in this period, though the historical contextualisation of literature for children had preceded it by many years.

In this chapter, attention will be paid both to the development of increasingly specialised historio-critical writing and the beginnings of the varied range of critical approaches to children's literature which have developed over the years. In general, the focus will be on writing before about 1990, by which date criticism of children's literature was well on the way towards being a 'respectable' area of academic study.

Nostalgia

Many of the early writers on children's literature took as their starting point the books which they themselves had loved as children. The results of this are twofold: firstly, there is in these volumes an inevitable lack of discussion of contemporary literature; and secondly, their approach, being coloured by childhood memories, is unavoidably tinged with more subjectivity than is normal in academic studies. Such studies also tend to rely heavily on a biographical approach towards the authors concerned, rather than literary criticism proper.

One of the most popular writers in this area during the middle part of the twentieth century was Roger Lancelyn Green. As an author, he produced children's versions of Greek myths and the legends about King Arthur and Robin Hood; his own fiction for children was also largely based on these classic sources. Additionally he wrote biographies of Lewis Carroll and J.M. Barrie, and of C.S. Lewis, his own mentor at Oxford University.

Although by no means the earliest venture into writing about children's literature, Green's compilation, *Tellers of Tales* (1946), which provides relatively brief accounts of a wide range of children's authors, is paradigmatic of the attitude taken by many writers about children's literature in the early years. Ostensibly addressing a child readership (he explicitly states that the book is not meant for the scholar (p.246)), Green suggests that, like himself as a boy, young readers may want to know more about the authors of the books they enjoy. Nevertheless, his book also provides useful information about these authors for adult readers, including students of the subject, supplying as it does 'Bibliographical Notes'; these comprise a list of works, with dates, by the authors discussed, together with a rather subjective selection of 'authorities'. Green's guiding principle when choosing whom to write about is that these are the 'most important' British writers for young people during the previous one hundred years; he does not, however, give any indication of his criteria for deciding which authors fit this descriptor. Only one of them, A.A. Milne, was alive at the date of publication, though Green does find an excuse to mention in his introduction his other living favourites: Arthur Ransome, whom he ranks as 'little lower than the angels' (p.16), and two authors he describes as 'lesser known': J.R.R. Tolkien and the now forgotten Geoffrey Mure. By its nature, this is clearly not an academic work, yet it epitomises an approach to children's literature which was all-pervasive at the time – writers are ranked, and discussion of their work is characterised in Green's case by adjectives such as 'delicious' (p.21), 'glorious' (p.62) and 'wonderful' (p.219). Inevitable in a book by a storyteller are the many anecdotes which enliven the accounts of the various authors.

The liberal humanist approach

Many of the critical approaches now prevalent in children's literature, as indeed in literary studies as a whole, have been of relatively recent inception. Though literary criticism in English prior to the twentieth century features such great names as John Dryden, Alexander Pope, Samuel Johnson and Matthew Arnold, it often appears to have been somewhat incidental to a writer's main literary output, and seldom involves close textual analysis. Not until the first third of the twentieth century, with the endeavours of critics such as I.A. Richards, F.R. Leavis, L.C. Knights, G. Wilson Knight and T.S. Eliot, do we see the replacement of an emphasis on biographical information about authors, together with musings on extra-textual issues,[1] by a presentation of theoretical perspectives on literature, from a liberal humanist perspective, based on close reading of the texts. Richards, whose *Practical Criticism: A Study of Literary Judgment* (1929) exposes the often bizarre misreadings made by readers deprived of information about the authors of poems presented to them, was influential in causing generations of university lecturers to insist that their students prioritise close reading of texts over knowledge about the lives of the authors concerned.

Many of the early writers who took writing for and about children seriously had either been taught by F.R. Leavis himself or had imbibed his principles during their own university studies, from lecturers who were themselves strongly influenced by his liberal humanist approach. Notoriously, *The Great Tradition*, first published in 1948 (though Leavis' influence on generations of English scholars preceded its publication by many years), begins, 'The great English novelists are Jane Austen, George Eliot, Henry James and Joseph Conrad – to stop at that comparatively safe point in history' (1993: 9), a clear indication of his provocatively evaluative approach.

A notable instance of this Leavisite inheritance is Peter Coveney's study of the literary portrayal of childhood throughout the ages, first published in 1957 as *Poor Monkey*, with a revised edition appearing in 1967 under the title *The Image of Childhood*. This second edition carries an introduction by F.R. Leavis himself, who takes the opportunity to expound his own views about the significance of childhood in literature. Although he is not talking about children's literature per se, he inevitably alludes to writers such as Blake, Wordsworth, Dickens and Twain whose work figures (sometimes on the periphery) in the syllabuses of studies in children's literature. This introduction affords Leavis the opportunity to present his elevated moral understanding of the function of literature: he argues that the child can in some texts, even those by the same author, be 'now a symbol of growth and development, and now a symbol of retreat into personal regression and self-pity' (p.32).

Thus he distinguishes between writers who 'went to the child to express their involvement with life, and those who retreated towards the symbol from "life's decay"'. He concludes, 'It is perhaps not remarkable that through writing of childhood there should be those who wanted to go back to the beginning to begin again, and others who wanted just to go back' (p.35).

This explicit moral perspective underlies much of the early writing about children's literature, and could also be seen to reflect a polarity between critics who seek to present literature from the past as a foundation for the future, and those, like Green, who just want to look back to what they themselves enjoyed as children. Coveney's own adherence to the principles of his mentor is made explicit in his 'Epilogue' where he expresses the hope that his book 'will at least have suggested some of the criteria upon which the immense proliferation of literature concerned with children in more recent times may be assessed' (p.337).

Following in the wake of the criticism of Leavis and Richards, early writing on children's literature tended to employ a book-centred approach, to abjure an overly biographical emphasis, and to evidence a desire to establish in children's literature an analogue of the Leavisite 'great tradition'.[2] A notable instance of this characteristic is the work of Fred Inglis (*The Promise of Happiness: Values and Meaning in Children's Fiction*, 1981), the first chapter of which, entitled 'The Terms of Reference', begins with words intentionally echoing Leavis: 'The great children's novelists are Lewis Carroll, Rudyard Kipling, Frances Hodgson Burnett, Arthur Ransome, William Mayne, and Philippa Pearce – to stop for a moment at that comparatively safe point on an uncertain list' (p.3). This tribute makes evident Inglis's desire to emulate the master by apparently attempting to set up, from the classics of the past, a standard by which later children's authors could be judged. The moral basis of this endeavour is indicated when he goes on to ask 'who would not want his or her child to read the best books ... we try to say what some of the best books are like, so that we can hand them on to our sons and daughters' (p.3).

Inglis continues to reveal his Leavisite standpoint as he presents his arguments: firstly 'that true judgments as to values are possible; secondly to try to show that the best prose is itself evidence of human goodness and a way of learning how to be virtuous; thirdly to suggest how the intrinsically human habit of fiction-making is essential to the making and maintaining of identity' (p.4). He claims that 'the best children's books awaken our innocence' (p.8) and that 'To study what is excellent helps towards excellence' (p.15).[3]

The titles of some of the chapters which follow reveal how Inglis attempts to fulfil his aims; in particular, Chapter Four, 'The lesser great tradition', which is summarised as 'A critical study of the best of

Victorian and Edwardian children's novels – *Alice,* girlhood and Oxford – Beatrix Potter and Victoriana – *The Secret Garden* and Romanticism – *The Railway Children* and political economy – *The Wind in the Willows,* home and friendship' (p.viii) could be said to encapsulate many of his aims. His final chapter, 'Resolution and independence', puts forward Dickens as 'the model to set before children's novelists' (p.ix).[4]

More space has been devoted to Inglis than perhaps he deserves, especially within the context of the way in which the criticism of children's literature was soon to develop. The justification for this is that he epitomises an approach which was for a long while normative in literary criticism generally but has now come to seem outdated – an approach which Leavis, and in turn Coveney and Inglis, could be said to inherit from Matthew Arnold. Its tendency to equate good writing with good living may seem naïve today but provided an important part of the rationale for literature teaching in the earlier part of the twentieth century. It also appears that approaches such as Green's have an implicit assumption that 'good' children's literature leaves the reader with a positive view of human nature, and, if not precisely a happy ending, a sense of hope for the future – an assumption that could be said to underlie much early writing on the subject, perhaps particularly if it had a pedagogical emphasis.[5]

Green's work was followed shortly afterwards by an equally personal response to children's literature from the distinguished children's author, Geoffrey Trease. In his *Tales Out of School* (1949), his progressive engagement with political ideology is as evident as it is in his own fiction. He asserted that 'children's enjoyment was not the sole or even the main criterion of a good children's book', and that because children are likely to be influenced by what they read, their mentors should both insist that they read the best and steer them away from the worst.[6] By 1964, when he came to update his work, he felt that his strictures on the limitations of the class-bound perspective of many children's authors of his time had borne fruit.[7]

Historical approaches

The main critical approaches to children's literature for about three quarters of the twentieth century were either historical or pedagogical. The somewhat idiosyncratic books by Green and Inglis had in fact been preceded by a more scholarly and systematic text devoted to the history of children's literature which appeared in 1932, J.F. Harvey Darton's *Children's Books in England: Five Centuries of Social Life.* Unlike the majority of literary historians at that time, Darton took children's books as worth study in their own right, though he died before he extended his study much beyond 1900. He was aware of the original nature of the task he had set himself, in recounting 'the story of English Children's Books ... as a continuous whole' rather than simply collecting interesting facts about it. He attempts rather 'to show, what was the actual determining cause, what the practical human circumstances, of a book's first appearance' (p.v). The thoroughness of Darton's presentation, together with the bibliographical material that he almost apologetically included, meant that in due course his book came to be recognised as an indispensable resource for anyone seeking to learn about children's literature. As indicated by Kathleen Lines, the editor of the second edition (1958), the original edition of only 1500 copies had been slow to permeate into libraries and schools, though by the time that it went out of print in 1945, it had been acclaimed for its scholarship.

The publication of Darton's major work also in due course heralded the publication of other scholarly historical texts, notably *A Critical History of Children's Books* (1953) by Cornelia Meigs with Anne Eaton, Elizabeth Nesbitt and Ruth Hill Viguers, and Percy Muir's *English Children's Books* (1954). The middle of the twentieth century can, in retrospect, be seen as the beginning of a scholarly interest in the discipline, accompanied by a quasi-governmental emphasis on the need to provide lists of suitable reading for children, partly to help them build up their own collections.[8] The production of the second edition of Darton's book was probably triggered by these and other scholarly studies which appeared during the 1950s, signalling the increasing concern about the subject. Its pages are physically smaller in size than those of the first edition, and the book in fact makes relatively few changes to the original text, keeping the original pagination as far as possible but adding additional sections. It incorporates Darton's own corrections, and adds a short list of 'Some Books of General and Specific Interest Published since 1932', together with brief supplements to the various chapters consisting of a few additional primary texts.[9]

The activity of the 1950s signals the beginnings of a change in the status of children's literature studies. During the next decade, perhaps the most significant addition to the list of historio-critical texts is John Rowe Townsend's influential *Written for Children: An Outline of English-Language Children's Literature* (1965). Like Darton's work, this popular and accessible survey has appeared in several editions, this time updated by the original author himself, who undertook it in addition to his large output as a children's author. In the Foreword to the 1990 edition, Townsend recounts how, in the original edition, he had 'tried to give a brief and readable account of prose fiction for children in Britain from the beginnings to the (then) present day' (p.xi). In particular, in the later editions, Townsend attempts to update Part Four of the book, which deals with post-Second World War literature; in the 1990 edition, however, he states his resolve to 'draw a line at the end of 1989' (p.xi).

Townsend's pragmatic test of whether or not to include a particular book is 'survival': 'I have tried to concentrate on work that was in print and likely to remain so' (p.xi). He observes, however, that (at the time of writing) too many good books 'are going out of print at an alarming rate' (p.xii).[10] All editions, however, reiterate his statement that his book is 'a study of children's literature, not of children's reading matter' (for instance 1974: 14 and 1990: xii). He also makes explicit that despite an attempt to see the work within its socio-historical context, his standards are 'essentially literary' (1990: xi). This belief that there is such a thing as an absolute literary standard can perhaps be traced back yet again to the influence of F.R. Leavis.

In comparing the approaches taken in these two major histories of children's literature, perhaps what Townsend has to say about Darton's work is the most effective way of illustrating their differences. Discussing the significance of the children's publisher, John Newbery (1713–67), Townsend says:

■ The late J Harvey Darton, whose *Children's Books in England* (1932) is still the most authoritative study of the subject over the period up to Queen Victoria's death, refers briefly to 'Newbery the Conqueror'. According to Darton, the year 1744, when the first Newbery children's book was published, was 'comparable to the 1066 of the older histories.' This was undoubtedly written with tongue in cheek, and Newbery was not in fact the first in the field. (1974: 30) □

Thus Townsend, while paying explicit homage to Darton, manages subtly to direct the reader's attention to the fact that his own work supplies the period missing from Darton's tome; he also tactfully corrects, without any air of negative criticism, what could be seen as an error in the earlier writer's chronology.

Similarly, a little later, while discussing the work of Frances Hodgson Burnett, Townsend manages to dissent without rancour:

■ Harvey Darton refers to *Little Lord Fauntleroy* [1886] as being supreme among the namby-pamby books, and adds that it 'ran through England like a sickly fever. Nine editions were published in as many months, and the odious little prig in the lace collar is not dead yet.' But this is not quite fair comment: Cedric Errol is neither odious nor priggish. (1974: 87) □

Townsend goes on to list many instances of Cedric's positive behaviour, thus displaying closer reading of Burnett than Darton had bestowed on the text.

In 1982, between the 1974 and 1990 editions of Townsend's work, the third edition of Darton's book appeared, edited this time by Brian Alderson and lavishly illustrated with pictures that make a very useful addition to the text. Alderson indicates that a fairly slight change to the pagination has been necessary but that alterations to the text are minimal. Despite his increased provision of scholarly sources, his book seems intended to enhance the reputation of the original author, rather than to pinpoint his limitations, something borne out in his Preface, where he claims that Darton's work 'is unsupplantable, for it is rooted in an experience and a quality of mind that are beyond the attainment of more recent generations' (1982: ix).

Not long after the first edition of Townsend's work, Frank Eyre's 1952 pamphlet was replaced by a longer study, *British Children's Books in the Twentieth Century* (1971). Although it could be claimed that this title suggests a more comprehensive study than was possible at a date when the twentieth century was not even three quarters complete, it is evidence of the desire to acknowledge contemporary children's literature in a less piecemeal way than had been the case for the additions to Darton's study. Eyre's principal object, in both the shorter work and this one, is 'to examine the main trends in the development of British children's literature during the first seventy years of this century and to call attention to outstanding books' (1971: 10). Eyre writes from the background of his experience in publishing books for children, together with a wide involvement with the book selection committees of the British Council. His perspective is also widened by a period of working in Australia: he appears to be the first to pay specific rather than incidental attention (though only in appendices) to books produced outside mainland Britain or the United States. The stance in this very useful reference book is, as might be expected from an author in the publishing industry, one of describing output rather than analysing content in depth.

The last history of children's literature to appear before 1990 is Mary Jackson's *Engines of Instruction, Mischief, and Magic: Children's Literature in England from Its Beginnings to 1839* (1989). In her Preface, Jackson cites the work of Darton (whose terminating date she shares) and others as indications of why her labour might appear superfluous but goes on to state her reasons for adding to the bulk of such histories of children's literature:

■ First, what were the various conditions and events, beliefs and ideas, that lay behind book trade developments, and how thoroughly did they account for the trade's evolution? ... And second, when, how precisely, and with what consistency did children's books come under the influence of adult literature (or influence it in turn?). (1989: x) □

Jackson goes on to show how, as a consequence of her emphases, her book differs from those of the earlier historians, noting for instance how 'the prevailing class bias of [Darton's] time prevented him from assessing fairly, I feel, the cultural and marketing implications of chapbook popularity' (p.xi).

The genres of children's literature

From 1970 onwards, the field of children's literature studies rapidly became more densely populated, and many writers tended to focus on particular genres rather than to attempt to look at the whole range of texts.[11] One of the first such studies is Margaret Blount's *Animal Land: The Creatures of Children's Fiction* (1974), a relatively early investigation into one of the most popular and distinctive areas of children's literature. The non-academic nature of her book is signalled by its dedication to, among others, 'Paddington Brown [and] The Velveteen Rabbit, Wherever they are'. Although Blount's book clearly arises out of her own fascination with these stories, she does pose some interesting questions about the reader's response to those humanised animals which are incorporated into an otherwise realistic world (in, for instance, Beatrix Potter's *The Tale of Peter Rabbit*, 1902), as distinct from such animals existing in their own world (as in Richard Adams's *Watership Down*, 1972); nevertheless, her book does not really tackle this subject at any depth. Rather, it represents an attempt to bring together accounts of the range of literature that focuses on animals, from a largely descriptive angle.[12]

Perhaps inevitably, given its importance in the development of children's literature, together with its potential for both nostalgia and historio-cultural analysis, the genre that has been most fertile as far as critical attention is concerned is that of the school story. This attention occurred in a period when the boarding-school story, so integral to the early development of children's literature (notably in the case of *Tom Brown's Schooldays*, 1857), was diminishing numerically as a proportion of the overall number of children's books published, though not perhaps to the extent representing a decline as forecast by Frank Eyre (1971: 82, 84).

In spite of the fact that girls' school fiction has often been viewed as having an inferior status to that featuring boys' schools, one of the first studies of school fiction is Mary Cadogan and Patricia Craig's *You're a Brick, Angela! The Girls' Story 1839–1975* (1976). Its somewhat eye-catching title accurately implies the expectation of an audience looking for enjoyable reading rather than critical insights, but the book also reveals the wide knowledge of its authors and lays the foundations for more academic studies to follow. Cadogan and Craig make the slightly questionable claim that 'a separate comprehensive body of girls' fiction did not come into being until the end of the last century' (p.9).[13] They state their intention 'to relate each book discussed to the context of its own time, and also to indicate how it is regarded now. This has involved the suggestion of certain criteria on which girls' fiction may be assessed' (p.9). Nevertheless, their judgments involve a good deal of subjectivity: they suggest that authors such as Angela Brazil and Dorita Fairlie Bruce are 'unintentionally funny but nonetheless good' (p.9, emphasis original) but that others, such as L.T. Meade, are not. The whole question of quality occupies them in several places in the text; within the Introduction they go on to say, 'We have had to be selective in the choice of books for analysis in depth; but we have found that certain writers stand out ... some are just remarkably good or bad, some are completely original, others exemplify, more or less consciously, the predominant attitudes of their own time' (p.11). They revert to the same theme near the conclusion of the book, adding a timely touch of gender equality: 'In the end, it is the polarities of "good" and "bad" that are important; and distinction in writing for children, or anyone else, is a quality which, like all others that have involved the exercise of reason or imagination, is not sexually determined' (p.372).

A claim as questionable as that quoted above about the rise of girls' fiction, this time about the primacy of Thomas Hughes' *Tom Brown's Schooldays* (1857), occurs in the first full-length study of the boys' school story, Isabel Quigly's *The Heirs of Tom Brown* (1982): Robert Kirkpatrick points out that Hughes' book 'had been preceded by at least 60 others' (*The Encyclopaedia of Boys' School Stories*, 2001: 1). Among the most notable considerations of boys' school stories within the period covered by this chapter are P.W. Musgrave's *From Brown to Bunter* (1985) and Jeffrey Richards' *Happiest Days: The Public Schools in English Fiction* (1988), both of which, unlike Quigly's, not only give an account of the development of the genre, but also use the fiction as evidence of social mores, Musgrave from a sociological standpoint, and Richards from that of social history. As Richards observes:

■ The importance of novels to historians is nowhere better exemplified than in the public school story. For it appeals directly to the emotions as well as or often instead of to the intellect. It repeats and ritualises the messages, providing social and cultural sanction for a set of attitudes. It furnishes role models and conduct validation. (1988: 3) □

Richards' justification for the critical study of fiction in fact presages the work of later critics of children's literature, such as Maria Nikolojevna.

Another genre receiving attention at the time is that of the adventure story; Margery Fisher's *The Bright Face of Danger* (1986) challenges the distinction between adult and children's fiction by observing how many 'adult' authors, such as Rider Haggard and Conan Doyle, have been popular with younger readers, and goes on to discuss their romanticisation of history, their characterisation of heroes (and occasionally heroines) and the whole question of the incorporation of issues upon which, in the best books, such as those of Rosemary Sutcliff, readers are given the opportunity to decide for themselves on the morality or otherwise of the actions of the characters.[14]

An alternative mode to that of focusing on genre, of narrowing the field of children's literature studies, is to relate a particular critical stance to a body of literature produced within a limited period of time. One of the most distinctive and influential texts to do this is Humphrey Carpenter's *Secret Gardens: A Study of the Golden Age of Children's Literature* (1985). Carpenter relates how twenty years previously he had formed the impression that 'the great children's writers from Lewis Carroll to A.A. Milne formed some sort of identifiable literary movement' (p.ix), a notion intensified by his work on the encyclopaedic *The Oxford Companion to Children's Literature* (1984); he admits that his study is selective, omitting authors such as Stevenson and Kipling whose 'work scarcely touches on the themes that preoccupied their more puzzling contemporaries' (p.x). After a preliminary survey of the largely didactic fiction available to young readers prior to the middle of the nineteenth century, Carpenter advances his major theme, that of the quest of a number of children's authors for an ideal world, a 'secret garden', in reaction against contemporary society. This emphasis means that he focuses on a particular kind of fantasy, that which embodies security; for instance, he makes the distinction between the idealised landscapes of Barrie and Milne, and that of Tolkien, marked by the latter's experience of the First World War and thus lacking this element of security: 'instead there is a constant threat of physical violence' (p.211). Carpenter's work is sometimes seen as possessing an implicit middle-class bias, but his identification of an underlying similarity between such writers as Carroll, Grahame, Barrie and Potter is based on an argument that has needed to be taken into account in all subsequent studies of these writers.

Conclusion

This brief survey of critical and historical writing on children's literature up to 1990 reveals how during a period stretching from shortly before the Second World War to near the end of the twentieth century, the subject had not only become academically respectable but was also attracting a wide range of critical input. Many of the trends to be detected subsequently had their beginnings during this period, notably a much greater understanding of the effects of social and ideological context on what was produced for child readers. It had progressed from a tendency for writers to justify their choice of books to discuss by reference to what they enjoyed as children towards an approach as scholarly and increasingly theoretical as that taken in any other branch of literary criticism. In parallel with this development there was a similarly increasing sophistication in the way in which the potential audience for children's books came to be perceived, as is noted in the next chapter.

CHAPTER TWO

Child Readers

Introduction

Traditionally, adult writers about children's literature have tended to be divided into 'book' people and 'child' people, the former starting from a background of literary studies, the latter being classroom orientated and looking at the texts in the context of their suitability for 'real' children.[1] Despite its flaws, this simplistic distinction (there are many writers about children's literature who have their feet in both camps) embodies an element of truth, and to this extent it is convenient in this chapter to focus on attempts to take into account the children who in most instances form the primary audience for the literature being discussed.

Criticism focusing on the child reader

Much of the earliest writing about children's literature took the form of an attempt to provide guidance for parents and teachers about the suitability of texts for the children under their care. By the second half of the twentieth century, this had developed beyond the blatant moral didacticism to be found in many nineteenth-century directives, such as Charlotte Yonge's *What Books to Lend and What to Give* (1888) and Edward Salmon's *Juvenile Literature as it is* (1888), towards a broader approach based on a discussion of the extent to which children's texts might have a positive effect on their readers' linguistic, literary, imaginative and moral development. The evolution of this approach, which has frequently been classroom-centred, into criticism written from a broader perspective, is to some extent the result of the establishment in 1970 of two important journals: *Signal*, engendered by Nancy and Aidan Chambers, in the January of that year; and *Children's Literature in Education*, established by Sidney Robbins, a Senior Lecturer at St Luke's

College Exeter, in March. The latter journal, as stated by the editors of a compilation of journal pieces (*Writers, Critics, and Children*, 1976) was the result of a conference, 'Recent Children's Fiction and Its Role in Education', held at Exeter in 1969, which had the objective of encouraging 'the keener consideration of [post-war] books and the responses of young readers' (1976: ix).

Another consequence of the movement which inspired both the foundation of these two journals and a series of subsequent conferences at Exeter and elsewhere, was the publication of three influential compilations of material on children's literature by prominent writers and critics: *Only Connect: Readings on Children's Literature* (1st edition 1969), edited by Sheila Egoff, G.T. Stubbs, and L.F. Ashley; *Children and Literature* (1973), edited by Virginia Haviland; and *The Cool Web: The Pattern of Children's Reading* (1977), edited by Margaret Meek, Aidan Warlow and Griselda Barton.[2] In their Introduction, Meek et al. refer positively to *Only Connect*, particularly because it affirmed that 'reading and writing stories for children was an activity of creative significance which adults could take seriously' (1977: 3). They suggest, however, that Egoff et al. had left unexamined certain questions, notably those concerning the nature and extent of the benefits that children derive from reading and the way in which writers, publishers and librarians perceived the child audience. In effect Meek et al. proclaim the centrality of the reader rather than simply that of the book (1977: 4). Their Introduction goes on to acknowledge the change of climate in the world of children's books during the period immediately prior to the publication of their collection: teachers were asking questions about the purpose of reading; universities were moving into the world of children's books and relating this study to various other academic disciplines; and the Schools Council had inaugurated two research projects focusing on children's reading.

The Cool Web itself is divided into four sections, entitled 'The Reader', 'What the Authors tell us', 'Approaches to Criticism' and 'Ways forward'. Other than pieces written by the three editors themselves, the material largely consists of previously published papers or excerpts from longer works – mostly from the 1960s and 1970s but some of earlier date – so the task of the editors was evidently one of selecting, on the basis of their own wide knowledge, from what had already been written about children's literature and forming it into a coherent whole in line with their own value-system, as indicated in their Introduction. Those from whom contributions are drawn include prominent educationalists and psychologists (such as James Britton, R.L. Gregory and D.W. Harding), experts on literature (such as Barbara Hardy and Elizabeth Cook), and a considerable number of authors of both adult and children's fiction (notably C.S. Lewis, Geoffrey Trease, Alan Garner and

Philippa Pearce). Inevitably the collection is open to the charge of lack-ing unity, but it could be claimed that it served an inspirational function in demonstrating that further work in the burgeoning field of children's literature studies could 'draw on the insights of all relevant specialisms and still not lose sight of the child' (p.331).

The many studies related to children's literature which follow in the wake of *The Cool Web*, particularly in relation to its emphasis on the role of the child reader, could be broadly divided into two categories. Firstly, there are those which look at the response of readers, young and old, to texts – taking as their mentors the increasing number of theorists who focus on the response of the reader. Secondly there are those which, while not being confined to suitability for classroom use, have the needs of the young reader in mind.[3]

Reader-oriented criticism

During the second half of the twentieth century, the quasi-objective stance taken by many critics towards the assessment of literary merit was increasingly questioned, and a number of theorists began to focus on the role of the reader. One of the first to emphasise the fact that the act of reading involves what she terms a 'transaction' between the reader and the text, was Louise Rosenblatt; throughout the earlier part of her career she produced a number of articles about this interaction, prior to the publication of *The Reader, the Text, the Poem: The Transactional Theory of the Literary Work* in 1978. Consequently, other theorists were already responding to her ideas before these appeared in book form. Norman Holland's *The Dynamics of Literary Response* (1968) takes on board some of Rosenblatt's insights and reinforces the growing aware-ness among critics of the importance of recognising that response is a creative act by the reader.

Equally influential on children's literature, however (and probably the most frequently cited of these theorists), is Wolfgang Iser, whose *The Implied Reader* (1974) puts forward a phenomenological approach to the reading process. He claims that a literary work can be said to be 'vir-tual' until 'the convergence of text and reader' brings it into existence (1974: 275). Such an understanding of reading allows for the fact that 'different readers can be differently affected by the "reality" of a par-ticular text', so that reading is recognised as 'a creative process' (1974: 279). This creativity is particularly evident in the way in which differ-ent readers, or even the same reader at different points in time, fill 'the gaps left by the text itself' (1974: 280). He examines how the reader's understanding of what is being read develops during the actual reading of units as small as a single sentence: 'it is the [continuous] process of anticipation and retrospection that leads to the formation of the virtual dimension, which in turn transforms the text into an experience for the reader' (1974: 281). Although all Iser's illustrations are drawn from adult literature, his stress on the active, creative nature of reading has proved attractive to many educationalists, particularly in relation to the 'gaps' that readers need to fill.

A theorist who further explores such insights is Stanley Fish, whose provocatively titled *Is there a Text in this Class?* (1980) confronts the recognition that the emphasis on the individual nature of the reading experience poses questions as to whether any readings can ever be rejected as deficient, a dilemma he seeks to resolve by putting forward the concept of the 'interpretive community'. This he defines as a group comprising those who share the strategies involved in the production of the texts concerned (1980: 24); it is likely to be formed of other writers who have a similar cultural and temporal background to the writer of the text.

Subsequently a number of other theorists have been responsible for bringing this emphasis on the role of the reader into their studies of young readers: two of the most significant of these are Arthur N. Applebee and J.A. Appleyard. Applebee's *The Child's Concept of Story* (1978) is not directly dependent on the work of the reading-response theorists mentioned above, but his research into the interaction between children and stories is frequently cited by those who incorporate some of the insights of these theorists, particularly those of Iser, into their consideration of children's literature. Drawing on the seminal work of D.W. Harding,[4] which emphasises the distinction between the role of the participant and that of the spectator (into which category most reading of literature falls), Applebee studied the responses to story of children aged between two and seventeen. He notes the tendency for the youngest children simply to retell the story to the best of their recollection, the gradual development of a more sophisticated response when children begin to adopt the strategies of summarising and categorisation, and their eventual arrival at the ability to distinguish between objective and subjective reactions to the story material.

In his *Becoming a Reader: The Experience of Fiction from Childhood to Adulthood* (1990), Appleyard pays tribute to Applebee's 'ground-breaking' work, and also indicates how his own study is informed by 'an interactional or transactional view of reading such as might be assembled from the works of Iser, Rosenblatt and Holland'. Despite any differences of emphasis between these three theorists, he finds a 'useful convergence' in the way in which they all view the act of reading:

■ [It] is primarily an encounter between a particular reader and a particular text in a particular time and place, an encounter that brings into existence the story, poem, or work in question. The story is not the same as the text on the page, nor is it simply the reader's uniquely personal response to the text. Rather the story is an event that has roots both in the text and in the personality and history that the reader brings to the reading. (1990: 9) □

From this basic position, Appleyard posits a number of stages typical of reading development: the Reader in early childhood as Player; the Reader in later childhood as Hero and Heroine; the Reader in adolescence as Thinker; the Reader at the college stage as Interpreter; and the Pragmatic Reader, who, with the maturity of adulthood, can make use of all these strategies. Despite the dangers of generalisation, Appleyard's stages form a useful template for the development of approaches to reading, though as he himself observes: 'the precise division of roles proposed here ... [is] less important than the general thesis that the way we organize our experience as readers and the meanings we give to it change significantly as we grow older' (1990: 19).

More recent studies have also looked at the phenomenon of 'resistant reading' or 'reading against the grain', where readers who are already competent may, implicitly or explicitly, reject the 'dominant', expected interpretation of what they read. Readers at Appleyard's 'Pragmatic' stage, who are able to institute their own reading strategies, may for instance deliberately adopt a feminist, a Marxist or a psychoanalytic stance, while being aware that this is not the way in which the original author expected the text to be read.[5] Such independence is not necessarily confined to more experienced readers: Alan Kendall's 2008 study of readers between sixteen and nineteen challenges 'demonising' representations of this age group, and puts forward instead a view that their reading of non-quality texts is far from passive, displaying a playfulness and resistance to the dominant adult culture.

The work of writers such as Applebee and Appleyard, following in the wake of Iser and the others mentioned above, has served to consolidate a situation in which it is impossible to pontificate in general terms about children's books without at least paying some attention both to the implied reader and to the impossibility of arriving at any objective or detached reading of any text, perhaps particularly in the case of young readers.

Bringing together the child and the book

The title of this subsection pays homage to a seminal work (also discussed in Chapter Four, because of its writer's dual background in psychology as well as literature): Nicholas Tucker's *The Child and the Book* (1981). Tucker's endeavour to bridge the gap between what literary critics say about specific texts and 'the factors most likely to affect children's response to literature at different ages' (1981: 232) involves generalisations; what some later writers have perceived as its lack of precision has inevitably been subject to adverse criticism (discussed later in this section). Nevertheless, it can be seen in retrospect as part of a body of work which attempts, however partially, to place the child's response, rather than that of the adult critic, at the centre of the appraisal of literature for children.

In one way or other, either as author or publisher, Aidan Chambers has been responsible for much of the increased emphasis on children as readers. His own *Booktalk: Occasional Writing on Literature and Children* (1985) is an assemblage of lectures and essays, but, despite the 'occasional' nature of these writings, as acknowledged in the book's subtitle, there is a unity in Chambers' approach. This results to a considerable extent from his focus on the reader and the frequent references to the work of Iser. One of the most influential essays in this collection is entitled 'The Reader in the Book'; originally a talk given at Bristol University in 1977, it was published in *Signal* later the same year and subsequently appeared in a variety of other publications (1985: 34). In it, by analysing passages from texts by Roald Dahl, Arthur Ransome and Lucy Boston, together with briefer references to a wide range of other children's authors, Chambers examines the way in which writers appear to seek to evoke certain responses in their readers. He determines that authors addressing young readers are likely, consciously or otherwise, to adjust their style, the point of view, the sympathies they establish, and especially the tell-tale gaps they leave to be filled, to the likely ability of their young readers; he describes these readers as being 'unyielding ... [in the way that] they want the book to suit them, tending to expect an author to take them as he finds them rather than they taking the book as they find it' (1985: 37). Chambers suggests that:

■ the concept of the implied reader ... offers us a critical approach which concerns itself less with the subject portrayed in a book than with the means of communication by which the reader is brought into contact with the reality presented by an author. It is a method which could help us to determine whether a book is for children or not, what kind of book it is, and what kind of reader (or, to put it in another way, what kind of reading) it demands. (1985: 49) □

The influence of this essay is acknowledged by Barbara Wall[6] in *The Narrator's Voice: The Dilemma of Children's Fiction* (1991), in which she develops Chambers' notions about authorship by an analysis based on a number of children's texts of the role, not only of the implied author as signposted by Chambers, but of the (actual or implied) narrator and narratee, whose relationship, she suggests, 'is the distinctive marker of a children's book ... [and] has changed markedly in the last one hundred and fifty years' (1991: 9). She progresses from this towards a useful distinction that she draws between children's fiction which apparently addresses only the child reader (single address); that which addresses the child and the adult reader but recognises that they have quite distinct perspectives (double address); and that which encompasses both audiences at the same time (dual address) (1991: 9).

Another important piece in *Booktalk* is Chambers' 'Tell Me: Are Children Critics?', written in conjunction with a group of classroom teachers and later expanded into a book under the same title (1993). The writers establish the importance to children of the opportunity to form their own judgments about books in an environment where the emphasis is not on learning the 'right' answers, or indeed answering particular kinds of questions about the text, but learning through actually talking about the books. As an eight-year-old child is quoted as saying, 'We don't know what we think about a book until we've talked about it' (1985: 174).

Some of the most influential of the other texts in this area emanate from the Thimble Press (the small publishing firm initiated by Aidan and Nancy Chambers); as well as producing the journal *Signal* mentioned earlier, Thimble published several important short monographs which attempted to bridge the gap between the literary and the pedagogical approaches. The earliest of these was Margaret Meek's[7] *How Texts Teach What Readers Learn* (1988), which makes evident the vast range of implicit knowledge a potential reader needs to acquire in order to derive meaning from a text. Reading a popular picturebook with a young boy whose lack of phonic skills was a concern to his teacher, Meek and one of her students were able to elucidate the fact that:

■ understanding authorship, audience, illustration and iconic interpretation are part of the ontogenesis of 'literary competences'. To learn to read a book, as distinct from simply recognizing the words on the page, a young reader has to become both the teller (picking up the author's view and voice) and the told (the recipient of the story, the interpreter). (1988: 10) □

The focus on the child audience, and the sophisticated skills which literature demands from its readers, formed the basis for a series of books published by the Open University from 1983 onwards in their 'English, Language, and Education' series.[8] Although these books anticipate a readership of teachers and are consequently pedagogic in their remit, the extent to which they emphasise the response of the reader and incorporate many of the insights of Iser and others cited above is manifest.

More significant within the academic and literary critical arena is the work of Peter Hunt. His two compilations of critical material – *Children's Literature: The Development of Criticism* (1990) and *Literature for Children: Contemporary Criticism* (1992) – include substantial pieces by Meek, Chambers and Tucker. These collections overlap chronologically with Hunt's single authorship book, *Criticism, Theory and Children's Literature* (1991), and it is evident that all three texts result from his familiarity with the work of a wide range of children's literature criticism from the earliest period onwards. In the Introduction to his single-authored work, Hunt makes his own position clear: 'In terms of children's books, I shall be advocating a new critical approach: "childist" criticism as a parallel to "feminist" criticism' (1991: 16). He expands on this statement in his final chapter, entitled 'Criticism for Children's Literature', citing a paper by Lissa Paul (included in his 1990 collection and first published in *Signal*), 'What Feminist Theory knows about Children's Literature'. Hunt observes that, just as women in the past have learned interpretive strategies consonant with male-dominated society, it is possible that, as they learn to play 'the literary/reading game, children are progressively forced to read against themselves as children' (1991: 192). He sees picturebooks and poetry as crucial areas in this search for the response of the child reader. In relation to the first of these, Hunt gives attention to texts by John Burningham which often involve the possibility of reading on several levels; this lack of direct authorial control, Hunt suggests, renders such books 'closer to the comprehension patterns of an orally based reader than the vast majority of texts that set out to be "for children"' (1991: 195). About poetry, he opines that 'it is only in the least important area of poetry, the ostensible subject-matter, that any distinction ... can be made between what is appropriate for children and what for adults' (1991: 197). The conclusion to this search for authentic child reading is his questioning of the 'deep-seated idea that the dominant value-structure is intrinsically valid, rather than being just another sub-species'[9] and his putting forward at least the possibility that recent and accessible texts should form the bulk of what is taught to children (1991: 200).

Before considering a view of children's literature criticism counter to those quoted above, it is convenient to look briefly at two other Thimble Press monographs: one of these is by Peter Hollindale, who had in 1988 received the Children's Literature Association award for his article 'Ideology and the Children's Book';[10] the other is a development by Lissa Paul of some of her earlier work. In his *Signs of Childness in Children's Books* (1997), Hollindale, like Paul, draws out the similarity of positioning between the female reader and the child reader: 'A male reader cannot read a novel by Margaret Atwood as a woman reads it, just as an adult cannot read a novel by Roald Dahl as a child reads it'

(1997: 10). However, as he observes, unlike feminist literature written by women, most children's books are not written by children. As part of advancing his argument, Hollindale finds it convenient to resurrect two terms previously encountered only rarely: 'childness, the quality of being a child' (p.47), and 'childly', an adjective relating to behaviour which is natural and appropriate to a child (pp.52–53). The use of such terms in the discussion of children's literature, he argues, enables the adult critic to engage in the debate without any tendency to be patronising or condescending. He puts forward a range of questions designed to facilitate the exploration of the childness of texts (and thus the determining of whether or not they can be seen as part of the corpus of children's literature), such as the extent to which child characters are psychologically realistic, consistent, and differentiated from adult characters (pp.88–89). Other aspects upon which to interrogate a text include its use of language and narrative voice; such features can help a critic determine whether the implied reader is indeed a child (pp.94–5).

Paul's *Reading Otherways* (1998) expands on her earlier work linking the feminist response to an adult text with the reading of children's literature. She carries out a close examination of some classic children's texts, and like Hollindale poses questions (pp.16–17), with the objective of focusing on aspects (notably that of relationships) which indicate how the author is positioning the child reader.

The stance taken by nearly all the critics named above is censured by Karín Lesnik-Oberstein, in her *Children's Literature: Criticism and the Fictional Child* (1994), for failing to take into account the incompatibility between, on the one hand, the search to determine how child readers actually behave in relation to their reading matter, and, on the other, the fact that references in critical material to any such reader inevitably apply only to a construct created by the adult literary critic. Lesnik-Oberstein focuses mostly on Peter Hunt's *Criticism, Theory, and Children's Literature* (1991), in which he seeks to apply some of the approaches of adult critical theory to children's literature, since he claims, like Chambers, 'that adult literary theory can be illuminated and explained through the issues of children's literature criticism' (1994: 148). Lesnik-Oberstein suggests that:

> ■ some of the adult literary theory Hunt engages with questions the very ideas necessary to children's literature criticism: selection or canonization of books, the assumptions surrounding the influences books have, the generalizations of reader response and the notion of readers as audience. (1994: 150) □

She complains that in the attempt to understand what happens when children read, Hunt creates the notion of a 'real reader', without displaying an awareness that this is just as much a construct as are the students and critics he dismisses from his scrutiny because they are reading in a 'deviant' way (1994: 150). While disrupting the notion of the 'canon' of children's texts because of its links with political and power structures, and asserting the importance of the choices and modes of reading of the individual, Hunt, she claims, nevertheless himself asserts the importance to children's books of 'literary' standards (1994: 153).

It is probable that children's literature criticism can never totally escape from this paradox – while seeking to be attentive to the variety of ways in which children actually read, it is almost impossible to avoid the generalised concept of 'the child', whether as an individual reader or as the audience to whom a specific book appears to be addressed. Indeed, the whole issue of what is a children's book is one which cannot be rigidly determined, given the changes in the concept of childhood that have occurred in different periods and cultures. As Hunt observes in a recent exploration of the works and stated motivations of several 'classic' children's authors:

■ the fact that the writer is an adult inevitably turns [the children's book] into something less pure, whether that is a wrestling with the difficulties of writing for children (as with A.A. Milne), or a skilful exploitation of the form (as with Blyton and Dahl). Perhaps the only 'pure' children's book is one written by a child, *for* a child, and that is something that adults should never read. (Butts and Hunt 2013: 130) □

Locating the response of the child reader

Since we are presumably never going to have a child literary critic who already has a reputation comparable to that of the adults who pontificate about the genre, perhaps all that can be done is to explore, in both quantitative and qualitative terms, the evidence we have about children's actual reading.

Quantitative investigations

During the twentieth century, educationalists began to take an increased interest in what children actually read. As the Introduction to the Schools Council booklet, *Children's Reading Interests* (1975),[11] states, most of 'the child's learning of English takes place outside the five or six English lessons on each week's timetable' (1975: 7). This survey of the voluntary reading of 8000 children therefore was initiated in recognition of the fact that such reading has an inevitable effect not only on language skills but also 'on the child's attitudes and values and on the whole picture he [sic] builds up of the world around him' (1975: 7). The research team, under Frank Whitehead, acknowledges the existence of earlier, smaller studies before presenting the results, in both tabular and title format, of this survey. *Black Beauty* and *Little Women* top the lists, but, predictably, Blyton's fiction also figures strongly. The 1975 results are today largely of historical interest, but some of the 'Discussion' chapter is more generally relevant. For instance, it states that 'there are some children (almost always boys) who turn to books as a source of information or knowledge' (p.40) – a situation which later surveys have tended to take as a starting point for further research on gender differences in reading. Among the other matters they put forward for further investigation are the problem of non-readers, the influence of the primary school on the reading of secondary school pupils, and the importance of the teachers' familiarity with the literature available for young readers.

It would not be appropriate to list here all the surveys of children's reading since 1975, but it is of interest to note how much wider their remit has been than that of earlier investigations. For instance, the questionnaire of *Young People's Reading at the End of the Century* (1996)[12] was addressed to members of the entire age range of compulsory schooling; additionally, it not only asks young people about the influences on their reading choices and the sources of books they read, but also, for older pupils, looks at the relationship between their reading and their understanding of their own physical and social development. Later surveys have been carried out in conjunction with Loughborough University, and by the National Literacy Trust, whose 2011 findings suggest that relatively few young people in today's computer- and mobile-phone-focused society confine themselves to paper-based reading.[13]

The information provided by such surveys is probably primarily of interest to publishers, librarians, and educationalists, though they inevitably throw some light on the conditions in which the more traditional reading of fiction takes place. Of more direct interest to those concerned with the reading of literature are the studies of individuals, whether these take the form of the observation of children's response to their reading (or in the case of the very young, of adults reading to them), or the recollections of adults about reading they themselves did as children.

Individual listeners and readers

Appleyard makes extensive reference to a number of studies of the response of young children to stories told them by adults, giving accounts of the records made about Carol White (1956), Rachel Scollen (1981), and Anna Crago (1983), and referring also to Dorothy

Butler's influential study of Cushla, a brain-damaged child whose intellectual development was greatly enhanced by parental reading (Appleyard 1990: 23–28; 197). Such studies can be very illuminating about the effects of story; more recently a fully documented account of her own children's developing response to books has been provided in Virginia Lowe, *Stories, Pictures and Reality: Two Children Tell* (2007). This is based on detailed handwritten notes she made at the time, rather than tape recordings, as this method enabled her to incorporate additional details, as well as avoiding the time-consuming process of transcribing tapes. As Lawrence Sipe[14] comments, her study is of particular interest since one of the children studied is her son, whereas previous such studies have focused exclusively on girls; he also notes the importance of the way that this extended study of the children up to the age of eighteen allows her to 'address various aspects of the fiction/reality distinction'.

Several studies have focused on small groups of young readers, paying heed to their individual responses while pursuing an overall research project involving the group to which they belong. Perhaps inevitably, the slant of such projects has often been educational and socio-ethnographic rather than literary, but insights about children's responses to specific texts also form an important part of their data. Shirley Brice Heath's investigation[15] of reading and storytelling behaviour in communities differing in ethnicity and class, involved both talk and the creation of journals by the children, thus providing an insight into their understanding of what reading involved. Meredith Cherland,[16] with an interest primarily in the differing responses of boys and girls, made use of transcripts of small group discussions of a range of children's texts, as well as of her own observations and interviews of participants. Perhaps the most informative in this context is the research project of Beverley Naidoo,[17] whose explicit reference, in her Introduction, to the Reading Response theorists mentioned above reveals that her focus in examining the responses of the children she worked with was one of recognising the importance of the role of the reader. She quotes Rosenblatt's use of the term 'transaction', which acknowledges what the reader brings to the text, in relation to her project to explore the responses of a group of children in an almost exclusively white area to four texts chosen because of their foregrounding of issues of racial tension. One of the significant parameters of her analysis is to measure the extent to which the degree of empathy aroused in the young readers is increased by the reading of these texts (1992: 136). The evidence which Naidoo interprets is derived from her own observation together with a good many transcripts of tapes of the children discussing their reading and a number of written responses.

Personal recollections

Another area which has added to knowledge about the response of young people to literature has been the increased value placed on personal recollections of childhood reading. Francis Spufford's *The Child that Books Built* (2002) tells his autobiographical story of the reading development of a book-addicted child from his earliest incursion into independent reading to his encounter with adult-addressed texts at the age of thirteen. While inevitably personal and somewhat idiosyncratic, this account also makes use of educational psychology in order to derive more general conclusions about stages of development, from the tangled 'forest' of neurons of the very young infant towards an ordered 'greenwood' (2002: 34). He acknowledges the important role of the local library in his own reading development, and also gives an interesting account of how books such as C.S. Lewis's 'Narnia' saga provided a 'window onto imaginary countries … an alternative to reality' (2002: 82).

Even the academic study of the history of children's literature has not been exempt from incorporating observations about children's reading. Seth Lerer's *Children's Literature: A Reader's History from Aesop to Harry Potter* (2008) draws not only on his scholarly studies of philology and medieval literature, but also on his own reading, together with that of his son (pp.318–19), charting the boy's progress from board books to 'Harry Potter' and beyond.

Building on the trend to look at the experience of reading, the Open University set up the Reading Experience Database (RED) in 2011. This project has now become international, embracing much of the English-speaking world. The UK section comprises over 30,000 records, described as being from 'the famous and the ordinary, the young and the old, men and women', which 'illustrate the diversity of reading experience and practice as well as patterns within particular periods and across time'.[18] Consulting this resource allows researchers to discover not only how individuals read certain books, from the children's literature canon and elsewhere, but also the reading backgrounds of specific authors.

A further source of information about what children actually read is to be derived from studies of what has been published, and its popularity among young readers. Evidence about the actual publication of children's fiction and its popularity is to be found in Kimberley Reynolds and Nicholas Tucker's 1998 study, *Children's Book Publishing in Britain since 1945*, described as 'the first sustained attempt to construct the story of modern children's book publishing in Britain' (p.xiii). They discuss the increased marketability of children's literature and examine issues then current, such as the rise of graphic novels and of the role of other media.[19] More recently, *Popular Children's Literature in Britain* (2008), edited by Julia Briggs, Dennis Butts and Matthew Grenby, after presenting the historical backdrop to the present publishing scene, gives some attention to the astronomical sales of Enid Blyton, Roald Dahl and J.K. Rowling, all of whom have in turn topped the lists of authors popular with children. In relation to the last of these, Julia Eccleshare accounts for the popularity of the Harry Potter series by suggesting that its advent coincided with a market searching for an author like Rowling, who would provide a readable series with so many elements attractive to children.

The 'real' child is likely always to prove elusive, but the statistics both about the sale of children's books and about the book choices made by children, as reflected by what they buy and what they borrow from libraries,[20] provide some solid evidence about what is enjoyed by them. This in turn has a significant effect on what publishers are prepared to spend money on producing, which inevitably then has a marked effect on what is available for young readers, as well as on the teachers and parents who are likely initially to be the agents in making this body of literature familiar to its implied audience. What seems certain is that critics of children's literature will never again be able to arbitrate authoritatively about which books are suitable for children, without an awareness of the actual position in this respect of the child readers themselves. Central to this positioning of the child reader is the relationship between authorial stance and the chosen mode of narration, an area which is the focus of the next chapter.

CHAPTER THREE

Narrative and Children's Literature

Introduction

It could be claimed that, like the majority of books about children's literature, the preceding chapters of this volume have started from the unquestioned assumption that we all know what constitutes children's literature. John Rowe Townsend's pragmatic definition, which simply identifies a children's book as one appearing on the children's list of a publisher,[1] has been queried by many theorists, without any universally recognised resolution of the problem having ever been reached. Barbara Wall (1991) quotes Neil Philip's criticism of Townsend's implicit acceptance of the total reliability of the publisher's classification:

■ The distinction between adult literature and children's literature ... would be more valid if one could reliably decide *after reading*, on technical, structural, linguistic or thematic grounds, whether or not a book was for children: especially if such a decision convincingly reversed publishers' judgements on occasion. (1991: 1, quoting Philip 1984: 15, italics original) □

Wall goes on to propose that her own study, based on recent work on narratology, offers 'a method of deciding whether or not a book is a children's book' (1991: 1). Her analysis of the approaches to narratives, both those of classic children's texts and of books featuring children but clearly addressed to adult readers, foregrounds the centrality of the relationship between authorial stance and the voice of the narrator, and more particularly the effect this has on how the implied child reader is positioned.[2]

In the second half of the twentieth century, a number of theorists attempted to bring insights derived from linguistics, folklore and anthropology into the analysis of adult fiction. Since it is impossible here to do justice to the abundance and complexity of such theory, the work of these writers will be mentioned briefly, where relevant, as a context for those children's literature critics, including Wall, who are concerned with the special characteristics of the discourse of that narrative fiction which is written for an implied audience of young readers.[3]

The narrator and the addressee in the children's book

In establishing a working definition of what is involved in narration, Barbara Wall quotes Shlomith Rimmon-Kenan who describes it as 'a *communication* process in which the narrative as message is transmitted by addresser to addressee'.[4] In the case of children's literature, questions can arise about both these key participants in the narration process; Zohar Shavit observes that:

> ■ One of the most powerful constraints [that children's literature is subject to] is the special and often ambiguous status of the addressee in a children's book, since it must appeal to the child reader and the adult, who is regarded in culture both as superior to the child and as responsible for deciding what is appropriate reading material for the child. ... This forces the children's writer to compromise between two addressees who differ both in their literary tastes as well as in their norms of realization of the text. (1986: 93) □

Shavit claims that many authors, rather than simultaneously addressing both of these audiences, in fact choose to focus primarily on either the adult (in many canonical texts), or, in the case of popular fiction, the child.

Barbara Wall (1991: 4) confronts the question of audience by developing a model of narrative text devised by Seymour Chatman,[5] and subsequently used by Rimmon-Kenan:

| Implied author → Narrator → Narratee → Implied reader |

Real Author   **Real Reader**

Whereas Chatman 'believed that not all narratives have narrators', and Rimmon-Kenan 'found implied author and implied reader to be dispensable terms', Wall states that:

> ■ Since I need to discuss not only the ways in which real adult authors address real child readers, using narrators, adult or child, who address child narratees, but also the ways in which implied authors sometimes set up implied adult readers in texts ostensibly addressed to children, I find that I need all six terms. (1991: 4) □

She claims that the real author and the real reader, though not found within the pages of a work of fiction, are 'the physical parties to the transaction', while the narrator and narratee are, in current children's fiction, likely to be covert rather than the overt figures frequently to be found in the work of writers as recent as C.S. Lewis and Roald Dahl. Wall sees the implied author[6] as 'the all-informing authorial presence, the idea of the author that is carried away by the real reader from his or her reading of the book', and:

> ■ The implied reader is ... the reader for whom the real and implied authors have, consciously and unconsciously, shaped the story, who is always there, and whose presence and qualities ... can be deduced from the totality of the book. (1991: 6–7) □

She emphasises that 'While the presence of the implied author pervades the text and colours and controls the reader's response, at any and every given moment it is the narrator who "speaks" ... [and] it is the narratee to whom the narrator speaks' (1991: 7–8). She describes how, as a result of questioning some of the assumptions made by Aidan Chambers in his 'provocative' article, 'The Reader in the Book' (1977),[7] she came to realise that 'the narrator-narratee relationship, rather than that of implied author and implied reader, is the distinctive marker of a children's book'. Wall links this distinction with her basic contention concerning the identification of books intended for children:

> ■ That it is possible to demonstrate that narrators are always addressing someone, and possible to decide whether that someone is a child or an adult, or neither one nor the other specifically, or neither one nor the other consistently, enables those who wish to do so to determine empirically which books are for children and which are not, and whether it is possible for books to be both for children and adults at the same time. Consciousness of audience is at the heart of the narrative process as it is undertaken by writers of stories genuinely for children. (1991: 22) □

Wall's argument hinges on her usage of the terms 'double', 'single' and 'dual' address; she claims that the first of these modes tended to be the one most frequent in Victorian children's fiction, and the second is that most prevalent today. She exemplifies double address, the alternating of narratee between child and adult, by referring to Barrie's *Peter Pan*,[8] and demonstrates how the narrator sometimes assumes that his narratee is as lacking in knowledge as a child, and at other times asks him[9] to recall what it was like to be a child (1991: 22–23). Single address, on the other hand, Wall illustrates with reference to the work of Arthur Ransome, who, despite his emphatic denial that he was a writer for children, nevertheless throughout his twelve children's novels consistently adopted the stance of 'a friendly adult talking seriously and without condescension to children – and a narrative style [appropriate to this persona]' (1991: 30). He succeeded in doing this because 'he simply put himself in the place of the children he was writing about and described what they saw and did, felt and thought. He has no viewpoint apart from theirs' (1991: 30). Dual address, 'a stance in which the narrator addresses child and adult narratees genuinely in the same voice', seems to be relatively rarely attained; Wall suggests that T.H. White captures it occasionally in *Mistress Masham's Repose* (1946), but she finds it more consistently present in fairytales, as a result of the oral tradition (p.40),[10] and also in some modern writers, such as Lucy Boston in her six-novel 'Green Knowe' series published between 1954 and 1976 (1991: 34, 226–7).

Wall's analysis of the narrative of a range of literature shows how her approach can indeed be a very valuable tool for discerning the extent to which a particular text can truly be termed 'children's literature', and recognising the merits of books which are indeed written 'to and for' children (1991: 190). For instance, unlike many of her contemporaries, Wall is prepared to acknowledge positive qualities in Enid Blyton's considerable output, remarking on the competent storytelling and the mastery of the voices of children: 'the narrator briefly recounts an action and then slides imperceptibly into the thoughts of the character, so that it appears as though the narrator is commenting on the action in the voice of the child character' (1991: 191). In his detailed study of the work of Blyton, David Rudd frequently draws on Wall's analysis, and, like many subsequent critics, demonstrates the utility of this approach to narrative.

In her Introduction, Wall states that she is writing about children up to the age of twelve or thirteen, not young adults (1991: 1). A recent article by Louise Salstad offers a development of the classification of narratorial stance to the older age range. Salstad asserts:

■ I would assign the type of address in which the narrator directs himself [sic] to child, adolescent and adult narratees at different times the term 'alternating triple address'. That in which the narrator addresses a narratee in one of the three age groups while the implied author addresses an implied reader in a different age group or groups, I would call 'split triple address'. When the narrator addresses the narratee, either covertly or overtly, in a tone appropriate to all age groups, or when the narrator confidentially shares the story in a way that allows him, whether child, adolescent or adult, a conjunction of interests with a narratee who could reasonably be child, adolescent or adult, I propose use of the term 'triadic' address. (2003: 219–220) □

Salstad makes use of her threefold classification in her discussion of series fiction for adolescents by a Spanish writer, Elvira Lindo, demonstrating how the Manolito Gafotas series of novels, which began publication in 1994, succeed in addressing readers of different ages, sometimes concurrently and sometimes alternately, because of their use of different age groups of narratee. She claims that this factor accounts for their success: they are 'texts that successfully, as far as real readers are concerned, construct a child narratee and implied readers in all three states of life' (2003: 228).

While the technicalities of Salstrad's analysis may well be too complex for its widespread use, the fact that she draws attention to the likelihood of texts, particularly those for young adults, simultaneously having addressees of several different age groups certainly opens up possible alternative approaches to reading even well-established texts. It also suggests the utility of further development of Wall's study beyond the age group to which it directly refers. The question of narration in crossover texts will be pursued further in Chapter Eleven.

'Childness' and children's literature

Like the other critics of children's literature mentioned above, Peter Hollindale admits the difficulty of defining the subject that they all claim to be talking about. As well as considering Townsend's attempt at definition, he looks at others based on the appeal to children, either now or in the past, the linguistic suitability to this audience, and the establishment of meaningful connections with child readers. He toys with the possibility of using the term children's literature to denote a 'reading event' rather than a text as such, but finds it insufficient unless qualified by reference to a text, because of its over-dependence on the individual child's reading competence and choice. Finally, he essays his own:

■ Children's literature is a body of texts with certain common features of imaginative interest, which is activated as children's literature by a reading event: that of being read by a child. (1997: 27–30) □

This definition includes something that Hollindale claims to be essential to this transaction, 'childness', the quality of being a child; he cites a speech by Polixenes in Shakespeare's *The Winter's Tale* (I: ii) which refers to his son's 'varying childness'. This, Hollindale suggests, refers to 'shared ground ... between child and adult': for the child it is 'the presentness of his condition', and for the adult it is 'participant reconstruction, made up from observation, and play, and memory, and values, and hope which he invests in childhood and the future represented by his son'. Hollindale goes on to argue that:

■ childness is the distinguishing property of a text in children's literature, setting it apart from other literature as a genre, and it is also the property that the child brings to the reading of a text. (1997: 47) □

He elaborates:

■ I propose 'childness', therefore, as a critical term with wider relevance. For the child, childness is composed of the developing sense of self in interaction with the images of childhood encountered in the world ... For the adult, childness is composed of the grown-up's memories of childhood, of meaningful continuity between child and adult self, of the varied behaviour associated with being a child, and the sense of what is appropriate behaviour for a given age.... This compound of cultural and personal attitudes is articulated in a text of children's literature, and the *event* of children's literature lies in the chemistry of a child's encounter with it. (1997: 49, italics original) □

The other aspect that Hollindale associates with children's literature is that of 'an interest in story, and in linear narrative' (1997: 62), since, he claims, 'the natural procedure by which we establish the continuity of our individual identities is by linear narrative' (1997: 68). Censuring contemporary critical theories which deny the continuity of selfhood, Hollindale claims that stories are essential in order for children to grow:

■ effective writers of children's literature are often those who retain the childhood intensity and urgency of storying, whose childhood is alive in memory and present existence because it is still essential to their mature procedures for articulating the self in time. (1997: 70) □

Hollindale goes on to support the practical utility of his adaptation of the term childness by an analysis of some modern children's novels, including two by Robert Westall. These, he claims, reveal the writer's sensitivity to changes in the nature of childness between 1975 and 1991.

Bakhtin and the positioning of the child reader

A number of theoretical works on narrative by Mikhail Bakhtin[11] were published in Russia during the middle years of the twentieth century but translations of these did not become widely known in Western literary critical circles until somewhat later. As Robyn McCallum points out,

■ His theories of narrative, in particular his formulation of concepts like polyphony, intertextuality and parody ... provide ways of analyzing narrative strategies and techniques that have gained popularity in contemporary children's and adolescent fiction. (1999: 10) □

Bakhtin regarded the novel as a dialogic form which by its nature involves a variety of voices, themselves derived from a variety of linguistic and social backgrounds. Even if only a single person is represented as speaking, the use of language itself constitutes a form of dialogue. This is made particularly evident through the concept of intertextuality, defined by John Stephens as 'the production of meaning from the interrelationships between audience, text, other texts, and the socio-cultural determinations of significance' (1992: 84). Stephens goes on to demonstrate how any text which is 'the immediate object of attention' ('the focused text') may have a variety of relationships to other texts. These may take forms such as direct quotation from an earlier work, use of a well-known story framework, reference to an archetype, the use of particular genres and conventions, the citing of historical narratives, artworks and so on (Stephens 1992: 84–5). McCallum quotes Bakhtin as remarking that: 'The intertextuality of discourse entails that "no living word relates to its object in a *singular* way: between the word and its object, between the word and the speaking subject, there exists an elastic environment of other, alien words about the same object, the same theme"' (1999: 14, italics original).

It is easy to see that the concept of intertextuality goes far beyond the mere tracing of literary influences. In the case of children's literature the situation becomes more complex. Because children may not have been exposed to the earlier texts to which an author makes direct or indirect allusion, the relationship between them and the focused text is by no means straightforward. Using well-known writing for children, including fairytales, Stephens shows how intertextuality can create a construct in which 'readers are enabled to experiment with subject positions different from those of their everyday lives ... [it may also] act as a critique of current social values' (1992: 116). Finally, Stephens claims that 'intertextuality frequently takes the specific form of parody or travesty of a pre-text'; this 'interrogat[ion] of official culture' he describes, again using Bakhtin's terminology, as 'carnivalesque' (1992: 120–1). Stephens distinguishes between texts which offer 'time out' from adult imposed norms but 'incorporate a safe return to social normality'; others which 'dismantle socially received ideas', thus provoking the reader to question such ideas; and texts which 'are endemically subversive of social authority, received paradigms of behaviour and morality, and major literary genres associated with children's literature' (1992: 121). Such strategies force readers to ask questions and to refrain from automatic identification with major characters, so that they will assume a subject position outside the text and even in opposition to 'society's official structures of authority' (1992: 156).

Further application of the work of Bakhtin to literature for young people occurs in McCallum's *Ideologies of Identity in Adolescent Fiction* (1999). Building on the way in which Bakhtin and others emphasise that 'an individual's consciousness and sense of identity is formed in dialogue with others and with the discourses constituting the society and culture s/he inhabits [so that] the formation of subjectivity is thus always shaped by social ideologies' (1999: 3), she analyses a range of fiction addressing teenage readers. She suggests that the novel, because of its diversity of narrative techniques, allows readers to take on a variety of possible subject positions and potentially to be actively involved in the production of meaning. While some texts may restrict the reader to a passive stance by means of an over-determined lack of dialogic elements, others can encourage young readers towards a range of such positions, thus equipping them with:

■ a wide range of reading strategies and skills for ascribing meanings to texts and for ascribing experiences in the world with meaning ... [and thus] facilitat[ing] a questioning of conventional notions of selfhood, meaning and history. (1999: 259) □

In effect, McCallum lauds texts which enable the young reader to develop the potential for 'resistant' reading, and thus a degree of autonomy appropriate to today's society – a society very different from earlier periods when conformity to established norms was reinforced by the 'single address' mode characteristic of the fiction then usually offered to the young.

As a preamble to the discussion of several genres of children's literature which follows in Part Two of the current book, it is useful also to consider here another narrative concept derived from the work of Bakhtin, the chronotope. Maria Nikolajeva suggests that this is best defined as '"a unity of time and space" presented in a literary work' (1996: 121), and claims that specific forms of chronotope are unique to particular genres. The concept enables her to distinguish between, for instance, fantasy, which has a link with reality and our own time and space, and fairytale, in which 'both time and space are beyond our experience' (1996: 122). Furthermore, her analysis enables her to claim that:

■ narrative structures in children's literature are becoming more and more complicated. From relatively simple structures with a concrete place and a logically arranged, chronological action in epic stories, the chronotope develops into an intricate network of temporary and spatial relationships, which better reflect our own chaotic existence. (1996: 151) □

Thus it could be claimed that some of the theoretical ideas designed by the Russian theorist have proved to be powerful tools in the analysis of literature addressed to an audience younger than that he would have envisaged. They also help illuminate the ways in which literature and culture have changed throughout the past century.

Ideology and the responsibilities of children's authors

The changes in society and culture over the last half century, together with an increased appreciation of the extent to which young readers are acculturated by and through literature, have led educationalists and others working with young people to appreciate the importance of an awareness of the means used by writers to convey, explicitly or implicitly, what they consider to be appropriate attitudes to society and their role in it. Thus attention has been focused on how the ideological stance of an author is, often covertly, embedded in a children's text. Peter Hollindale[12] states that:

> ■ Our priority in the world of children's books should not be to promote ideology but to understand it, and find ways of helping others to understand it, including the children themselves. (2011: 36) □

Hollindale goes on to present a distinction between three levels of ideology. The first, which he terms 'active ideology', occurs when the author deliberately sets out to influence the reader, for instance towards anti-racist or anti-classist attitudes. As Hollindale observes, such writing can be seen as crudely didactic:

> ■ If writers present as natural and commonplace the behaviour they would *like* to be natural and commonplace, they risk muting the social effectiveness of stories. If they dramatize the social tensions, they risk a superficial ideological stridency. (2011: 38, italics original) □

As Hollindale indicates, those writers who opt to present their views less overtly take the risk of being misunderstood, something which, as he demonstrates, has occurred when 'the greatest anti-racist text in all literature, *Huckleberry Finn*' has been misread: 'you cannot experience the book as an anti-racist text unless you know *how to read a novel*' (2011: 38–39, italics original).

Hollindale's second level is passive ideology: 'the individual writer's unexamined assumptions' (2011: 39), which tend to 'reflect the writer's integration in a society which unthinkingly accepts them'. Thus it is likely that young readers will also take them for granted unless such assumptions are drawn to their attention. Still more likely to be invisible to young readers is Hollindale's third level, in which the ideology is latent within language itself: in the 2011 edition, he terms this third level 'organic ideology'.

Hollindale elucidates the three levels of ideology by an analogy with the human body. Our decisions on how to use our bodies, by adding to our original capacity such activities as playing games or driving a car, can be seen as paralleling active ideology. The bodily processes we take for granted because we share them with all other human beings – eating, drinking, sleeping and so on – can be regarded as equivalent to passive ideology, and only become visible to us when there are problems with them. Organic ideology he represents as similar to the changes in our bodies as we grow, develop, age and ultimately die. He claims:

> ■ Similarly, the organic ideology of the world we live in changes and dies. We may re-imagine the organic ideology which rules our forefathers, but we can never reoccupy it … Noticed or not, it seeps irresistibly into language, the way we write and the way we read. (2011: 42–3) □

Hollindale concluded the earlier version of his paper with a series of questions which can help readers to determine the ideology behind any chosen text (1991: 19–22). The later version, however, follows these with a detailed analysis of Nesbit's *The Railway Children* as an illustration of ideology in practice (2011: 52–75). This is insightful and thought-provoking and provides an excellent example of practical criticism.

Referring to the 1988 version of Hollindale's paper, Stephens describes it as 'the most comprehensive exploration of ideology and children's literature so far published', but indicates that more 'sophisticated narratological insights' are needed, something Stephens seeks to provide in his own work (1992: 11). Murray Knowles and Kirsten Malmkjaer (1996) also examine the question of ideology, but from a more explicitly linguistic perspective. Before summarising Hollindale's work (basing their synopsis on Hunt 1992: 9–11), they provide a brief account of a study, not specific to children's literature, by J.B. Thompson, which lists a number of modes and strategies which convey ideology and may be carried by narrative: 'As Thompson points out, narratives provide particularly fertile ground for the portrayal of social relations and the unfolding of consequences of actions "in ways that may establish and sustain relations of power"' (1996: 47),[13] while fiction in general affords a variety of opportunities to exercise further strategies. To illustrate their own categorisation, Knowles and Malmkjaer go on to provide detailed linguistic analyses of two children's texts: *Jane and the Dragon*[14] in connection with 'Collocation … the tendency for certain words in spoken and written texts to appear in the vicinity of others' (1996: 69); and Frances Hodgson

Burnett's *The Secret Garden* (1911) as a site for consideration of how the three linguistic systems embodied in the clause[15] perform the function of conveying the author's intended meaning. Their analysis, which draws on the work of Michael Halliday, is too detailed to be summarised here, but succeeds in demonstrating how 'linguistic analyses can be a powerful means of support for textual interpretation' (1996: 80).

A natural consequence of the recognition of the extent to which children's books can be instrumental in conveying ideology is the question of how far literary merit and challenge to the younger reader can justify the inclusion in the school curriculum of texts with controversial aspects. Such texts today may just as easily be ones which challenge the equality values of society as those which were a cause of concern to previous generations because of their explicit language about matters deemed to be unsuitable for young readers. This raises the topic of censorship: Nodelman and Reimer comment that 'Many adults are far more interested in determining what children should *not* [italics original] read than what and how they should read' (2003: 101). Distinguishing this from the positive process of selection is not always easy, but Nodelman and Reimer claim that their discussion of ideology 'suggests that ignorance is always likely to do more harm than knowledge can' (2002: 102). A key step, they claim, is for those who believe that censorship is to be resisted to be aware of any tendencies they themselves may have towards finding certain material disturbing. David Booth, in *Keywords* ((eds) Nel and Paul 2011: 26–30), traces the history of attempts to impose censorship on children's reading, but also shows how children's literature has 'provided a venue for resistance to censorship' (2011: 28).

Concern today is likely to be expressed over books that may convey a negative stereotype or inadequate image of certain groups, whether in terms of 'race', gender, sexual orientation or any other quality. Given the range of possible areas that may be regarded as causing offence, and the likelihood of future changes in society's perception of individuals and groups, what is needed is greater awareness by young readers. As Pat Pinsent points out:

> ■ in the long run, the only possible answer is to make children into critical readers, able to detect and withstand all forms of prejudice, however subtly they are conveyed. Paradoxically, one of the most effective ways of doing this is to help them to work through books which may not always be perfect in their adherence to contemporary views about equality. (1997: 41) □

Conclusion

It is evident that social attitudes are often most clearly displayed by the ways in which narratives are received and convey meaning, and that this is nowhere more important than in the instance of literature which anticipates an audience of children. In our rapidly changing society, affected by the many recent alternative modes of creating narrative, it is particularly interesting to note that, although in the recent past stories were likely to reach most young readers through the medium of print, many such tales have been shaped by having been told orally during countless previous periods. In an age when rapid technological developments are constantly causing changes in the material available to young people, it is salutary to observe the ways in which narrative in the past was affected by the far-reaching technological development of printing. Walter Ong explores the transition from orality to literacy, observing for instance how writing restructures consciousness. Among other aspects, he looks at the differences between oral and literate cultures in relation to narrative. He claims:

> ■ Although it is found in all cultures, narrative is in certain ways more widely functional in primary oral cultures than in others... [Because in them] knowledge cannot be managed in elaborate, more or less scientifically abstract categories ... oral cultures use stories of human action to store, organize and communicate much of what they know. Most ... oral cultures generate quite substantial narratives or series of narratives ... [which] are often the roomiest repositories of an oral culture's lore. (1982: 140) □

Ong goes on to point out how narrative 'can bond a great deal of lore in relatively substantial, lengthy items that are reasonably durable' (by contrast with short sayings such as proverbs, or 'nonce' occurrences like speeches). Some of the means used to fix narrative in the memory or attract the listeners' attention have had a considerable effect on plot and characterisation (for instance, the creation of 'flat' rather than 'rounded' characters). He claims that 'technologies of the word do not merely store what we know. They style what we know in ways which made it quite inaccessible and indeed unthinkable in an oral culture' (1982: 155). If then such significant changes in thought and narrative have come about over a relatively short period, it is to be expected that current and future developments in multimedia communication will have at least as notable an effect.

The focus in this and the two preceding chapters has largely been on the relationship between the author and narrator on the one hand and the real or implied reader on the other. In the four chapters which constitute Part Two, some of the more distinctive genres of children's literature will be examined.

PART II

Genres

CHAPTER FOUR

Fairytales[1]

Introduction

Some of the earliest scholarly approaches to children's literature emerged from work in the areas of child psychology and psychotherapy. It was perhaps inevitable that the main field of such explorations should be that of the fairytale, given Freud's emphasis on the formative role of childhood in the development of the psyche, together with the association of these stories with infancy.

An additional determining factor was that stories of this nature seem to be universal in their provenance, something which had also attracted attention from scholars of anthropology and folklore, who were fascinated by the similarities they detected between material from a variety of different cultures. In 1910 Finnish anthropologist Antti Aarne (1867–1925) produced a typology of folk tales[2] (including fairytales as a substantive element) based on the analysis of episodes; this, further refined by the American scholar Stith Thompson (1885–1976), became a relatively widely used instrument for those studying the tales. The Aarne–Thompson classification uses categories such as 'Animal Tales' and 'Jokes and Anecdotes', with most fairytales being described as 'ordinary tales'.[3] A number is allocated to each tale type as defined by a series of episodes: examples include 'The forbidden chamber', 'The children and the ogre' and 'My mother slew me', 'My father ate me'.[4] By contrast, the Russian formalist critic, Vladimir Propp (1895–1970), preferred to concentrate on the characters involved in such tales, listing these under the heading 'dramatis personae' and featuring for instance the villain, the helper and the hero. He also listed thirty-one functions in which, based on his analysis of one hundred tales, he claimed there was evidence for the involvement in the plots of such characters, also asserting that while not all the functions occurred in each tale, the order in which they did occur was universal.[5] Propp's classification of recurring character types and motifs in fairytales seemed to lend itself to analysis using Jungian archetypal patterns.

Universalist readings of fairytales have subsequently, however, been challenged by other critics, notably Jack Zipes. Some of this later criticism will also be examined in the current chapter.

The Freudian approach

Sigmund Freud (1856–1939) himself is well-known for having made use of myths (especially that of Oedipus who notoriously killed his father and married his mother) in an attempt to explain human behaviour. It is hardly surprising that those who looked at psychoanalysis from a Freudian perspective should turn their attention to those stories which are frequently presented to young children and in many instances verge on myth, which are called fairytales even though many of them do not include any beings from the world of 'faerie'. The best-known analysis of fairytales is that of Bruno Bettelheim (1903–1990), whose focus in his widely read *The Uses of Enchantment* (1976) was not on the pure play of children's imaginations, but on the bibliotherapeutic value of such tales in helping child readers to achieve maturity. His most influential work can be seen as arising from his desire to engage with earlier critics who had questioned the suitability of fairytales for children, and as a result of whose endeavours, he asserts, many children were deprived of the chance to meet fairytales other than in 'prettified and simplified versions which subdue their meaning and rob them of all deeper significance' (1978: 24). In attempting to understand the importance of these stories in relation to the inner life of the child, Bettelheim recounts how he himself came to realise that 'these tales, in a much deeper sense than any other reading material, start where the child really is in his psychological and emotional being' (1978: 6). Unlike modern stories, 'fairy tales [reveal] that a struggle against severe difficulties in life ... is an intrinsic part of human existence' and that it is possible to emerge from this struggle victorious (1978: 8). Later in the book he describes how:

■ Fairy tales underwent severe criticism when the new discoveries of psychoanalysis and child psychology revealed just how violent, anxious, destructive, and even sadistic a child's imagination is. (1978: 120) □

But 'those who outlawed traditional folk fairy tales', rather than acknowledging that for this reason tales which include violent elements were speaking to 'the inner mental life of the child ... decided that if there were monsters in a story told to children, these must all be friendly – but they missed the monster a child knows best and is most concerned with: the monster he feels and fears himself to be ...' (1978: 120).

Bettelheim consistently uses Freudian terminology in his explication of the underlying meanings he detects in the stories. For him, a triumph over a monster can be seen as

■ symbol[ising] the difficult battle we all have to struggle with: should we give in to the pleasure principle, which drives us to gain immediate satisfaction of our wants or to seek violent revenge for our frustrations ... or should we relinquish living by such impulses and settle for a life dominated by the reality principle, according to which we must be willing to accept many frustrations in order to gain lasting rewards? (1978: 33–4) □

Similarly Bettelheim's explications of 'Jack and the Beanstalk' and 'Snow White' emphasise the Oedipal motifs to be detected in parent figures, to the extent that tales like these 'permit the child to comprehend that not only is he jealous of his parent, but that the parent may have parallel feelings ... [and to reassure] the child that he need not be afraid of parental jealousy' (p.195).

Explanations such as these have seemed to some critics to provide an over-simplistic interpretation of the tales and to that extent, contrary to Bettelheim's intent, can seem a crude and mechanistic assessment of their value. Jack Zipes, whose work will be looked at in more detail later in this chapter, describes Bettelheim's analysis of 'Beauty and the Beast' in Freudian terms as 'unhistorical and too glib' (1983: 32). This somewhat reductive critique makes too little allowance for the way in which Bettelheim succeeded in redirecting critical attention towards these stories, and the extent to which his influence has shown little sign of diminishing in the more than forty years since his study appeared.

Maria Tatar's extensive work on fairytales challenges Bettelheim by reducing his emphasis on children's innate propensity for negative behaviour; she also shows how adults have used the tales, particularly in the nineteenth century, as means of controlling children. She has also extended Bettelheim's work by revealing the potential bond fairytales can create between adult and child readers (1993). Tatar's earlier study explores the extent of the violence in the Grimms' tales, while, paradoxically on a number of occasions the brothers deliberately avoided referring to everyday elements of the original tales such as pregnancy (1987; 1999: 366). One of her most important achievements in the field, however, is in grouping and providing introductions to a number of stories, from various origins, in *The Classic Fairy Tales*; she also provides a valuable series of excerpts from various theorists, including those mentioned above.

Despite the many subsequent adverse comments concerning Bettelheim's *The Uses of Enchantment*, notably by Jack Zipes and Marina Warner, it probably remains the best-known work of criticism on the subject of

fairytales. While his book may not have the validity sometimes attributed to it in the past, it has the merit of being controversial and thus
demanding attention, even if some of his contentions are finally rejected.

Jungian approaches

Carl Gustav Jung (1875–1961), originally associated with Freud, went
on to present an alternative approach to psychoanalysis, one that
employs a good many concepts which have been found useful by those
with a particular interest in literary studies. Again it is scarcely surprising that his followers should apply some of these concepts to fairytales.
One of the earliest of such studies is by Marie-Louise von Franz (1915–
98) whose pioneering text, *The Interpretation of Fairy Tales* (1970),[6] based
on a recording of a series of lectures she had given at the Jung Institute,
traces the history of fairytales from a Jungian perspective, asserting, for
instance, that fairytale is a form of 'decayed myth' (1982: 17); she goes
on to apply some of Jung's concepts, notably 'animus' and 'anima', to
chosen tales. Some years later, in describing the genesis of her book, she
observed that, with minor exceptions, 'no interpretations of fairy tales
had been published by Jungian authors at that time. That is why it was
my primary intention to open up the archetypal dimension of fairy tales
to the students'.[7] Talking of later Jungian scholars, she warns that some
of them have made too literal an identification between fairytale figures
and ordinary humans, and cautions:

■ in contrast to the heroes of adventurous sagas, the heroes and heroines
of fairy tales are abstractions ... archetypes ... In a personalistic interpretation, the very healing element of an archetypal narrative is nullified.[8] □

In her original work, we can see instances of her own practice in this
respect: for example, she relates the frequency of the figure of the King
in such tales to the centrality of the 'self' and the need for development
of its faculties, but warns that any such readings have to be taken in a
general rather than specific manner (1982: 37).

As von Franz indicates, subsequent to her original work there have
been many books interpreting fairytales from a Jungian angle. A recent
example is Susan Hancock's *The Child that Haunts Us* (2009), which
explores the application of Jungian psychoanalytic criticism both to fairytale and to fantasy more generally. Hancock prefaces her own analysis
(focusing on 'miniature' characters), with a useful account of relevant
archetypes: Anima, Animus, Child (whose relationships also bring in
references to the Mother, the Wise Old Man and the Wise Old Woman),
Shadow and Trickster.

Approaches related to child development

Not all explorations of the use of psychological approaches in relation to fairytales start from a psychoanalytic perspective; critics whose focus embraces the educational aspect are often more interested in developmental psychology, notably the work of Jean Piaget (1896–1980).[9] Nicholas Tucker's 1981 study, *The Child and the Book: A Psychological and Literary Exploration*, the subtitle of which reveals its combined perspectives, claims that Piaget's work helps to explain the continuing appeal of stories to children. Since children possess 'both a lasting desire to understand and be able to predict the course of familiar events, and also a natural curiosity that will want to investigate anything new' (1981: 42), they are likely to be attracted to 'fiction ... [which] usually portrays a simplified, cut-down version of reality which young minds may find particularly easy to understand ... they will also require a version of events that they can both grasp and sympathise with' (1982: 4). Such qualities are certainly to be found in fairytales.

In his chapter on fairy stories, myths and legends, Tucker starts by recalling the debates about the age of children for whom fairytales are suitable, with Froebel recommending them for kindergarten children and Montessori delaying their presentation until the age of seven (1982: 67). Rather than allocating a specific age range, Tucker applies insights from Piaget's developmental stages to show how stories shaped by 'regular chunks of repetition' in language and plot may be particularly appropriate to younger children who may feel at home in an environment which is 'often clear-cut and predictable' (1982: 73). At a slightly older age, the magic element of many stories may chime in with their imagination 'that they, or their parents, have the power to control physical events by the force of their wishes alone' (1982: 73). Some stories seek to 'explain natural phenomena in terms of human intervention long ago – a mental process described by Piaget as "artificialism" – which is certainly easier for the young to understand than any scientific explanation' (1982: 74). Tucker claims that 'magic in fairy-tales and magical beliefs in children themselves can both be arbitrary processes, appealed to at one moment, and ignored in favour of a more recognisable reality in the next' (1982: 74). The presence of 'humanised animals and magical human beings' supports the 'idea of a morally coherent and humanly motivated universe [which is] fundamental to a small child's outlook'; the development of an appreciation that the moral order is not organised like this is, according to Piaget, an important developmental stage (1982: 75–6). By catering for the 'mixed stage' (1982: 77), fairytales can be an invaluable resource.

David Gooderham (1995) also presents an analysis based on children's stages of development, in his case arguing for a classification dependent on perspectives contributed both by a Freudian theorist, Erik Erikson, and by a Jungian, Ravenna Helson. Since the examples he draws on are relevant to a wider range of fantasy texts than simply fairytales, some further information about his work is provided in Chapter Five.

Marxist/cultural materialist and feminist criticism

One of the most important and prolific theorists concerning the fairy-tale is Jack Zipes, whose original specialism in Germanic studies provided him with a wider perspective on the development of the fairytale than that of a number of other researchers.[10] Unlike many scholars, including those cited above, he exhibits a distrust of psychoanalysis; in a recent interview he states, 'I am very wary of Jungian and Freudian psychology and don't believe that they offer fundamental explanations of how tales, especially fairy tales, originate and are disseminated'.[11]Rather, his life's work has been devoted to showing how storytelling reflects human adaptation to changing environments of all kinds. He claims:

■ Tales emanate from concrete experience that stimulates the mind and imagination. They are *historically* [italics original] specific articulations of shared experience ... The fact that there are amazing similarities in tale types throughout the world has less to do with a collective unconscious or archetypes in our imagination than with natural and culturally defined human responses and reactions to similar manifestations in environments.[12] □

This fundamentally Marxist/materialist perspective has characterised Zipes's work from its beginning. His first major contribution to the criticism of fairytale, *Breaking the Magic Spell* (1979), was one of the earliest critical works in English to adopt a Marxist perspective; in it he emphasised the importance of researching the oral folk tale, which he claimed was adapted, from the late seventeenth century onwards, into a literary genre. Here, and in *Fairy Tales and the Art of Subversion* (1983), he illustrates how Perrault and others from the late seventeenth and early eighteenth century, such as Madame d'Aulnoy and Madame Leprince de Beaumont, were responsible for 'the literary "bourgeoisification" of the oral folk tale, and paved the way for founding a children's literature which would be useful for introducing manners to children of breeding' (1991: 27). In the later text, he illustrates this process with reference particularly to 'Beauty and the Beast', the treatment of which by Bettelheim occasions the negative critique of his work as 'unhistorical' which is quoted above. Zipes continues:

■ The pseudo-Freudian approach to literature suggests that children are born with basic fears, anxieties, and wishes. But if we examine the development of the individual and family in different societies in relation to the civilizing process, we can see that instinctual drives are conditioned and largely determined through interaction and interplay with the social environment. (1983/91: 32) □

Later chapters give attention to the way in which the oeuvres of the Brothers Grimm (the subject of a later study by Zipes), Hans Andersen, George MacDonald, Oscar Wilde and Frank Baum were all the product of interaction between the writers and the social contexts in which they wrote. Additionally, a substantial chapter is devoted to how fairytales were used in twentieth-century Germany as instruments of socialisation, both within the Weimar Republic (by both conservatives and radicals) and by the Nazis. The 'Nordic cultural heritage' was idealised:

■ In regard to the family, the elements of fertility, the assertive courageous prince, the virtuous self-sacrificing mother, and industrious children could be viewed as the qualities which went into the making of an ideal Germanic family. (1983/91: 151) □

Zipes shows how, despite this ostensible exaltation of the family, in fact:

■ the Nazi interpretation of the tales stressed elements which suited their policies, i.e. community and race over family, the king and realm over all. (1991: 151) □

In the final chapter of this book, headed 'The Liberating Potential of the Fantastic in Contemporary Fairy Tales for Children', Zipes goes on to describe 'two major types of experimentation which have direct bearing on cultural patterns in the West' (1983/91: 180): the transfiguration of the classical fairytale and 'the fusion of traditional configurations with contemporary references' (1983/91: 180), citing among other fairytale creators the feminist groups who have transformed the inadequate portrayal of female characters which is all too frequent in the traditional tales.

In the same year as the original publication of *Fairy Tales and the Art of Subversion,* Zipes also produced the first edition of *The Trials and Tribulations of Little Red Riding Hood,* though a revised and expanded edition 'intended to strengthen [his] argument' appeared in 1993. Zipes contends that 'Perrault transformed a hopeful oral tale about the initiation of a young girl into a tragic one of violence in which the girl is blamed for her own violation' (1993: 7). He illustrates his thesis with a substantial collection of versions dating from 1697 to 1990, claiming that the tale was in effect transformed into a 'story of rape' (1993: 14), though he also exemplifies the way in which it has subsequently been reframed by feminists and others in order to establish 'principles of social justice and gender equality that have not been satisfactorily practiced [sic] in Western societies' (1993: 343). In his Prologue, Zipes gives some attention to another writer who attempted to set 'Red Riding Hood' in a historical focus, Robert Darnton.[13] While applauding Darnton's insistence on the importance of taking into account 'the material conditions that brought about distinct world views in folk tales', Zipes claims that Darnton bases his conclusions on a debatable version of the tale, one that lacked a happy ending, and thus he 'distort[s] a female perspective as expressed in the oral tale' (1993: 3–4).

A similar motivation to restore the gender balance is to be detected in another collection of tales edited by Zipes, *Don't Bet on the Prince* (1986): he states his aim here as being:

■ to bring together material which will enable us to understand the vitality of the fairy tale and the significance of the transformations which have taken place in the last 15 years. (1986: xiv) □

His title provides an ironic reflection of the way in which Prince Charming or some similar figure is expected to step in to rescue a heroine incapable of saving herself from oppression, as in 'Cinderella'.[14]

As Zipes makes clear, a number of traditional tales had already been adapted by feminist writers before the 1986 publication of *Don't Bet on the Prince*.[15] Alongside these was an increasing amount of criticism from feminist writers such as Sandra Gilbert and Susan Gubar (*The Madwoman in the Attic*, 1979) and Karen Rowe ('To spin a yarn: The female voice in folklore and fairy tale', in Ruth Bottigheimer's *Fairy Tales and Society*, 1986).[16] The best-known study from a feminist point of view, however, is Marina Warner's *From the Beast to the Blonde* (1994).

The main focus in the first part of Warner's study is on the storytellers, frequently women, whose situation inevitably mirrors the societies from which they were drawn. She observes:

■ Prejudices against women, especially old women and their chatter, belong in the history of fairy tale's changing status, for the pejorative image of the gossip was sweetened by influences from the tradition of the Sibyls and the cult of Saint Anne, until the archetypal crone at the hearth could emerge as a mouthpiece of homespun wisdom. (1994: xx) □

Like Zipes, Warner has little that is positive to say about Bettelheim's ahistorical treatment of the material. For instance, in discussing the many tales in which stepmothers are present, she quotes at some length his Freudian analysis which sees this feature as a means to enable the child to 'split' the 'benevolent and threatening aspects' of their parents, so that:

> ■ The fantasy of the wicked stepmother not only preserves the good mother intact, it also prevents having to feel guilty about one's angry thoughts and wishes about her. (Bettelheim, *The Uses of Enchantment*, quoted by Warner 1994: 212) □

Warner describes this theory as 'extremely persuasive' as 'a convincing emotional stratagem', but deplores the fact that it 'has contributed to the continuing absence of good mothers from fairy tales in all kinds of media, and to a dangerous degree which itself mirrors current prejudices and reinforces them'. In particular, his argument and its diffusion have:

> ■ effaced from memory the historical reasons for women's cruelty within the home and have made such behaviour seem natural, even intrinsic to the mother-child relationship ... This archetypal approach leeches history out of fairy tale. (1994: 213) □

Warner goes on to claim that:

> ■ the absent mother can be read literally as exactly that: a feature of the family before our modern era, when death in childbirth was the most common cause of female mortality, and surviving orphans would find themselves brought up by their mother's successor ... When a second wife entered the house, she often found herself and her children in competition – often for scarce resources – with the surviving offspring of the earlier marriage, who may well have appeared to threaten her own children's place in their father's affection too. (1994: 213) □

Another related field that Zipes is concerned with is that of socio-cultural criticism, particularly in relation to the 'culture industry' as applied to retellings or film versions of fairytales. One of his main targets is the 'Disneyfication' of stories of both literary and oral provenance. His essay 'Breaking the Disney Spell'[17] asserts that Disney, from a stance dominated by a 'radicalism of the right and the righteous', 'changed our way of viewing fairy tales ...[in order to] reinforce the social and political status quo' ((ed.) Tatar 1999: 333). In an analysis (Tatar 1999: 343–5) of 'Puss in Boots', he shows how the 1922 Disney film changed the focus of Perrault's story from the cat to the young man, no longer a peasant as in the original version, but a form of entrepreneur, a figure particularly dear to American society at that date and probably also representing Walt Disney's own ambitions. Similarly, in the films featuring heroines (*Snow White, Cinderella, Sleeping Beauty*), the young women 'are helpless ornaments in need of protection' (p.349), while the active work of cleaning up the world, which is intended to reveal Disney as on the side of justice, is performed by male figures, such as the seven dwarfs. Zipes concludes by listing a series of ways in which Disney himself, and later his corporation, changed the fairytale, basically making the stories one-dimensional, possessing a simplicity that denies the work of all the theorists on the subject. While there is some justice in Zipes' negative criticism, it could be argued that his approach ignores the multi-modal pleasures of animated film: instead he treats the film adaptations of these tales as mere repositories of written narratives. In his 1997 volume, Zipes extends his study of 'the culture industry', widening his scope to consider other areas (even including a basketball game) where he feels that the original impulse of storytelling has been distorted.

Zipes' more recent work, as presented in *Why Fairy Tales Stick* (2000) and *Relentless Progress* (2009), suggests reasons, based on understandings of the brain, evolutionary psychology, and the theory of memetics, for the prevalence and lasting impact of fairytales. This is conveniently summarised by Zipes in the interview with John Smelcer mentioned above:

■ The theory of memetics generally maintains that a meme is an informational pattern contained in a human brain (or in artifacts such as books or pictures) and stored in its memory, capable of being copied to another individual's brain that will store it and replicate it. □

■ Though memetics remains a hypothetical, if not speculative science, it seems to me that it offers a viable way to explore how the brains of humans function to store and disseminate tales, and among the tales we tell that deal with profound human and social problems are fairy tales which deal with sibling rivalry, jealousy, rape, violence, incest, infertility, reproduction, abuse, etc. The fairy tale is a hybrid genre that has evolved over thousands of years, and it offers a unique narrative mode that has developed and expanded with new means of technology. Today, certain fairy tales can be found throughout the world in startlingly different variants that bear resemblances to one another.[18] □

Paradoxically, Zipes would appear here to be celebrating a quality that he has previously deplored.

In his 2009 volume, Zipes applies this theory to the well-known tale, 'The Frog Prince', describing the evolution of this story and the various versions supplied by the Grimms, and comparing them with others still extant, including cinematic treatments of the story. He concludes that:

> ■ 'The Frog Prince' exists as meme in millions of brains ... as long as men and women, whether heterosexual or homosexual, develop mating strategies that stem from their natural dispositions and mental capacities to make sexual choices influenced by changing social codes, 'The Frog Prince' will play a role in the discourse about mating as a social symbolic act that will enable us to understand the ramifications of decisions that we seem to make freely and decisions that are made for us. (2009: 119) □

It is evident that, whether or not readers accept his arguments, Zipes has contributed a vast amount to theoretical studies of a genre established from time immemorial but still incredibly powerful today.

Conclusion: Studies by writers of children's fiction

Other theoretical studies of fairytales are less easy to classify under the above headings. Three of the most distinguished writers of these studies are at least as well-known for their fiction for young people as for their criticism on the subject. The scholarly work of Katharine Briggs (1898–1980) has provided the foundation for many academic studies of fairytales. Her 'encyclopaedic surveys ... [trace] the connections between literature and folk belief, particularly fairy lore, during the centuries of transition between medieval and modern times' (Suzanne Rahn, in (ed.) Zipes 2000: 63). Briggs is also well-known as a writer of children's fiction, her two novels having been 'drawn from the depths of her scholarship in British fairy lore' (Zipes 2000: 63). J.R.R. Tolkien's influential essay 'On Fairy-Stories', based on a lecture given in 1938 and originally published in 1947, is, despite its title, really a broader study of the fantasy genre which throws light on his own fiction. Partly in response to the work of Tolkien, his friend and fellow writer, C.S. Lewis, also wrote several essays which again probably throw more light on his own writing than on the subject in general. Consequently, the work of both these important theorists, alongside that of other writers about fantasy, is discussed in Chapter Five.

CHAPTER FIVE

Fantasy

Introduction: The value of fantasy

'Fantasy doesn't really relate to the real world.' Thus Joanna Trollope, author of a reworking of Jane Austen's *Sense and Sensibility*, is quoted in *The Sunday Times* (6/10/13) as saying. Fantasy stories, she also observes, give 'little moral guidance' to the young.[1] While Trollope seems to be taking a narrow view of fantasy, confined to series such as *Twilight* and *The Hunger Games* that address teenagers, there is no doubt that children's fiction presenting what might variously be termed as imaginary, make-believe, magic or mythic worlds has attracted censure from at least the eighteenth century. In spite of this, a number of writers and critics have argued that this perennially popular genre is in some instances the best or indeed the only way to express truths and perceptions that lie beyond consensus 'reality'. A markedly contrasting view to that of Trollope was stated by Salman Rushdie in a BBC Television programme in 1990: 'Fantasy is not escapism: it is a way of defining and dreaming the world.'[2] Consistent with this more positive approach is the way in which fantasy is often used as a vehicle for psychological, philosophical or religious explorations, instead of the socio-historical data more appropriate to realistic fiction.

Like many other important entities, fantasy is easier to recognise than to define, for attempts to do so usually demand a complementary encounter with the equally elusive meaning of such terms as 'reality' or 'realism'. It could be claimed, however, that it is only at the borders between genres that definitions start to matter. In some senses, as Peter Hunt observes, 'all fiction could be called fantasy, as it necessarily presents a version of the world differing from pragmatic reality' (2001: 271). Children's literature itself might be regarded as necessarily fantasy, since 'all adults writing about childhood are describing a world they can no longer directly experience' any more than authors can enter their own invented worlds (Matthew Grenby 2008: 145). In the attempt to narrow the perspective from all fiction or all children's fiction, while allowing discussion of a wide range of material, the focus in the current chapter will be on all forms of departure from a consensual understanding of the everyday world other than fairytale.[3] This breadth is in line with the approach of Kathryn Hume who states, 'By fantasy I mean the deliberate departure from the limits of what is usually accepted as real and normal' (1984: xii). In contrast, Colin Manlove gives a fairly detailed definition of fantasy as 'a fiction evoking wonder and containing a substantial and irreducible element of supernatural or impossible worlds, beings or objects with which the mortal characters in the story or the readers become at least partly on familiar terms' (1975: vii). While he justifies the minutiae of his definition in relation to his chosen subjects,[4] who straddle the boundaries between children's and adult fiction, its general applicability is perhaps more debatable, and it seems easier here to allow such details to emerge in the course of discussion of specific writers.[5]

In her Preface, Hume challenges the 'western cultural bias in favour of imitation' (1984: 12) which she finds implicit in, for instance, Erich Auerbach's *Mimesis: The Representation of Reality in Western Literature* (1953); later she indicates how her study is intended to illumine some of 'the numerous ways in which fantasy's complex power over our imaginations can be exploited' (1984: 196). Hume's illustrative material is generally drawn from literature for adults; Karen Coats observes that a good deal of theoretical writing about fantasy (such as Tzvetan Todorov, *The Fantastic*, 1975, and Rosemary Jackson, *Fantasy: the Literature of Subversion*, 1981) has relatively little to say about children's literature, though in some cases their work may be applicable to fiction which anticipates a young adult audience (2010: 85).

Even if much theoretical writing about fantasy has little direct relevance to children's literature, some of what is said concerning its value is nevertheless applicable here. In particular, it seems worth quoting at some length from Hume's summative comments: she refuses to regard fantasy as a separate genre, claiming instead that 'fantasy and mimesis seem more usefully viewed as the twin impulses behind the creation of literature'. She suggests that while mimesis, even if it does not involve fantasy, can perform its function of being a mirror to the similarities between our world and that portrayed in fiction, fantasy has other possible contributions to make:

■ [Fantasy] provides the novelty that circumvents automatic responses and cracks the crust of *habitude* [italics original]. Fantasy also encourages intensity of engagement, whether through novelty or psychological manipulations. In addition, fantasy provides meaning systems to which we can try relating our selves, our feelings, and our data. In other words, it asserts relationship. Fantasy also encourages the condensation of images which allows it to affect its readers at many levels and in so many different ways. And it helps us envision possibilities that transcend the purely material world which we accept as quotidian reality. □

■ Novelty, intensity, relationship, condensation, and transcendence of the material and the materialistic: without these qualities, literature would only be able to affect our sense of meaning in limited, rational ways – and ultimately, meaning is not a rational matter. Reason can only deal with the material universe, and few people get enough intensity or assurance from that to find scientific truth an entirely satisfactory frame of meaning. (1984: 195–6) □

Hume's analysis of the potential of fantasy to free the faculties of the human mind without its being anchored to materiality or scientific explanations probably helps explain the appeal to writers exploring the nature of humanity and our situation in the universe. Many of the fantasy writers whose work will be considered in what follows certainly seem to have taken advantage of such qualities of fantasy. In this they are heirs to a tradition which embraces Homer, Virgil, Dante and Milton, whose imaginations were not bounded by the confines of everyday life.

In relation to these epic writers, it is worth note that Ann Swinfen also cites the author of *The Divine Comedy*: 'To Dante ... the imaginative faculty ... was divinely inspired, offering a dimension of creativity going beyond man's empirical experience' (1984: 3). By their nature, epics such as his transcend the limitations of the here and now – and it is not irrelevant to link them with writers such as Tolkien and Pullman whose invented worlds present their protagonists (and their readers) with the kind of questions about human nature and the meaning of the universe which could not be posed by fiction whose horizons were those of the material world. Like Hume, Swinfen refuses to collude with the viewpoint that fantasy has no link with the 'real' world; she claims:

■ Fantasy is about reality – about the human condition ... its major difference from the realist novel is that it takes account of areas of experience – imaginative, subconscious, visionary – which free the human spirit to range beyond the limits of empirical primary world reality ... The fundamental purpose of serious fantasy is to comment upon the real world and to explore moral, philosophical and other dilemmas posed by it. (1984: 231) □

Perhaps, however, the major justification for fantasy literature is its primacy in all periods before the rise of realist fiction at the end of the sixteenth century, and the fact that, even since that date, it has not only been the mode chosen for influential literary works,[6] but has also intruded – sometimes in the form of dreams, ghost stories and other flights of fancy – into novels otherwise almost exclusively realist.[7] Perhaps the single common element to all fantasy is that it is, as indicated by John Stephens, 'a *metaphoric* mode, and realism [is] a *metonymic* mode' (1992: 248; italics original).

The range and classification of fantasy

While from some points of view any attempts to categorise different types of fantasy might seem to be an idle exercise (albeit one in which scholars have frequently indulged), the reason for attempting it here is that, given the impossibility of referring to criticism about each individual author, observation of the aspects considered worth critical discussion for particularly prominent authors of a specific type of writing can help provide guidelines for others from the same or related sub-genres. An endeavour therefore will be made here to distinguish between the varieties of fantasy most popular in children's literature from the middle of the twentieth century onwards, as a means to present some of the critical approaches that have been taken. The broad definition of fantasy given above inevitably means that subdivision into different kinds is both essential and controversial: disagreement about the placing of individual texts is inevitable, and any schema should be seen as merely a framework for discussion.

The number of possible classifications is potentially vast. David Gooderham argues for a division dependent on a combination of insights derived from the Freudian psychologist Erik Erikson (1950) and the Jungian Ravenna Helson (1973). He presents an analysis based on children's stages of development, concluding that there are 'a number of fantasy elements which occur in many and varied relationships in these texts' (1995: 182). He identifies these as: incorporation (metaphorically indicated by womb-like enclosures); disappearance, reappearance, power, magic; the heroic; invention and achievement; and devotion and self-realisation. More than one of these, he observes, may occur in a single literary text. His classification has perhaps most to offer in a pedagogical context; while there may indeed be developmental aspects to the kind of fantasy appropriate to specific age ranges, it is convenient here to employ a more widely established classification, while recognising that some texts will cut across any imposed categories.

The term 'high' fantasy is often applied to fantasy totally set in a secondary world, in which characters and their deeds tend to resemble those of epic. This terminology is not used here, despite consideration being given to such texts, because it seems to imply that fantasies excluding any interaction with 'our' world are in some way superior to those where characters may move from one world to another, or those confined to 'our' world. My headings resemble but are not identical with those presented by Peter Hunt:

■ 'other world' fantasies; ... future fantasies (often merging into Science Fiction ...); books in which magic intrudes into the contemporary world ... ; dreams ...; excursions into other, parallel worlds ...; animal fantasies.... (2001: 271)[8] □

My starting point is the distinction between fantasy which in one way or another presents secondary worlds, and that which confines the 'make-believe' to a significant alteration in certain aspects of 'our' world (such as the laws of nature, the limitations or varieties of species, the time/space continuum, etc.). I have subdivided this further in order to take into account some of the modes of fantasy most frequently encountered in children's literature. Illustrative critical material is, with the exception of Tolkien, drawn from discussion of post-1950 texts, significant in their own right as well as being representative of the form of fantasy under discussion. It should however be emphasised that no system of categorising fantasy can be absolute; not only will every theorist arrive at a different grouping, but also many of the individual texts defy any rigid categorisation, so that arguments could be adduced for placing them in different categories. Critical texts about specific authors often raise more general questions concerning the kind of fantasy that is being discussed; comment more specific to these texts, notably that of a biographical or bibliographic nature, has been omitted from consideration.

Other-world fantasies

Texts entirely or partially set in secondary worlds have the scope to pose questions of a theological and philosophical nature, whereas fantasy set in 'our' world may be limited by the exigencies of daily life. The conditions within invented worlds have to be fully elucidated in the text, and such books are often furnished with maps. This means that readers are not confronted with the implicit demand of historical fiction, of knowing something about the 'real' time and space setting. Instead, readers are free to empathise with characters placed in a fictional situation, without any barriers being created by the knowledge that it all happened in a 'real' past about which it is possible to learn.

The total fictionality of the worlds created by writers such as J.R.R. Tolkien, Ursula Le Guin and Michelle Paver enables them to examine issues such as loyalty, betrayal, ambition and the role of women, without the need to provide a setting in place and time which could distract readers from such issues. Nevertheless, to imply that such fantasies are in some way superior to those in which some at least of the characters originate from 'our' world appears artificial, given that similar issues are explored within both the primary and secondary worlds portrayed by C.S. Lewis and Philip Pullman. As Farah Mendlesohn observes about Diana Wynne Jones, some of whose fiction portrays other worlds, 'Fantasy – like science fiction – provides the playground for thought experiment' (2005: xv). Nor do all critics take a positive view of Tolkien's exclusivist brand of fantasy: Pullman cites with approval Goldthwaite's observation in *The Natural History of Make-Believe* (1996) that 'such fantasy is both escapist and solipsistic: seeking to flee the complexities and compromises of the real world for somewhere nobler altogether ... The result is a hollowness, a falsity' (2001: 661).

Tolkien, sub-creator and theorist

While disavowing any suggestion of superiority, it is convenient to look first at fantasies in which the secondary world is totally distinct from today's world. Sometimes, as in Tolkien's stories about 'Middle-Earth', it is suggested that the events occurred in some remotely past period before recorded history; a similar device has been used more recently by Michelle Paver in her six-novel 'Chronicles of Ancient Darkness' (2004–9). Ursula Le Guin's 'Earthsea' series (1968–2001), consisting of five novels and a short-story collection, is set in a cluster of islands where the existence of wizards and dragons is taken for granted, as indeed is the need for a school for wizards.

There is little doubt, however, that it is the work of Tolkien which has received the greatest critical attention. This is partly because of his eminence as a philologist and literary scholar during his Oxford career, but also, arguably, because his books have been turned into major commercial cinematographic ventures. Tolkien created his own mythology: both *The Hobbit* (1937) and *The Lord of the Rings* (1954–5) are set in a secondary world to which access is impossible for present-day humans. Although the latter saga was not addressed primarily to young readers, its three volumes have certainly been read by many of them, though these have probably subsequently been outnumbered by those experiencing his invented world through films and computer games.

Tolkien also contributed very significantly to the theoretical understanding of fantasy.[9] Despite its title, his essay 'On Fairy-Stories', which originated in a lecture given at the University of St Andrew's in 1938, is really about his own understanding of fantasy, underlying his own fiction. He himself indicates that it 'may ... be found interesting, especially by those to whom *The Lord of the Rings* has given pleasure' (1975: 9).

The kinds of imaginative writing that for various reasons he excludes from consideration (*Gulliver's Travels* (1726), beast fables, dreams etc.) are evidently those which differ as fantasies from his own brand. He claims that the stories that truly relate to the world of 'faerie' create in readers a desire for a richer and more beautiful world, even if its inhabitants include such dangerous elements as dragons (p.44). Another characteristic is the sense that such worlds are separated from us by an immeasurable abyss of time (p.36); any elements which were originally historical (as in the case of Arthurian Romance), have been transformed and combined with elements from other stories, as if all these constituents had been in 'a Pot of Soup, the Cauldron of Story' (p.32). He goes on to present his own views about the 'sub-creative Art' of fantasy, which 'is founded on … a recognition of fact, but not a slavery to it'. He relates the human propensity for this kind of sub-creation to the divine: 'we make … because we are made: and not only made, but made in the image and likeness of a Maker' (p.37).

Perhaps the section of Tolkien's treatise most often cited is that relating to what he sees as fantasy's essential elements: Recovery – seeing with a fresh eye what might appear trite and everyday in 'our' world; Escape – from grim 'realities' such as hunger, poverty, pain and death; and the Consolation of the happy ending, or in a term Tolkien coined, the *Eucatastrophe*: 'It does not deny the existence of *dyscatastrophe*, of sorrow and failure: the possibility of these is necessary to the joy of deliverance; it denies… universal final defeat [thus] … giving a fleeting glimpse of Joy' (p.68). In his Conclusion he spells out explicitly the link for him as a Christian between this Joy and the Gospel story (*evangelium* or 'good news') which 'begins and ends in joy' (p.71) (italics original).

Despite Tolkien's conviction about the link between, on the one hand, divine creative and redemptive activity, and, on the other, the sub-creation engaged in by writers of fantasy, relatively little literary criticism of his own fiction has considered it from a religious perspective.[10] Essays in the two collections edited by Neil Isaacs and Rose Zimbardo (1968 and 1981) present some early material from his contemporaries as a basis for critical discussion and look particularly at *The Lord of the Rings*, exploring for instance the presentation of heroism and the effect of Tolkien's philological expertise on aspects of his novels. Collections of this kind can be of particular value to the student; in combining the insights of a wide range of well-respected scholars, they often present a better-rounded picture of a writer than those journals which specialise in the work of a single author, with a tendency to attract contributors with a 'single-issue' focus on the writer concerned.

Other essential critical reading on Tolkien includes Paul Kocher (1972); this has the merit, for the student of children's literature, of examining *The Hobbit* in itself instead of merely as a forerunner to the longer trilogy. Kocher also engages to some extent with the question of religion. The focus in Thomas Shippey's analysis (1982) is linguistic, while the second edition of Brian Rosebury's *Tolkien: A Cultural Phenomenon* (1992; 2004) adds scrutiny of the films and other media to his previous book-based perspective. William Gray (2009) provides a valuable link to literature in other languages by exploring the relationship between some major English writers of fantasy and German Romanticism. More recently, *A Companion to J.R.R. Tolkien* (2014), edited by Stuart Lee, includes contributions from many eminent Tolkien scholars. Although its scope goes well beyond Tolkien's writing for children, the way in which his fiction is placed within an academic, literary, linguistic and more general context makes it an essential source of information for the student of Tolkien. Essays in this collection also give attention to film, television and game adaptions of his work.

Secondary worlds entered from 'our' world

It should be evident that the substantial critical attention given to the fiction of Tolkien both pinpoints the importance of 'other world' fantasy and indicates some of the directions which the criticism of fantasy has taken. Invented worlds such as Tolkien's offer scope for exploring the nature of the universe in which we actually live. The same is true of fantasies where the human characters start from 'our' world and, whether deliberately or accidentally, enter, through some kind of portal, one or more secondary worlds which differ from ours in key aspects; because of these links with the more familiar, this kind of mixed fantasy is by its nature probably more immediately accessible to younger readers.

Among the many distinguished writers of popular fantasy texts which set the world of everyday 'reality' against world(s) which differ from it in such aspects as history or the kind of inhabitants, are C.S. Lewis, Alan Garner, Diana Wynne Jones, Susan Cooper, Philip Pullman and Helen Dunmore.[11] As well as inspiring a good deal of critical comment, many of these have also written important essays about fantasy in general and their own fiction within this genre. One of the most relevant of these is Lewis's essay, 'On three ways of writing for children',[12] which probably provides more insights into his own fantasy than do most of the studies about it. He claims that to write a children's story because 'a children's story is the best art-form for something you have to say' is not only one of the best ways to write for children, but also the only one he himself could ever use (1980: 208). He goes on to assert the value of fantasy for all age groups, emphasising that it is far from being escapist: rather, by not deceiving the reader into thinking it depicts reality, it facilitates a deeper understanding of this world and of character.

Lewis's seven-novel 'Narnia' saga (1950–6), and to a lesser extent his 'Perelandra' space trilogy, published between 1938 and 1945 and certainly accessible to teenagers, have attracted a good deal of critical attention, particularly given his reputation as a religious polemicist and the undoubtedly theological messages which his books convey, even in light of his rebuttal of any suggestion that they are allegorical. Probably the most illuminating of these studies, and the ones which raise the most issues relevant to other fantasy writers, are those by Peter Schakel (1979) and Colin Manlove (1987). Schakel's book is probably the first to treat the Narnia books from a predominantly literary point of view; he makes use of the work of Northrop Frye to trace thematic patterns. Manlove focuses on similar aspects, charting some of Lewis's use of symbolism; additionally, like Gray in his later study, he suggests some well-supported links between Lewis and MacDonald. Susan Hancock links her Jungian readings of Tolkien and Lewis with an identification in the work of the former of 'idealising and sublimating aspects of the feminine'; Lewis's saga, on the other hand, shows, she suggests, 'a lack of reconciliation between male and female' (2005: 54). More recently, a volume on Lewis has appeared in the 'New Casebooks' series; edited by Michelle Ann Abate and Lance Weldy, it not only embraces traditional approaches to criticism such as textual analysis, but also scrutinises the transfer of Lewis's work to film and new media. A rather more negative approach to Lewis has notoriously been taken by Philip Pullman, whose very different attitude towards religion perhaps accounts for his distaste at being often grouped with the older author as writing the same kind of fantasy. Pullman describes the Lewis who wrote the Narnia books (as distinct from the writer of 'On three ways of writing for children') as a 'paranoid bigot' (2001: 660), because of what he sees as Lewis's rejection of the physical pleasures of this world.

Pullman's comment about Lewis, together with his unfavourable opinion of Tolkien, quoted earlier, perhaps illuminates his own writing more than that of his predecessors. He goes on to demand from fantasy a connection with the everyday, with 'people [who] behave like us, with the full range of human feelings' (2001: 662). There is no doubt that the major part of the critical attention paid to Pullman's own work focuses on the *His Dark Materials* trilogy (1995–2000), although he has written many other books for young readers, including other fantasy novels.[13] The omission of Pullman's other works does not however apply to Nicholas Tucker (2003), who not only sets the trilogy in the context of Pullman's other writing, but also usefully provides the text of the essay which Pullman has declared to be a major influence, Heinrich von Kleist's 'On the Marionette Theatre' (1810; translated by Idris Parry). Pullman's ambivalent attitude towards the genre of fantasy as such is exposed by William Gray; he begins by quoting Pullman's reluctant agreement to his stories being called fantasy at all; his dislike of the term relates to his often repeated insistence that his work presents characters with real human feelings in real situations (2009: 153).

There are several collections of essays on Pullman; the studies in the collection edited by Millicent Lenz with Carole Scott (2005) scrutinise areas such as the relationship between fantasy and human nature, the use of intertextuality and the theological and science fiction affiliations of his writing. Burton Hatlen's chapter on Pullman's relationship to Tolkien and Lewis also makes a link with one of Pullman's main sources, Milton's *Paradise Lost* (1667; 1674), while Pullman's debt to Blake forms the subject of Susan Matthews' contribution. Other recent appraisals of Pullman's work include a special issue of *The Journal of Children's Literature Studies* (7(1), March 2010) which carries a paper by Anne-Marie Bird, one of the most perceptive commentators on his text. The most recent contribution to Pullman scholarship is a volume in the Palgrave 'New Casebooks' series; as well as discussing areas such as religion, gender and the filming of the first book of the trilogy, this includes an interview with Pullman himself.

It is arguable that fantasy involving worlds entered from the everyday is not only the most popular variety with young readers but also the one which has attracted some of the major talents among children's writers. It is impossible here to do justice to criticism concerning notable children's authors such as Alan Garner and Diana Wynne Jones,[14] both of whom have not only created imagination-gripping secondary worlds but have also provided illuminating essays about their own fantasy. Farah Mendlesohn discusses Jones's extended critical papers, which address both her own work and that of Tolkien, looking particularly at the qualities of the hero character (2005: xvii–xxii). Mendlesohn concludes her monograph with an epilogue which describes Jones' oeuvre, both critical and creative, as 'a thirty-year-long argument about teaching children to read and about what reading and reading the fantastic mean' (2005: 196).

A collection of writing by Alan Garner (1997) mostly comprises lectures he has given at conferences; it reveals a good deal about the background to his own writing but does not provide general criticism on fantasy as such. The most important critical discussion of Garner's own writing is Neil Philip's *A Fine Anger*. Although this study was published as long ago as 1981, the fact that Garner has written relatively little children's fiction since that date means that it has by no means become outdated. Only his early novels, *The Weirdstone of Brisingamen* (1960), *The Moon of Gomrath* (1963) and *Elidor* (1965), really belong to the type of fantasy currently being discussed;[15] all of these, Philip claims, reflect how Garner transmutes the folklore and historical sources which underlie his writing: 'the research is a way of validating and containing the vision' (1981: 64).

Charles Butler's *Four British Fantasists* (2006) associates Garner and Jones with Penelope Lively and Susan Cooper as authors who 'share a profound concern with time, myth, magic, the nature of personal identity, and the potency of place' (2006: 7). Interestingly, they all have in common the experience of having been a child during the Second World War, and having studied at Oxford during a period when both Tolkien and Lewis lectured there[16] (though Garner left without completing his degree). Butler suggests that the significance of the two older writers lies less in their direct influence than in the literary reception of the writing of the younger group, and the way in which the prestige of Lewis and Tolkien provided a kind of licence to invent secondary worlds. Butler shows how these fantasy worlds are deeply rooted in British myth and legend, and concludes that they all offer the reader an experience of how, in our lives, the 'border between the mundane and the magical ... blurs and shifts' (2006: 274). Finally, an alternative slant on Garner's work is provided in Nicholas Clark's exploration of the poetic, artistic and musical sources of inspiration for *Elidor* (*Journal of Children's Literature Studies*, 8:2, July 2011).

This-world fantasy

'Magic' elements in our world

Several of the writers named above, notably Susan Cooper and Alan Garner, have set many of their fantasy books in a world recognisably our own but altered by the incursion of magic individuals or events.[17] An interesting slant on those fantasies for young adult readers which are set in 'our' world and yet confront characters with extraordinary events is provided by Alison Waller. On the basis of a study of works by Garner, David Almond and others,[18] she claims: 'Young adult fantastic realism combines the characters and events of contemporary or recognisable adolescence found within teenage realism with some aspect of the consensually impossible, supernatural or unreal' (2009: 17).

The emphasis in the current sub-section is on texts where the world is recognisably familiar, but peopled by characters who differ in some significant way from ordinary humans. David Almond's novel, *Skellig* (1998), presents as an incursive fantasy character a non-stereotypical angel who at first glance resembles a tramp but whose powers are finally displayed in his healing of the little sister of Michael, the protagonist. In a discussion of Almond's work, Jean Webb shows how this experience enables Michael and his friend Mina to be open to the spirituality latent in a world which superficially seems bounded by rationality (2006: 247). Elsewhere Geraldine Brennan focuses on Almond's treatment, in this and other novels, of loss and death within a context both of familial change and of adolescent development. She shows how novels such as these can help adolescent readers to face up to real-life uncertainty (2001: 126–7). Many other examples could be adduced to illustrate how fantasy in which human characters are confronted with strange elements outside their normal experience provides a good deal of scope for critical interpretation, often related to adolescence, an age group on the threshold of adulthood.

One of the best-known examples of this kind of fantasy is Mary Norton's five-novel 'Borrowers' series (1952–82), in which Arriety and her family are just a few inches tall and live beneath the floorboards. Although the central idea is attractive to younger children, there is no doubt that issues of adolescence, though not the only ones addressed, are paramount. Additionally, post-Swift, the very invention of miniature people who are in all other respects similar to ourselves enables writers to present a satirical view of the everyday world, as suggested by Humphrey Carpenter, who describes the first volume in the sequence as a 'social parable' (1985: 216). While not rejecting this perspective, Sarah Godek claims that 'Norton deconstructs the illusion of reality', presenting the story within a framework that questions 'not so much its veracity as whether it is ever possible to determine the "truth"' (2005: 98). Susan Hancock's discussion reveals the complexity of the depiction of the central character, Arriety, who can be seen as exemplifying 'the adolescent in that liminal stage of growing away from family and gaining confidence in her own, separate and individual life'; she is also associated with images of the natural world and metaphorically acts as a unifying factor between widely varying versions of humanity (2009: 104–6). These differing perspectives are not mutually exclusive but serve to illustrate the potential of fantasy to 'interrogate all that we take for granted about language and experience' (Lance Olsen, quoted by Godek 2005: 97–8).

There is no doubt, however, that the texts in this category which have attracted the most attention in recent years are the seven Harry Potter novels[19] by J.K. Rowling, published between 1997 and 2007. Critical and commercial interest has been such that several studies were published before the saga was completed. Some of the contributions in the collection edited by Lana Whited (2002) look at antecedents for Rowling's work, both in mythology and in the school story genre, including previous instances of schools for witches and wizards (as found in the novels of Ursula Le Guin, Jill Murphy, Diana Wynne Jones and Anthony Horowitz). Another early study, by Suman Gupta,[20] focuses on *'the political and social implications of the Harry Potter phenomenon'* (2003: 7, italics original). A critical compilation edited by Elizabeth Heilman (2003), which appeared in its first edition before the chronicles of Hogwarts were complete, has subsequently been updated (2nd ed 2009) to include references to the later books. Heilman's focus is on 'how the books and the Harry Potter phenomenon fit into contemporary culture'; thus attention is also given to their interpretation in other media (2009: 8). A recent volume in the 'New Casebook' series, edited by Cynthia Hallett and Peggy Huey (2012), also looks at the films, together with a range of topics including fairytale, gender, mixed race and sexuality.[21]

It is apparent that criticism has evolved in order to come to terms with an age in which popular texts are likely to be turned into films and computer games, sometimes even before a series is complete. The extent to which comment on commercial factors has become a part of the critical response to literary texts is even more manifest here than with Tolkien and Pullman. It is perhaps relevant in this context to mention briefly the cultural phenomenon which gave rise to Joanna Trollope's adverse remarks about fantasy quoted at the beginning of this chapter, Stephanie Meyer's four-novel series, *Twilight* (2005–8). In it, vampires and werewolves, creatures which owe their origin to gothic and horror fiction and are seen as posing a threat to 'our' world, are portrayed in the context of school stories and teenage romance. Films and computer games are part of the spin-off from such series, which tend to appeal mostly to the adolescent age-group. Critical comment,[22] which has focused on societal themes as revealed in treatment of topics such as eroticisation and identity within these series, suggests that they have more relationship to the 'real' world than Trollope surmises.

Animal and toy fantasy

It could be claimed that the anthropomorphic portrayal of animal and similar characters is really a subset of the category above, but it is so prolific in children's fiction that it deserves specific attention.[23] This group is itself open to subdivision, as its exemplars range from texts for young children which present animals in a totally human environment (such as Judith Kerr's *The Tiger Who Came to Tea*, 1968) to those which set them in something approaching a natural habitat but with abilities and language which appear to be beyond those of 'real' animals (such as Richard Adams' *Watership Down*). While examples from all periods of children's literature abound, in the second half of the twentieth century the most notable instances are perhaps to be found in picturebooks.

Patricia A Ganea and others,[24] basing their conclusions on research carried out on children aged three to five, have suggested that such texts create confusion in their readers' minds: 'Presenting animals to children in ways that are similar to how humans act and behave is likely to be counter-productive for learning scientifically accurate information about the biological world ... [and to] influence children to adopt a human-centered view of the animal world.' Their research also suggests that it is the text rather than the pictures that creates this kind of effect.[25] They are not the first to make this charge: C.S. Lewis in fact countered it more than sixty years previously; in his article 'On Three Ways of Writing for Children' (1952) he suggests that 'talking beasts [provide] an admirable hieroglyphic which conveys psychology, types of character ... more briefly than novelistic presentation ...'. Such books, he claims, do not give children a false impression of the world, because children do not in fact expect the real world to be like the stories, whereas ostensibly realistic tales such as those about school may indeed deceive readers about what to anticipate from life (in (eds) Egoff et al. 1980: 212–4).

The classic critical text in this area is Margaret Blount's *Animal Land: The Creatures of Children's Fiction* (1974). Even though inevitably some of her material is dated and there is no consideration of later texts, it provides a starting point for studies of more recent texts. Blount suggests that not only do adults enjoy writing such stories, as 'an animal fantasy is a kind of imaginative launching ground that gives a built in power of insight to narrative', but also that such stories have always been sources of moral instruction (1974: 15). One of Blount's categories is that of toy fiction, an area amplified in a later study, Lois Kuznets' *When Toys Come Alive: Narratives of Animation, Metamorphosis and Development* (1994). This incorporates insights gained from areas such as psychology, anthropology and computer science. Her terms of reference allow her to provide a critique of the work of one of the most important writers in this sub-genre, Russell Hoban. As she observes, the 'playful parody' of *The Mouse and His Child* (1967) 'notes the failure of philosophic attempts to make sense of the universe ... Hoban uses his toy narrative to mirror and exploit the uncertainties of human life' (1994: 176). As is often the case, scrutiny of a specific text can throw light on issues explored in a range of others. More recently, Tess Cosslett (2006), despite limiting her chronological perspective largely to the nineteenth century, explores the cultural message of such stories so as to provide a useful starting point for those looking at more recent fiction.

Fantasies involving time

Time is one of the most frequently encountered themes in literature generally, and certainly features strongly in children's fiction. As Lisa Sainsbury comments:

■ Books dealing with time, whether as a subject in its own right or as part of thematic or metaphoric explorations, comprise an important body of writing for the young, despite the fact that understanding time poses numerous problems for children. (2005: 156) □

Conjectures as to why such a theme is so popular preoccupied many of the speakers in a conference in 2006 on the subject,[26] with the historical, dystopian and fantasy aspects being explored. It is suggested that in some ways such texts are a part of the process of children coming to terms with the universality of human experience, and what people living today have in common with those of previous generations.

John Rowe Townsend begins his chapter entitled 'Modern Fantasy (iii) On the margin' with the observation that

■ Much fiction that is essentially naturalistic, concerned with what actual people do in the actual world, puts a foot across the border into fantasy, in search of some degree of freedom that realism, strictly interpreted, would not allow. (1990: 234) □

The exploration of time may involve characters in time-travel to the past, a notable feature of the work of Edith Nesbit and also occurring in Alison Uttley's well-known *A Traveller in Time* (1939). Inevitably such fiction has intersected with the historical novel, and despite the lack of realism in the means by which the protagonists are propelled into the past, many such books seem to have a good deal of kinship with realism. Even Lucy Boston's 'Green Knowe' series could be described as a fusion between time travel and the ghost story, being anchored in a real location, Hemingford Grey, as described by Boston (1973) herself, while it presents encounters between the twentieth-century protagonist Tolly and his predecessors from the past.

A similar link with the realistic novel could also be claimed for dystopias set in an imagined future. Notable examples include 'The Changes' trilogy (1968–70) and *Eva* (1988), by Peter Dickinson, and Robert Swindells' *Brother in the Land* (1984), together with more recent texts such as *How I Live Now* (2004) by Meg Rosoff. The depiction of imagined and generally unpleasant futures reflects these authors' concern about current ecological and political issues which could result in threatening situations.

Probably the most notable children's book tackling the subject of time within a framework which fuses the everyday and the past is Philippa Pearce's *Tom's Midnight Garden* (1958). Its landmark position is highlighted by Margaret Meek:

■ If ... those professionals involved in children's literature are asked to name a book that typifies their attachment to this kind of writing, the chances are that *Tom's Midnight Garden* will be one of those chosen to

represent 'the best'. Since its publication in 1958 it has been acknowledged in canonical judgements as a classic. (2002: 76–7) □

Meek cites an earlier critic of children's literature, Margery Fisher, who
in 1961 praised Pearce's style for succeeding in making the garden
real to its readers. Meek also sees the book's eminence as a factor in
encouraging writers and critics to take the world of children's literature
seriously. Margaret and Michael Rustin's words about this text could be
seen as having a more general relevance to quality fantasy:

> ■ The author ... understands that what happens in imagination and play
> has a reality too, and can lead to growth and change without dramatic
> external deliverances. *Tom's Midnight Garden* doesn't need to be told in
> the realist mode ... nor do the children have to effect miracles to survive.
> Reparation and restitution take place in the mind, as well as in outward
> action. (1987: 36) □

Appositely, in a time context, Morag Styles predicts that Pearce's work
will be judged long into the future as 'the touchstone of deep, nourish-
ing, timeless fiction' (2007: 175).

Conclusion

Faced with the impossibility of doing justice to the considerable amount
of discussion concerning children's fantasy, I have focused in this chapter on some significant and potentially more general critical readings
of a relatively small number of primary texts. The intention is to throw
light on the kind of issues, frequently philosophical, theological or
psychological in nature, highlighted by fantasy texts; thus the critical
discussion relates both to the situation of human beings in the universe
and to their understanding of themselves and others. Many writers of
fantasy for children, such as Tolkien, Lewis and Pullman, have chosen a
medium which allows them to transcend everyday reality because they
felt that this was the best or perhaps the only way to confront teleologi-
cal issues unhampered by the bounds of everyday experience. Others
have found fantasy an appropriate medium to explore human personality and development. Either way, the texts discussed here are indicative
of how fantasy has proved one of the most important and enduring
modes of writing for children. The texts discussed in this chapter have
by and large relied on words to create fantasy worlds or elements. Conversely, the subject material of the next chapter, the picturebook and
the comic, frequently create equally non-realist themes, this time with
a visual emphasis.

CHAPTER SIX

Visual Texts

Introduction

Throughout the ages, children have been introduced to reading by means of texts bearing pictures as well as words, but it is only in recent years that critical distinctions have been drawn between books where the function of such pictures is merely to illustrate the verbal material, and those where, in one way or another, the pictures have a major role to play in the narrative and characterisation, a role which is complementary or sometimes even contradictory to the verbal text.[1] The artwork in both types of book is often of a high standard, frequently receiving its own plaudits from art critics, but the focus in the current chapter is on criticism concerned with the interplay between narrative (generally through word) and picture.[2] The development of such criticism has gone hand in hand with picturebook evolution itself, notably in the years since the publication of Maurice Sendak's *Where the Wild Things Are* (1963).

Until around the end of the twentieth century, it could perhaps have been claimed that the picturebook[3] genre was unique to children's literature. Paradoxically, however, such texts are likely to be more familiar to adults than is the case for most children's books: parents, carers and teachers are frequently the mediators of the verbal text to pre-literate children, and often enjoy drawing attention to relevant details of the pictures. Consequently the creative portrayal of the relationship between word and text by author-illustrators such as Quentin Blake and Anthony Browne finds an appreciative adult audience; similarly, picturebooks designated for a solely adult audience have appeared more recently, ranging from those depicting as monsters children who resist their parents' attempts to get them to sleep, to treatments of human mortality.[4]

Picturebooks are not of course the only genre in which young readers are exposed to the visual as well as the verbal. Discussion of performance and interactive media is postponed to Chapter Twelve, but consideration is given here to comics and graphic novels.

Critical approaches to picturebooks

One of the earliest critics to draw attention to the distinction between picturebooks and illustrated texts was John Rowe Townsend. In the 1974 edition of his oft-revised *Written for Children*, he observes that in the first edition (1965) he had confined his attention to 'prose fiction for children in Britain' (1974: 13); however, from the 1974 edition onwards, he has included several chapters on picturebooks. He also widens his remit to literature from other English-speaking countries, preceding his chapter on British picturebooks by another entitled, 'Picture books in bloom: U.S.A.'. The two picturebook artists who seem to have been most influential in the development of Townsend's thinking are Maurice Sendak and Edward Ardizzone,[5] perusal of whose work seems to have been instrumental in the formation of his rationale for the distinction he draws:

> ■ Although many contemporary illustrators are also picture-book artists, the two functions are not the same. Illustration explains or illuminates a text, helps (or, sometimes, hinders) the working of the reader's imagination, but is subordinate; it is the text that counts. In a picture book, the artwork has at least an equal role to that of the text, very probably the major part, and occasionally is unaccompanied by any text at all. (1974: 308) □

Townsend goes on to claim that 'the picture book is a genre on its own' (1974: 309) and rejects the kind of criticism which attempts to separate its 'literary and graphic elements' (1974: 308).

The ensuing twenty years were to witness the publication of many of the really significant theoretical studies of the picturebook genre, thus reflecting the simultaneous development of the picturebook itself, as a range of author-artists on both sides of the Atlantic explored its potential. One of the earliest critics to relate narrative theory to picturebooks was Stephen Roxburgh (1983–4),[6] while the journal *Word and Image* included two important articles on the subject in its April–June 1986 issue (2.2).[7] In one of these, 'The Object Lesson: Picture Books of Anthony Browne', Jane Doonan notes the variety of important themes and styles to be found not only in books by Browne but also in others by artists such as Michael Foreman, John Burningham and Raymond Briggs. In the other article, William Moebius, in 'Introduction to Picturebook Codes', analyses the significance to narrative of pictorial aspects such as page position, perspective, colour, frame and line.

Despite the value and interest of these and other short articles,[8] the most influential critic from this period is undoubtedly Perry Nodelman, whose *Words About Pictures* (1988) is the first book-length study of the modes used by picturebook artists to make narrative meaning. In his Introduction, Nodelman justifies the approach taken in his book:

> ■ Since the major task of the visual images in picture books is to communicate information, they make most sense in terms of an approach that focuses on the conditions under which meanings are communicated. Semiotics, which has its roots in linguistics, is such an approach; its prime interest is in the codes and contexts on which the communication of meaning depends. (1988: ix) □

Nodelman shows the extent to which cultural assumptions enter into interpretations, even by young children, of every picture, including the most apparently realistic ones, and suggests that 'picture books that tell stories force viewers to search the pictures for information that might add to or change the meanings of the accompanying texts'; thus a picturebook becomes 'a subtle and complex form of communication ... unusual as narrative in its supplementation of verbal information with visual and as visual art in its focus on the meaningful aspects of visual imagery'. He claims: 'Given their complexity, it seems clear that neither pictures nor the books they appear in can communicate directly and automatically' (1988: 18–21).

Having established the complementarity of pictures and texts – an interaction for which later in the book he uses the musical term 'counterpoint' (1988: 263) – Nodelman goes on to explore some of the ways in which this feature is displayed in a range of picturebooks, the majority of them published in the wake of Sendak's *Where the Wild Things Are* (1963).[9] He looks at the use of framing devices to create a sense of objectivity or heighten dramatic focus (p.51); the way in which colour can give solidity (p.69) or establish a mood (pp.141–146); and the positioning of objects and people on the page (pp.134–5). He also shows how directionality (usually in Western texts from left to right) is important in the understanding of action (pp.163–166). Following his consideration of how such means are used by picturebook artists, Nodelman goes on to discuss the relationship between the pictures and the words, challenging the facile assumption that 'they seem to mirror each other' (p.193) by referring to interpretations made by people exposed to only one of these modes: for instance, adults encountering only the verbal text of Sendak's *Wild Things* are likely to consider it to be more frightening than if they see the complete book. 'By limiting each other, words and pictures together take on a meaning that neither possesses without the other' (p.221). Sometimes the effect created may be one of irony, something which 'occurs in literature when we know something more and something different from what we are being told' (p.223). Irony can result from the difference of narrative standpoint between the text, which may appear quasi-objective or take the point of view of one of the characters, and the pictures, which by their nature are likely to be from a different angle. He concludes with what might appear to be an over-exalted claim for 'what picture-book art offers children ... objective awareness based on deep understanding that allows us first to know the world and then to love the world we know' (p.286).

Picturebooks and young children

It is evident that much critical writing about picturebooks was triggered by the very original approach taken by a number of picturebook artists,[10] particularly post-Ardizzone and Sendak. During this period, many such books were being used in classrooms in a variety of ways, and Peggy Heeks cites the 1957 Caldecott award winner, Marc Simont, as suggesting 'one basic division [is] between illustrations which complement the text, that is, extend it, and those which [merely] supplement or repeat it' (1981: 31–2). Probably the best-known piece of educational writing about a number of picturebooks[11] with significant interplay between verbal and visual text is Margaret Meek's short monograph, *How Texts Teach What Readers Learn* (1988). The development during this period within a teaching context appears particularly noteworthy since only a few years earlier, the otherwise all-embracing Bullock Report about English teaching, *A Language for Life* (1975), makes no explicit reference to the genre. Further evidence of pedagogical interest is attested to by Stuart Marriott's *Picture Books in the Primary Classroom* (1991), in addition to shorter pieces by Susan Fremantle and Sharon Walsh.[12] However the two books with the most significant contributions to the debate are Judith Graham's *Pictures on the Page* (1990)[13] and Jane Doonan's *Looking at Pictures in Picture Books* (1993).

Graham's major contention is that amid all the acknowledgement of the value of picturebooks from an aesthetic and educational point of view, 'what has been very much overlooked ... is the part that the illustrations in a picture-book may play in the literary development of a reader' (1990: 8). Basing her analysis on the work of theorists (such as Wolfgang Iser (1978)), who emphasise the need for readers to take an active role in the reading process, she shows how author-illustrators like Raymond Briggs, Pat Hutchins, and Anthony Browne, not only introduce children to the characters who populate the books, and the settings which these characters inhabit, but also facilitate awareness of story. Graham points out that rather than being detrimental to this understanding by distracting the reader's eye from the print, they help provide the knowledge that readers need to bring to the reading process (1990: 76). Acknowledging the seminal role of Sendak, she shows how a number of contemporary picturebooks[14] subtly incorporate 'social, political and moral themes' (1990: 106), inviting children 'to enter their imaginary worlds. They all share a belief that children want to think as well as to laugh' (1990: 107). Her conviction is that picturebooks have 'an essential role to play in the teaching of the literary conventions that all readers operate throughout their lives' (1990: 117).

By contrast, Doonan's focus is on the means by which the pictorial art of the picturebook communicates, and, as well as giving pleasure and facilitating the telling of the tale, enables the book to function as 'something which gives form to ideas and to which we can attach our ideas' (1993: 7). Looking at the use of colour, light and dark, scale, shapes, patterning and rhythms, she leads the reader through 'the use of picture books as part of an education in developing a visual sense generally and in being able to make meaning from visual information in particular' (1993: 48). She also provides a schema of lessons aimed at raising visual awareness in pupils in their early teens. Referring to some significant theoretical texts, she confesses to having some reservations about Nodelman's semiotic approach, feeling that 'grasping the meaning of a picture is [not] as neat as he suggests'. Nevertheless, she acknowledges the inspirational value of his work to teachers, admitting that it led her to formalise her own classroom practice, and thus to write her own book (1993: 80).

It would be fair to claim that between them, in different ways, Nodelman, Graham and Doonan have helped to educate a large number of teachers and others about the immense potential of picturebooks – especially those produced from the second half of the twentieth century onwards – in the literary and artistic education of people of all ages, not simply young children. Subsequently a number of compilations of articles on picturebooks and on young children's response to them have appeared, often including contributions by artists as well as educators. Notable in this enterprise have been academics from Homerton College, Cambridge. As early as 1992, several relevant articles appear in *After Alice: Exploring Children's Literature,* edited by Morag Styles, Eve Bearne and Victor Watson, while a fuller treatment occurs in *Talking Pictures: Pictorial Texts and Young Readers* (1996). The editors of the latter volume, Victor Watson and Morag Styles, describe it as a 'conversation about picture books' in which contributors 'have things to say about the reading lessons within picture books, about their cultural place and significance, about how they are made, and about how they become part of the lives and learning of young readers' (1996: 1). In their conclusion, they comment on how these essays, ranging over many disciplines, demonstrate that the complexity and multi-layeredness of picturebooks make them as intellectually engrossing to adults as well as children, offering 'the first steps towards enjoyment of literature, critical literacy, artistic education, and independent, wide-ranging readings' (1996: 181).

In recent years a significant degree of attention has been paid to analysing the responses of young children to picturebooks. Caution is necessary in generalising from any such results: what Nodelman has to say about 'self-fulfilling prophecies' (1988: 39) is as relevant to the danger of attributing undue sophistication in interpretation to children as it is to that of underestimating their abilities in this respect. There is also the danger of asking questions that invite a particular kind of response. A good many recent studies, while avoiding such pitfalls, have provided valuable documentation about variations and similarities in children's reading of picturebooks. A substantial part of *Talking Pictures* consists of three chapters in which Victor Watson charts the development over several years of two girls, initially both six-year-olds. Watson finds the many differences between their responses to picture and text revealing about the processes involved.

The contributors to Janet Evans' *What's in the Picture? Responding to Illustrations in Picture Books* (1998) also provide a good deal of evidence derived from recorded sessions with young children, while much of Evelyn Arizpe and Morag Styles' *Children Reading Pictures: Interpreting Visual Texts* (2003) is devoted to an account of a longitudinal study of young children's reactions towards picturebooks created by such illustrators as Anthony Browne and Satoshi Kitamura. This study, which attempts to combine pedagogical and theoretical aspects of the subject, analyses not only the children's verbal responses but also the drawings they produced in response to the pictures seen. Further investigations of children's responses are discussed by Sylvia Pantaleo, for instance in an article in *Early Childhood Research and Practice (ECRP)* (2005). Basing her findings on a project exploring the responses of first-grade children to eight picturebooks with metafictive devices, Pantaleo concludes that in the majority of instances their subsequent storytelling could be described as 'interdependent' rather than parallel, suggesting a very real interaction with the presented material. A later compilation edited by Janet Evans, *Talking beyond the Page* (2009), further explores the responses of young children, including those to wordless and postmodern picturebooks. The use of visual material with immigrant children is also explored. The second edition of Arizpe and Styles's *Children Reading Pictures* (2015) updates earlier research and includes a chapter by Margaret Mackey on digital picturebooks.

Further critical studies on the genre

It is evident that the multi-modality of picturebooks makes them eminently appropriate to a postmodern world in which a range of different voices and even media may carry narrative without any very obvious prioritisation being given to an omniscient narratorial voice, or indeed the printed text itself. Janet Evans contends that picturebooks work as an effective instrument to enable people to confront:

> ■ a 'postmodern' world: a world where society, culture and literature are in the process of challenging and changing life as it used to exist in the earlier parts of the twentieth century ... changes in the way people are able to make sense of texts, used in this sense to mean visual, dance, drama, music, song, media and IT as well as written texts. (1998: xiii) □

Several studies have looked at the postmodern characteristics of the work of some of the best-known picturebook artists, which in many instances predated the appearance of such qualities not only in the rest of children's literature but also in much popular fiction for adults. Post-modernist writing generally foregrounds the conventionality of text, something almost forgotten by many fluent readers as they get 'lost' in the story.

David Lewis was one of the earliest critics to elucidate this aspect of many modern picturebooks. In a short conference paper focusing on two contrasted books by John Burningham, Lewis suggests that 'the openness, playfulness and interrogative qualities of many picture book texts' work against the conventions which normally serve to convince readers of 'the verisimilitude of the events depicted be they fantastic or otherwise' (1992: 85, 81) and thus 'offer, for readers of all ages, the opportunity for a playful exploration of what is involved in the making and interpretation of literary fictions' (1992: 81). In *Reading Contemporary Picturebooks: Picturing Text* (2001), Lewis goes on to expand on this contention in what David Rudd (2003) in a review describes as 'a series of interconnected essays' on a number of picturebooks, drawing also on the views of children. Rudd suggests that this book, rather than replacing the seminal work of critics such as Nodelman and Doonan, could be seen as a 'more advanced text' than theirs (2003: 147).

These same qualities of picturebooks are highlighted in Laurence Sipe and Sylvia Pantaleo's *Postmodern Picturebooks: Play, Parody and Self-referentiality* (2008), a collection of essays by a number of distinguished scholars in the field. In a review, David Lewis remarks on the difficulty caused by the fact that 'no-one seems to agree exactly what constitutes postmodernism, so Sipe and Pantaleo ... suggest that individual picture books may be thought of as sitting somewhere on a continuum according to how many or how few postmodern features they appear to display' (2009: 91). Cherie Allan (2012) pursues the issue of picturebooks and postmodernism further, coining the term 'Postmodernesque' (by analogy with Bakhtin's 'carnivalesque') to refer to those elements of the postmodern tradition, such as metafictive devices, which have been imported into picturebooks but nevertheless implicitly provide a critique of the postmodern world. This is nicely summed up in a review by Mateja Latin and Dina Pavkovic: 'The postmodernesque picturebook is a picturebook about postmodernism' (*Libri & Liberi* 2013.2(2): 363).

Other twenty-first century critical texts and compilations, while not ignoring the postmodern qualities highlighted by Lewis and others, take on a wider critical agenda. Maria Nikolajeva and Carole Scott's *How Picturebooks Work* (2001) discusses the wide range of differing relationships between word and image in a number of modern picturebooks, giving a succinct account of current critical approaches to the genre, including a résumé of some of the attempts to establish a typology. Like other critics, notably Nodelman and Graham, they look at some of the narrative strategies fostered by picturebook artists, including setting, characterisation, and figurative language, as well as focusing on broader issues like mimesis and modality. Morag Styles and Eve Bearne's *Art, Narrative and Childhood* (2003), resulting from a conference held in 2000, also covers a wide range of topics, including the link between the picturebook and cultural concerns.[15]

Two twenty-first-century studies of children's literature attest to the fact that substantial attention needs to be given to picturebooks within all current critical discussion. Kimberley Reynolds' *Modern Children's Literature: An Introduction* (2005) includes two such chapters. Judith Graham's 'Reading Contemporary Picturebooks' looks at the intellectual and perceptual challenges posed by texts ranging from a wordless book to Lauren Child's *Who's Afraid of the Big Bad Book?* (2002) which is characterised by 'playful bending and breaking of literary rules and conventions' (2005: 225). This is followed by Lisa Sainsbury's analysis of politics and philosophy in the work of Raymond Briggs, which bears out Judith Graham's contention, noted above, that the picturebook can be an appropriate medium for the presentation of important social themes.

A limitation of some of the criticism highlighted above is that it focuses only on British, or in some instances, American illustrators. Reynolds' slightly later *Radical Children's Literature* (2007) includes, however, a chapter which draws on a range of international picturebooks to support the thesis that today's children, 'whose understanding of fiction and culture has been shaped by picturebooks such as those by Fanelli, Child, and Wiesner, can be expected to reach … radical conclusions about the nature of narrative when they become the authors and writers of the future' (2007: 44). Attention to picturebook artists from the rest of the world is also evident in some of the collections of papers given at the conferences of the International Board on Books for Young People (IBBY): these include perspectives supplied by Penni Cotton (2004 and 2008) about the European Picture Book Collection, and analyses of picturebooks from France, Sweden, Mexico, South Africa,

Greece, Australia and Taiwan, among others. Substantial attention is also paid in the later volume to the responses of the primary audience, young children.

Comics and graphic novels

Like the picturebook, stories told in comic strip format have always been associated with a child audience, and it is only in recent years that informed criticism of them has begun to appear. A major problem in the critical discussion of material produced in comic strip format is definition. Some of the best-known work of certain picturebook author-illustrators, such as Raymond Briggs[16] and Shirley Hughes,[17] makes use of conventions generally associated with the comic, notably speech balloons, while criteria for distinguishing between comics and graphic novels have not been rigidly established. Martin Barker, in *Comics: Ideology, Power and the Critics* (1989), suggests that defining comics simply in terms of their use of sequences of pictures is not enough; he claims:

■ All the following seem to me importantly part of their nature.

1. they appear at regular intervals;
2. they have recurring characters, with relatively predictable ranges of behaviour;
3. characters appear within distinct genres among other characters of the same kind involved in similar kinds of actions and events;
4. comics have accumulated a great number of conventions, which allow still frames to represent an enormous range of things. Among these: speech, movement, relationships, emotions, cause and effect, reader-involvement, and the fictional nature of the comic itself and its characters. (1989: 6) □

Barker brings insights derived from a variety of theoretical sources, notably Vladimir Propp (best-known for his typology of fairytales), into the analysis of comics ranging from the well-established *Beano* to more recent examples from the sub-genres of action and romance. He stresses the importance of production history and its relationship to the implied readers, and concludes by applying his theory of ideology, based on Proppian analysis of the 'form' of the cultural object (1989: 275), to comics produced by the Disney Corporation.

A notable study of comics is that by artist Scott McCloud (1993). Working within a comic-book format, he presents not only an account of the historical development of the genre but also explores its formal aspects and the vocabulary appropriate to describing these. An indication of the importance of this book is the recognition given to it by leading exponents of the graphic novel including Art Spiegelman (creator of *Maus*, 1991), who notes how it 'deconstructs the secret language of comics' and Neil Gaiman (creator, with Dave McKean, of *The Wolves within the Walls*, 2003).[18] A more conventional approach to comic history is taken by Roger Sabin, a cultural historian; his *Comics, Comix and Graphic Novels* (2001) traces the development of the genre from low-status material directed to a young audience towards the considerable variety available today. Writers such as Barker, Sabin and McCloud have shown the value of comics as an intrinsic aspect of the culture of childhood.

A sub-genre which seems to have enjoyed quite a short shelf-life is that of the girls' comic which experienced its heyday between 1950 and 1980; its attraction to a female audience has been seen as atypical, presumably fulfilling a social need for a group of readers whose roles were particularly subject to change in this period (see Mel Gibson, in (eds) Styles and Bearne 2003: 87–100). As Gibson observes, such comics were in due course largely subsumed into the girls' magazines, a much more traditional medium.

In a later article, in the *Routledge Companion to Children's Literature* (2010: 100–111), Gibson contributes to the debate about definition; she observes that while 'graphic novels ... share the grammar of comics [they contain] a single complete narrative' (p.101). She notes the extent to which the blurring of the barriers between the two comic-based forms and the picturebook as such is revealed by artists such as Briggs and a younger exponent influenced by him, Shaun Tan.

As well as his 'Dark Materials' saga, Philip Pullman has made use of comic/graphic novel approaches in his own writing; his first novel, *Count Karlstein* (1982), based on a play written when he was a middle-school teacher, has also been published in graphic novel format (1992) as a result of a collaboration with artist Patrice Aggs. Thus Pullman is well qualified to write about the art form in his chapter, 'Picture stories and graphic novels' in (eds) Reynolds and Tucker (1998). Pullman (after considering the possible origins of the term graphic novel in Will Eisner 1978), describes it as 'a lengthy comic: a single story in the comic strip format printed in one volume' (1998: 113). Mentioning the 'speech balloons, think bubbles, captions, and sound effects', he claims that: 'This graphic vocabulary is so natural-seeming, intuitive, reader-friendly, that it seems to have come to the understanding of most of us very early in our reading' (1998: 112); he goes on to look at titles ranging from *Rupert* of the *Daily Express*, through the *Eagle* and the work of Raymond Briggs, to a work universally hailed as a graphic novel, Spiegelman's *Maus* (1987). Pullman concludes by emphasising the necessity to take the graphic novel seriously as an art form. A more recent critical work, Jeet Heer and Kent Worcester's *A Comic Studies Reader* (2009) is one of the earliest to fulfil this plea, dividing the work analysed into four areas: history and genealogy, inner worlds, social significance and close scrutiny and evaluation.

It is evident that the whole critical field of visual texts is an expanding one and that material which until recently would have been regarded as of transitory interest or as having an appeal only to the very young is now receiving due scrutiny. Conversely, poetry and drama, the genres discussed in the next chapter, are probably the earliest to have been the subject of literary criticism.

CHAPTER SEVEN

Poetry and Drama

Introduction

It is paradoxical that while poetry has traditionally been seen as the most exalted form of literature, and theorising about it, by such eminent writers as Aristotle, Horace and Sidney, has formed the foundation for later literary criticism, there has been very little sustained study of poetry for children. Indeed, in a recently published guide, *The Routledge Companion to Children's Literature* (2010), it is allotted less than a single page, in contrast to longer discussions of such more topical issues as gender studies and race. In their contribution to this *Companion*, 'Sidelines: Some neglected dimensions of children's literature and its scholarship', Evelyn Arizpe and Morag Styles, with Abigail Rokison, comment: 'In many respects, it is outrageous that as significant a genre as poetry for children should be tucked away in a chapter dealing with Cinderella forms of children's literature' (2010: 133). This marginalisation of a body of work for children to which many major poets, both in the past and today, have contributed, seems to result partly from an all too prevalent fear of poetry among teachers, which has stood in the way of quality presentation in the classroom, and partly from problems of definition: what exactly is children's poetry? While poetry features in most of the histories of children's literature, the question of how, and indeed whether, poetry for children differs from that written with an adult audience in mind, is not always confronted. Even when it is, no definitive answer is given.

Consequently, much of what follows here is concerned with various writers' attempts to define the body of poetry they are considering. Only after some consideration has been given to this (generally inconclusive) debate, is it possible to look at critical discussion of the forms taken by children's poetry, such as oral rhymes or the sub-genre of 'nonsense' which is sometimes seen as especially characteristic of verse for the young. Criticism of the children's poetry of major writers such as

William Blake, T.S. Eliot and Ted Hughes is considered towards the end of this chapter, but scholarly discussion of the poetry about childhood by poets such as Henry Vaughan, Thomas Traherne and especially William Wordsworth, is, for reasons of space, beyond the scope of the current volume. Nor is it possible here to scrutinise critical material about other poems by these writers (such as Wordsworth's 'Daffodils') which have by now become part of the corpus of children's poetry. It is perhaps worth observing that such poems generally possess the quality of 'sense immediacy' which Neil Philip (see the following section) demands in poetry for children.

Another area, that of dramatic literature for children, sometimes associated with poetry though generally distinct from it, has also been given little critical attention – in this instance because there is in fact comparatively little dramatic literature specifically designed for young audiences (as distinct from adaptations from prose or other texts). Consequently a brief discussion of theoretical and critical writing which focuses on drama is also included here rather than forming a chapter in itself.

What is children's poetry? An unresolved question

Perhaps it is unreasonable to expect literary critics to be clear as to how children's poetry differs, if at all, from that written for adults, when the whole question of what actually constitutes a poem itself remains open to debate. Some interesting attempts to answer this question are recorded in Richard Andrews' *The Problem with Poetry* (1991), a volume in the Open University 'English, Language, and Education' series. The general editor of the series quotes the American poet Wallace Stevens as saying 'Poetry is a response to the daily necessity of getting the world right' (1991: ix). Less celebrity in its origin, but no less cogent, is a definition from an eleven to twelve-year-old pupil also quoted by Andrews: 'A poem is a collection of words which do not go right up to the edge of the page' (1991: 8). While the mature poet focuses on the poet's struggle to put into words something important yet defying clear expression, the pupil pays attention to one of the features characterising most poetry – what might be described as one of the ways to play the serious language game of poetry. Poets impose on themselves their own rules in this game, deciding:

- whether to rhyme, alliterate, use a particular rhythm or employ any other device affecting how the poem will sound;
- whether or not to conform to 'normal' syntax or punctuation;

- whether to write in an established poetic form with its own rules, such as the sonnet or the haiku, or perhaps to choose a shape that in some way mirrors the meaning they want to convey;
- whether to write a long or short piece, or indeed a short poem that is part of a longer work;
- how expansive or alternatively how elliptic their writing should be;
- what kind of imagery to use to illuminate any abstract matters.

All of these choices, and countless others, apply equally to poetry written for any age group; indeed Peter Hunt suggests 'that it is only in the least important area of poetry, the ostensible subject matter, that any distinction ... can be made between what is appropriate for children and what for adults' (1991: 197). While it could be argued that, in addition to differences in subject matter, there are variations in register between poems directed towards an adult audience with a width of reading sufficient to understand allusiveness (Eliot's *The Waste Land* (1922) demands a reader with a more comprehensive literary and philosophical background than does his *Old Possum's Book of Practical Cats*, (1939), such aspects tend in turn to arise from the differences in subject matter. Even the question of how accessible a poem is to young readers will vary not only according to the cultural and linguistic background of the reader, but also in relation to the period in which it was written. It is apparent that poems addressed to young readers of previous centuries need much more explanatory material for their contemporaries today.

The attempt to define 'children's poetry' cannot be totally independent from incidental reference to its history, a fuller account of which occurs in the next sub-section. First it is worth looking at attempts made by editors of collections of verse for children to supply definitions as part of the process of deciding (implicitly or explicitly) about the corpus of poetry on which they can draw. Inevitably their decisions are bound up with their own notions of what constitutes a child (and indeed what is 'suitable' for such an individual at the period in which they are writing). Janet Adam Smith's Introduction to her anthology, *The Faber Book of Children's Verse* (1953), is less tentative than later anthologies in claiming that 'nobody objects to being called a child up to the age of fourteen' (1953: 19) – a statement displaying a certitude which would be rare today. Her choice of poems seems to be largely based on answers from children of this age range to questions about what they enjoy; she also questioned an older age group about what they had enjoyed at that age. Her expressed aim in introducing children to her chosen poems – the education of the feelings – may also strike twenty-first-century readers as over ingenuous and idealistic.

Smith seems to envisage a child audience for her anthology, but the authoritative *Oxford Book of Children's Verse* (1973), chosen and edited by

Iona and Peter Opie, while not excluding the young reader, is clearly designed for an audience capable of appreciating the information provided about the origins of the material. Such an audience will be aware of the labour involved in the Opies' search for 'the original printing of each poem' (1973: xii). The Opies are clear in their aim of 'distinguishing the verse that was always for children from that subsequently adopted for children' (1973: viii). This methodology demands a high degree of scholarship and results in a fairly narrowly defined (though nevertheless substantial) body of work.

The Opies describe their anthology, which excludes all writers alive at the date of publication, as 'the grandchild of [Sir Arthur Quiller-Couch's] *The Oxford Book of English Verse'* (1973: vii), but Neil Philip's *The New Oxford Book of Children's Verse* (1996) does not appear to bear a similar relationship to any of the later incarnations of the adult Oxford volume. Rather, as noted in his Acknowledgement, it is intended to 'stand alongside [the Opies'] magisterial' work. No doubt part of Philip's intention was to bring their work up to date: nearly half of his contributors were alive at the date of publication, in contrast to the Opies' deliberate exclusion of living writers.

At the beginning of his Introduction Philip tackles the question of how he has interpreted his terms of reference:

■ This anthology is, as its title proclaims, a collection of 'children's verse'. This is a term that covers a multitude of sins. In practical terms I have taken it to mean verse written for children, or with them prominently in mind, or published for them with the explicit or implicit endorsement of the author. (1996: xxv) □

Yet, as Philip goes on to say, this apparently simple statement raises the whole question of how children's poetry differs from poetry in general. Ingenuously, but perhaps aptly, he states: 'This anthology is itself a full answer to this difficult question [What is children's poetry?], but it is not an answer that is easy to summarise', so he makes some attempt to answer it in a mere thirteen pages (as against his 339 pages of poems). While admitting that some of the best anthologies for children contain verse not specifically written for them, he nevertheless suggests that there is indeed a recognisable tradition of children's verse, one in which 'immediate sense perceptions have an overriding importance', a quality accompanied by 'a clarity of thought, language and rhythm' (1996: xxv–xxvi).

Philip goes on to attempt to reconcile two apparently conflicting but over-simplistic views of what constitutes children's poetry: the view which sees it as 'defined and perfected' in a period ranging from R.L. Stevenson to Eleanor Farjeon; and that which suggests that modern children need 'silly verse' instead of irrelevant 'nostalgia' (1996: xxvii). Rather than limiting his material to that which fulfils either of these perceptions of its nature, he claims that children's poetry needs 'the celebration of the child's world', a taking on board of serious themes, as well as the kind of nonsense created by poets as far apart in time as Edward Lear and Spike Milligan, and many others since then.

Philip indicates that he feels liberated by the fact that the work of the Opies[1] has freed him from the necessity of including any poem simply because of its historical importance; thus those few which occur in both volumes – as for instance is the case with Blake's 'Piping down the valleys wild' – clearly have both historical significance and immediacy of sense perception. In this context it is perhaps significant that Blake is an outstanding instance of a poet whose work is at the same time accessible to children and a source of profundity which has made it the subject of considerable discussion by literary critics. Thus, in effect, Philip comes back to his contention that the real answer to the question of what children's poetry is can only be seen by looking at the poetry itself.

The history of poetry for children

In examining how poetry is treated in histories of children's literature, it is convenient to start with Peter Hunt's *Children's Literature* (2001); though it is not a history of children's literature as such, it incorporates a good deal of historical material, and the short section on poetry is germane to the current discussion. Hunt quotes from Philip's Introduction, considered above, referring to what he terms Philip's 'robust defence of the form', while making manifest his own scepticism about the possibility of 'articulat[ing] "childhood" for children' (2001: 294); he also voices his own scepticism about the quality of much of the poetry which has been presented to them. He provides examples of verse that in its moralising or its sentimentality (or both) 'bypasses' childhood, before he concludes that, under the influence of the new media, 'we may … be returning to the oral roots of poetry, which did not differentiate audiences' (2001: 298).

In order to perceive, on the one hand, how poetry changed from being a largely oral form to the written mode in which it has generally been presented to children (at least those beyond the nursery rhyme stage), and on the other, the way in which it may indeed be reverting to its oral roots, it is necessary to look briefly at those histories of children's literature which either give some attention to children's poetry or actually focus on it. The earlier histories generally seem to rely on the simple definition – children's poetry is poetry that has been presented to children – rather than attempting to analyse any distinctive qualities. As indicated in Chapter One, it took a long time before children's literature was recognised as a 'respectable' field of study, histories of English literature tending to regard it as consisting of a few items to be tacked on after a proper perusal of adult texts. This marginalisation is compounded in the case of poetry.[2] Not only is children's verse largely unrepresented in the histories of poetry as such, but until recently it was also given little more than a passing glance by some of the historians of children's literature. For instance, Harvey Darton only seems to acknowledge any significance in nursery rhymes in a section largely devoted to fairytales. Significantly too, even in the twenty-fifth anniversary edition (1990) of his *Written for Children*, J.R. Townsend does not provide an update of his original Chapter 11, entitled 'Writers in rhyme', from the 1965 edition. He does, it is true, slightly amplify a later chapter, 'Virtuosity in verse', by giving increased attention to Ted Hughes, whom, together with Charles Causley, he describes as one of the 'distinguished British poets who have written most successfully for children' (1990: 297). Despite the somewhat patronising titles of these two chapters, Townsend observes that 'it is surprising to realise how much has been produced for children by good poets, and how much of it is still alive and enjoyable – by adults as well as by children' (1990: 103).

By the time that Morag Styles published her *From the Garden to the Street: An Introduction to Three Hundred Years of Poetry for Children* (1998), the world of children's literature studies was more than ready for such a history. In her Introduction, Styles, of necessity, foregrounds the question, 'What do we mean by children's poetry?', admitting that it is not easy to 'identify such as a thing as a child's poem' (1998: xv). While her book is in general concerned with poetry specifically written for readers between about five and twelve, she admits to also including some poetry 'shared with the adult canon' (1998: xv). She states, however, that it is important to her that poetry for children should be valued in its own right, and that it should not be 'disparaged as "talking or writing down" ... [It should be as] honest, vigorous and unsentimental as ... children generally are' (1998: xvi). Ultimately, Styles sees the whole debate about what children's poetry is, or indeed what poetry itself is, as 'unproductive'. She states that her aim is to 'include anything and everything that could possibly be classed as poetry – hymns, songs, playground rhymes, raps, verse forms and free verse, trivial or profound. I subscribe to the widest possible definition of poetry'. This all-embracing manifesto gives her the go-ahead to include verse which children may enjoy but in which adults can find little of value (1998: xxv).

Styles suggests that 'the young have been well catered for in poetry' (1998: xvi), and she examines how different periods have provided poetry appropriate to the then current notions of 'the child': 'If "the child" is essentially a cultural invention, then different human cultures have invented different children' (1998: xxii). Thus she finds that it is impossible to produce a history of poetry that fails to contextualise it within current concepts both of childhood and of poetry itself. Her title itself alludes to such changes: much of her book is devoted to 'the garden' (cultivated by those children's poets who were inspired by R.L. Stevenson's *A Child's Garden of Verses* (1885)), and beyond it to 'the street' of today, though perforce she also looks at the intensely devotional and didactic poetry of earlier periods. While she locates a mood not dissimilar to Stevenson's in much of the early twentieth-century children's verse, she conducts a spirited defence of the later, so-called 'urchin verse', of 'the street', and her epilogue presents some of the verse by Caribbean writers which became popular in England in the late twentieth century.[3]

Another area on which Styles focuses is that of women poets, who are often given little or no attention in critical literature. In fact, she explores this legacy not only in her own book but also in a chapter in a book she edited with Mary Hilton and Victor Watson, *Opening the Nursery Door: Reading, Writing and Childhood 1600–1900* (1997); this collection also includes information about a previously unknown eighteenth-century woman who wrote a good deal of verse for her own children, Jane Johnson.

Within a shorter compass than that of Styles, M.O. Grenby's *Children's Literature* (2008), which takes a generic approach to the development of children's literature, provides a survey of the verse; in it he makes a case for 'early collections of poetry for children … [being] … just as important in the history of children's literature as the much more celebrated mid-eighteenth-century prose innovations produced by John Newbery' (2008: 35). He observes that verse for children was much more pervasive in earlier cultures than it is today, and that, despite changing constructions of childhood, there is a striking element of continuity in form, tone and style.

Perhaps, however, one of the key points with which Grenby concludes his chapter should also bring an end to the inconclusive debate which has dominated so much critical writing about children's poetry. He states, 'What actually constitutes children's poetry has always been uncertain, and subject matter, original intended audience, language and genre do not offer certain guidance' (2008: 56). It is perhaps pertinent, however, to let the last words on what is children's poetry be those of children themselves: on the basis of a small research project involving a group of twelve and fourteen-year-olds, Stephen Miles found that 'It was neither the form nor the content that ultimately mattered to them, but the *intent* [italics original]: what really mattered was that the poet respected them as children'; he observes that 'we all need poems for the different parts of us' (in (eds) Styles et al. 2010: 31–2).

Oral verse

However heated the debate about what is, or is not, poetry for children, it has always been accepted that nursery rhymes are part of it; critical material in this area has concentrated instead on the characteristic features of such rhymes, together with the various attempts to determine their origins. The most important contributors in this area are Iona and Peter Opie, whose *Oxford Dictionary of Nursery Rhymes* (1951) confronts these questions. The Opies waste little time on definitions; instead, in their comprehensive Introduction, they applaud the vitality of oral tradition. They also reveal the origins of the vast range of their collected material to be popular songs, political lampoons, ballads, riddles and numerous other sources, few of which, other than lullabies, are specific to children. The volume is alphabetically arranged and copiously annotated.[4] While nursery rhymes may have initially entered the children's canon in a variety of ways, the fact that parents and carers were singing them to children must have been an important factor. Many of the rhymes were collected in written form from the eighteenth century onwards, which inevitably widened their availability. For them to become the property of children, however, demands memorability, of which the salient features are surely rhyme, rhythm and repetition, together with the frequent focus on individuals going about pursuits that children can empathise with, notably eating (Jack Horner, Jack Sprat, Little Miss Muffet and countless others).

Similar qualities of rhyme, rhythm and repetition are displayed in verse associated with another area of children's lives, the playground, but there the similarity ends. In this sector, too, the Opies have provided the indispensable source material: *The Lore and Language of Schoolchildren* (1959) and (by Iona Opie alone) *The People in the Playground* (1993).[5] As the Opies observe, what distinguishes this body of material from that in the nursery rhyme collections is the manner of its transmission: 'By its nature a nursery rhyme is a jingle preserved and propagated not by children but by adults ... a rhyme which is adult approved... The schoolchild's verses are not intended for adult ears' (1959: 21). The Opies' analysis relates to the development and regional variations of such verses, classifying them into such categories as chants which are specifically associated with games, as well as topics such as nicknames, friendship, customs and many others. In her later work, Iona Opie also looks at the more recent evolution of rhymes, and the way in which television jingles can be adapted to children's interests. As is indicated in the earlier volume, there is ample material here for study by folklorists and anthropologists.[6]

Later literary scholars have built on the comprehensive achievement of the Opies; as Styles observes in her chapter on the subject, such verse 'reminds us of the vibrancy of vernacular language and children's defiance of adult rules and strictures' (1998: 103). Some attention to nursery rhymes and other oral material is given in a more recent, conference-based collection, *Poetry and Childhood*, edited by Morag Styles, Louise Joy and David Whitley. In particular, Karen Coats looks at children's attraction towards rhyme: 'If it rhymes, it's funny' (2010: 121), and C.W. Sullivan III examines the way in which children's oral poetry often includes a scatological element (2010: 131–140).

Didacticism and entertainment

Because verses can be committed to memory, educational and religious material has often been presented to children in rhyme. The starting point for most historians of children's poetry lies with Puritan writers who versified religious texts[7] or drew morals from nature (as in Bunyan's *A Book for Boys and Girls* (1686). Isaac Watts is explicit about his motives in producing his *Divine Songs* (1715): 'What is learnt in Verse is longer retained in memory' (quoted in Styles 1998: 14). To take the seventeenth century as a starting point is, however, to ignore the fact that both moral precepts and information had been presented to children in verse long before this, and Seth Lerer's *Children's Literature: A Reader's History* (2008) builds on his specialisms in philology, the Greek and Roman classics, and medieval literature, in order to present some poetry, including twelfth- to fifteenth-century French and German versifications of Aesop (2008: 46–53) as well as Middle English verse dramas (2008: 64–70). These latter were intended both to instruct and to entertain, as recommended by the Latin writer, Horace. Lerer also finds evidence of verse deriving from children themselves, both marginalia in manuscripts and early printed books, and scraps of children's songs recorded by adult writers (2008: 70). Lerer's work reminds modern readers of the child consumers of this largely didactic verse. They foreshadow the later, more visible, young audience for both the didactic material and the less formal verse of chapbooks and ballads. Indeed, Grenby suggests that 'most children led a much richer poetic life in the seventeenth and eighteenth centuries than they do today' (2008: 36).

John Bunyan's *A Book for Boys and Girls* (1686) has some claim to be the first collection specifically intended for the entertainment and edification of young readers. Less scholarly analysis has been devoted to this than to his prose fiction or his theology, but it has been recognised as reflecting the influence of the emblem tradition on religious poetry (see Rosemary Freeman's magisterial work, *English Emblem Books*, 1970). Early editions of Bunyan's text were unaccompanied by illustrations, relying on the words to create their own pictures. Seth Lerer's comparison between the experience of reading the sequence of Bunyan's rhymes and Christian's journey in Bunyan's better known *Pilgrim's Progress* (1678) is apposite to the order in which the poems are presented (2008: 93).

Isaac Watts has a distinguished place in the development of the English hymn, but his verse for children is also remembered because of the parodies to which some of his poems are subjected in *Alice in Wonderland* – this in itself is a form of satirical comment from Lewis Carroll but also attests to his enduring appeal to later ages. As Styles observes, Watts' 'lyric gift' constitutes an important part of his appeal (1998: 15), notably in his employment of common hymn metres in these verses.

Eighteenth- and nineteenth-century texts such as the writings of Charles and Mary Lamb, Ann and Jane Taylor, and Lucy Aiken's collection *Poetry for Children* (1801, 1803) are frequently cited in the histories. Mary V. Jackson's *Engines of Instruction, Mischief, and Magic* suggests that these writers, together with the contemporary highly moralistic writers of prose, 'participated ... in the vast work of reestablishing the religious, social, and political verities necessary to bolster Church and State' (1989: 184). Nevertheless, she claims that the Taylor sisters in particular did write many 'lighter, comic, and occasionally truly poetic poems' (1989: 184), while the continuing popularity of Cecil Frances Alexander children's hymns, such as 'Once in Royal David's City' and 'There Is a Green Hill Far Away', attests to the fact that, as Styles comments, 'she was able to write for children with simplicity and directness in approachable language' (1998: 26).

Christina Rossetti continued the association between women poets and children's verse, but, paradoxically, the poem most likely to be found in children's anthologies, *Goblin Market* (1862),[8] was not written for children; as Roderick McGillis[9] observes, it 'manifestly contains the theme of sexual frustration' (1987: 209). His substantial discussion of its ambiguity, its links with fairytale, and its figurative language is longer than the section of his chapter devoted to *Sing-Song* (1872), a collection which is certainly addressed to young readers, but in which he finds the same preoccupations as the longer work.[10]

The majority of the other well-known late nineteenth- and early twentieth-century writers of verse for children tend to be remembered by the critics for their prose rather than their poetry; in some instances they are better-known for their adult writings than those for a younger audience. Certainly the critical attention devoted to R.L. Stevenson's *A Child's Garden of Verses* (1885) is minimal by contrast with that given to his prose writing, both for adults and for children. Styles' discussion seems rather to have the aim of introducing readers to his poetic oeuvre than subjecting it to analysis; she does, however, defend his work against the charge of intellectual dishonesty made by Goldthwaite (1996), who censures Stevenson for portraying childhood as 'a pleasant land of make-believe' (1998: 170) when his own childhood was certainly not idyllic. More recently, David Fergus in 'A major minor poet' (2012)[11] puts forward the possibility that in such lines as 'The world is so full of a number of things, / I'm sure we should all be as happy as kings' (written in a year when Stevenson had had a near fatal haemorrhage and was also threatened with blindness), he was writing ironically rather than with 'facile optimism'.

Whatever Stevenson's status, there is no doubt that the picture of childhood he presents has had a considerable influence on subsequent verse for children, perhaps most obviously in the case of A.A. Milne. Critical attention tends to be on prose writings featuring Winnie-the-Pooh rather than Milne's children's verse, his plays for adults, or his humorous pieces for *Punch*. Styles quotes critics – both those contemporary with Milne and subsequent to him – who regard his children's verse as over-sentimental, but she defends it on the grounds of its continuing appeal to children and Milne's mastery of metre and rhyme (1998: 232). In fact, as Ann Thwaite makes evident in her biography of Milne, 'there was a lot wrong with poetry for children in 1923' (the year when Milne was writing *When we were very young*), and Milne's collection, unlike the work of some of his contemporaries, addresses the child in 'rational English' (Thwaite 1990: 246), thus succeeding in enhancing the status of children's poetry.

Among the other esteemed children's poets of the earlier half of the twentieth century is Eleanor Farjeon, whose poetry is described by Humphrey Carpenter and Mari Prichard as 'slight but always technically deft' (1984: 183). Styles praises her 'lightness of touch' and the range of her work, including its 'lively narratives' (1998: 236). She also describes Farjeon's friend and contemporary, Walter de la Mare, as 'probably the most significant poet for children of all time writing in the Romantic tradition' (1998: 223), though his brand of fantasy was not highly regarded by contemporary arbiters of poetic taste, such as F.R. Leavis. Nevertheless, he received a good deal of critical attention during the 1920s and 1930s, and 'The Listeners' and 'Silver' are well represented in anthologies, not only those for children; they illustrate his effective portrayal of detail, together with 'his almost flawless command of metre and rhyme' (Styles 1998: 227–8). It could be said that virtually all of de la Mare's output is suitable for children, though that would not imply that all children would necessarily respond to it.

What seems to emerge from this rapid survey of much of the verse written for children is that, however children's poetry be defined, the qualities of vivid description appealing to the senses, and language

whose memorability is enhanced by rhyme and rhythm, are more relevant to its appeal to children than is its actual subject matter.

Children's poetry with greater appeal to the critics

Exceptions to the general neglect by many critics of the poetry considered in this chapter occur in relation both to nonsense verse and to the
work of major poets, some of whose output implies a young audience.

Nonsense poetry

To counterbalance both the didactic emphasis of much of the poetry
mentioned above, and the dangerous approach to sentimentality of
some of the rest, attention needs to be given to the criticism of nonsense
poetry. While it is undeniable that this sub-genre seems to have a particular appeal to children, Noel Malcolm, in *The Origins of English Nonsense*
(1997), claims that instances of nonsense verse which indirectly influenced its major nineteenth-century exponents, Edward Lear and Lewis
Carroll, are to be found in writing for adults as early as the late sixteenth
century. That there were other predecessors of these renowned exponents of the genre is made clear also by Grenby (2008: 43), but there is
no doubt that it flourished from the middle of the nineteenth century
onwards and became particularly attractive to the young. Lerer suggests reasons for this, both in the way that the work of Darwin made
evident the abundance of strange creatures that had preceded human
beings, and the contemporary discovery of an abundance of unfamiliar
languages, both ancient and modern. Lerer claims that the notion of
linguistic nonsense 'as a challenge to the logic of adulthood and the
laws of civil life ... [was] a new idea in Victorian England' (2008: 191).
He admits the impossibility of doing justice to the volume of critical
work on Lear and Carroll, but his discussion of their poetry provides a
useful starting point, particularly since he writes as a linguistic scholar.
He observes that Lear and Carroll present a world changed as if in a mirror or upside down – a perspective which resembles the kind of vision
which a child, not comprehending the grown-up world, might have.
Both these nonsense writers also relish the sounds of words and enjoy
placing incongruous but similar sounding words together: Lerer cites
Lear's pairing in a letter of the words 'carrots' and 'parrots' (2008: 202).
Lerer goes on to suggest that among those following in the nonsense
tradition of Lear and Carroll were the Dadaists, who 'made the absurd
[into the twentieth century's] defining aesthetic' (2008: 204). In his
concluding paragraph on the topic he remarks: 'Nonsense is more than
play: it takes us to the limits of expression' (2008: 208). This suggests

that it is an important, even essential, part of the serious language game that is poetry.

Children's Writing by Major Poets

Since it is not practicable to discuss here poems often included in children's anthologies by writers such as Wordsworth, Browning or Kipling, nearly all the major poets considered here who deliberately chose to address a child audience derive from the twentieth century. The exception to this is William Blake, discussion of whose *Songs of Innocence and Experience* (1794) has deliberately been postponed from its chronological slot. This is partly because to describe these poems as either didactic or entertaining would be simplistic, and partly because Blake seems to belong with a small number of other major poets who have written for children, notably Ted Hughes and Charles Causley, and indeed the rather different children's verse of T.S. Eliot. Though the verse they wrote for children usually receives less attention than the rest of their output, it demands the context of their total oeuvre. In some instances too, the question of definition arises again, though occasionally the classification has been made evident by the poets themselves.

Blake's *Songs* clearly possess both the 'immediate sense perception' demanded by Neil Philip, and the facility with rhyme and rhythm characteristic of so much verse that appeals to children. Many of his poems are written in the hymn metres popularised by Isaac Watts, and this apparent simplicity contrasts with the profundity of the questions addressed to the child. Styles cites Peter Ackroyd, Blake's biographer, who considers that the poet wrote solely with children in mind, before quoting Zachary Leader's verdict in his *Reading Blake's Songs* (1981): 'The deceptively simple and reassuring rhythms of nursery rhyme, folk-song, jingle, lullaby, ballad, and hymn, when combined with an equally child-like pictorial style ... [create] a children's book for adults' (Styles 1998: 42). Leader's in-depth analysis both of the verse and the pictures means that his book has to be the starting point for any study of Blake's verse for children.

The answer to the question as to whether any of T.S. Eliot's works are intended for children is in effect provided by the poet himself: *Old Possum's Book of Practical Cats* (1939), in its subject matter, its address (originating in letters to his godson), and perhaps above all its rhythm and rhyme, is very different from the works on which Eliot's reputation rests, such as *The Waste Land* (1922) or *Four Quartets* (1943). Nevertheless, Styles suggests that the use of this book as a foundation for Andrew Lloyd Webber's musical *Cats* (1981) means that the collection should be regarded as a book for adults rather than children (1998: 218), while Marion Hodge (1974) contends that the seedy criminal world rife in many of Eliot's adult poems and his demonstration therein of the imperfections of humanity have affinities with the behaviour of many of his cats.[12]

Unlike many of his predecessors as Poet Laureate, Ted Hughes took writing poetry for children very seriously. This is evidenced not only by the large volume of material he published for them but also in his own prose writing on the subject. His *Poetry in the Making* (1967) has much more to say about his own craft (albeit at an early stage in his career) than its subtitle: *an anthology of poems and programmes from 'listening and writing'* [lower case sic] would suggest. For instance, he tells of how, to him, his poems have their own autonomy, often coming to him unexpectedly (1967: 15). Hughes also emphasises the importance of myth to both poetry and prose, seeing it as a kind of mediator between the powers of the inner world, and the outer world of everyday life.[13] In a more recent study, Michael Lockwood traces how the style of Hughes' poems for children evolved from his early use of rhyme, through a period when he largely used free verse in his animal poems for young readers. His development culminated in a return to rhyme in his later verse, the quality of which Lockwood feels is not yet fully recognised.[14]

Despite considerable differences from Ted Hughes, a similarly mythic quality of the imagination is displayed in the work for both adults and children of Charles Causley; indeed, it is rather difficult to discern any significant differences in the addressee of most of his output.[15] As Styles observes, his use of rhyme and metre, unlike that of Hughes, is basically traditional, while J.R. Townsend sees him as a storyteller as well as a poet, whose 'work is imbued with the spirit of the old ballads and with folklore and legend' (1990: 298).

Writers such as Hughes and Causley have in recent years raised the status of children's poetry, and in the case of Hughes, himself poet laureate, paved the way for another poet who has written a good deal for children, Carol Ann Duffy, to be his successor in the post of Poet Laureate (now held for ten years rather than a lifetime). It is perhaps appropriate to the nature of children's literature that the Children's Laureateship, a post in the foundation of which Hughes was also instrumental, with Michael Morpurgo, is only held for only two years. As well as children's novelists and illustrators, two children's poets have (up to 2014) held this position, Michael Rosen (of whom more will be said in the next section) and Julia Donaldson.

The poetic idiom and the contemporary scene

The relationship of the language of children's poetry to everyday speech has been foregrounded in the last part of the twentieth century and the early years of the twenty-first. This is partly because of the important part played by Caribbean poets such as John Agard, Grace Nichols and James Berry, whose work, increasingly popular with children, has always been associated with performance. Another agent of this effect has been Michael Rosen who has not only made extensive use of spoken language in his many collections for young readers but frequently gives them memorable performances. This recalls the previously quoted remark of Peter Hunt about the importance of new media in facilitating orality in poetry (2001: 298). Rosen, given the official accolade of the Children's Laureateship (2009–2011), is also a scholar of children's literature who uses his own experience as a writer as a basis for consideration of educational issues. In 'Texts and Contexts: A Reading and Writing Memoir',[16] he emphasises the importance of children's poetry in a school curriculum which he considers rates feeling as less important than a kind of 'logical positivism ... [in which] every process is reduced to its component facts, chronology and logic'. He stresses the danger that poetry is merely 'slotted into the curriculum after tests at the end of term' (2010: 14). Both Rosen and Styles speak of the danger that the compilation and presentation in school of anthologies may minimise the children's opportunity to encounter the work of individual poets. Styles voices her concern in a talk entitled 'Keeping the flame alive in challenging times' given at a conference on poetry for children in 2011.[17] She emphasises the value of single-poet collections, which enable young readers to engage with the poet, and are not so subject to editorial choice as are anthologies.

Involving children with poetry also demands that they themselves engage in this struggle with words and meanings. A good deal of attention has been given in recent years to acknowledging children's own efforts in the area of creation, and while the pedagogical aspect cannot be to the forefront in this presentation of criticism, the way in which children are encouraged to write poetry, and the value given to it by their teachers, is scarcely peripheral to the debate. Sandy Brownjohn's *Does It Have to Rhyme?* (1980) released children, and teachers, from the necessity of writing with this constraint, although clearly the enjoyment that some of them feel in complying with this particular 'rule of the game' should not be overlooked. Certainly the conference referred to above, which took its title from the Brownjohn book, involved a good many speakers who took the poetic efforts of young people very seriously. Among these were David Whitley who poses the question of whether children writing poetry should again be taught to use rhyme and metre, and Kimberley Black on the interaction between word-based performance poetry and human rights. This latter paper, like the one by Emily Roach on children reading poetry by adult writers about death, brings up again the perennial debate as to whether certain subjects are unsuitable for children's poetry.[18]

Another feature of the contemporary scene in children's poetry is the recognition given to living poets who are writing for a young audience. Unless they have other employment, poets are dependent firstly on publication and then on sales for their income. Until the recent establishment of the Children's Laureateship, the most important form of recognition given to British writers of poetry for children was in prizes. Between 1979 and 2001, the Signal Poetry Award, under the aegis of the Thimble Press, run by Nancy and Aidan Chambers, was the most important of these. This not only rewarded the poets concerned but also generated interesting articles, published in *Signal,* about the winner and children's poetry in general.[19] The final issue of this prestigious journal[20] not only contains articles by Neil Philip on Ted Hughes' books for children (deploring the general absence of critical comment on this part of his oeuvre), and Richard Flynn on American children's poetry, but also and more relevantly in the current context, a short account by the children's novelist, Jan Mark, of the Poetry Award itself. She highlights the work of some of the winners but also conjectures as to whether it is possible to determine what children's poetry is. However, she concludes with a plea for excellence – a quality sought by the judges in the poems they reviewed 'because we all believed that children deserve nothing less' (2003: 141).[21]

Drama for children

If, as Peter Hollindale observes, 'drama ... [is] the Cinderella of children's literature' (1996: 219), then the paucity of criticism concerning this form of literature is scarcely surprising. In this section, only theatrical material created for performance by or for children will be considered. Since there are now so many modes into which texts originally created in a printed form can be adapted, this area is discussed in a later chapter, particularly since adapted versions of written children's literature are often multi-modal in nature.

Hollindale's article, quoted above, provides a succinct history of children's involvement in theatrical performance: for instance, companies of young actors were mentioned, largely pejoratively, in plays by Shakespeare and Jonson since they posed an economic threat to the adult companies; their flourishing, however, came to an end with Puritanism (1996: 211–215). A number of plays intended for the education and/or edification of children were published over the years (see Hunt 2001: 266 and Carpenter 1984: 415), but until the twentieth century none of them commanded a mass audience. Undoubtedly a turning point was the production of J.M. Barrie's *Peter Pan, or The Boy Who Wouldn't Grow Up* (1904).[22] Unlike plays based on earlier children's texts, such as *Alice in Wonderland*, the 'classic' children's novel did not appear in this instance until after the performance of the play, which itself arose out of Barrie's adult novel, *The Little White Bird* (1902). The character of Peter Pan, a small boy living in Kensington Gardens, features in one of the storylines in this book. The genesis of the play, and subsequently the children's novel based on the play and entitled *Peter Pan and Wendy* (1911), is described at length in Jacqueline Rose's seminal work of criticism, *The Case of Peter Pan or The Impossibility of Children's Fiction*; in it, Barrie's work is used as a springboard for the discussion of what Rose terms 'the fantasy which lies behind the concept of children's fiction ... the acknowledged difference, a rupture almost, between writer and addressee' (1984: 1;2).

Quite apart from its role in engendering one of the most famous prose works for children, the play of *Peter Pan* was influential in several ways. As well as inspiring a number of other playwrights to write for a child audience, it fostered an interest in the provision of theatres appropriate to the performance of such plays. The pioneering work of the US writer and director Charlotte Chorpenning (1873–1955) in Chicago set new standards for children's theatre, leading eventually to the establishment of specialist theatres, such as the Unicorn Theatre in London, and initiatives run by organisations including the National Theatre.

Amongst the relatively few playwrights who have written specifically for children and young adults, are Chorpenning herself and Aurand Harris in the United States, though many of their works are adaptations rather than originals. One of the few playwrights whose work for young people has attracted critical attention is Edward Bond, whose innovative and challenging writing has more recently given rise to a collection of studies, edited by David Davis (2005). The essays in his collection outline the responses of young people to Bond's work, thus linking with the role of drama in education and often taking the form of improvisation. In fact, despite the existence of scripted plays for young people, the emphasis among educationalists has tended to be on a child-centred participatory approach. An early proponent of this was Peter Slade, whose *The Child at Play: Child Drama* (1954) recounts his long experience in this field, with the intention of helping teachers to foster improvised drama. The successful outcome of his campaigning may be deduced from the fact that the short section on drama in The Bullock Report, *A Language for Life* (1975), while paying lip-service to performance based on a script, is almost totally devoted to the value of improvised drama as a means of language development. Other important exponents of dramatic work in the classroom were Dorothy Heathcote and the major disseminator of her approach, Gavin Bolton (1995), whose writing gave support to teachers lacking confidence in their ability to develop the full dramatic potential of their students. A greater emphasis on performance is, however, to be found in the work of David Hornbrook (1998), to the extent that the two schools of thought on the place of drama in the curriculum are often at odds. Jonothan Neelands distinguishes them thus: 'the product approach is often associated with "theatre" as a subject of study and the "process" approach with improvised forms of drama used as a method of teaching and learning across the curriculum' (2008: 4). He claims that the 'product' approach views its goal as the students' understanding of drama in its literary and performance modes, which contrasts with 'the assumption that the "process" approach grows out of forms of dramatic play associated with the early years of childhood and grows into more "adult" forms of theatre knowledge and practice' (2008: 5).

Peter Hollindale's short analysis of the place of drama in children's literature remains the most useful critical introduction to the subject. It concludes by deploring the lack of 'critical attention and institutional support' given to it, observing that 'it is arguably the most important children's art form of all, the one they are sure to live with, through the media of film and television, all their lives' (1996: 219). This aspect, which inevitably involves adaptation from and to other media, will be given some attention in the final chapter of the current volume. The focus in Part Three which follows is on some of the more theoretical areas which have received considerable recent critical attention.

PART III

Theoretical Approaches

CHAPTER EIGHT

Gender Studies and Queer Theory

Introduction

In tracing the development of literary criticism focusing on aspects of gender – both in general terms and in relation to children's literature – the role of feminist scholars, who were pioneers in voicing a raised awareness of bias, is fundamental. It was not until well after the publication of seminal texts in the field of feminist criticism that attention was given to 'masculinist' issues or the significance in children's literature of what had previously been seen as 'deviant' behaviour in the area of gender. The roots of early feminism, and the resulting attention to the ways in which books influenced, and were influenced by, sexist attitudes, can be traced back to the 1880s and before. Nevertheless, Maggie Humm claims that 'feminist criticism did not become recognised as representative of intellectual endeavour in the academy until second-wave feminism' (1994: 2). The term 'second-wave', which implicitly pays tribute to the earlier pioneers of female emancipation, is applied to, among others, Simone de Beauvoir (*The Second Sex*, 1949), Betty Friedan (*The Feminine Mystique*, 1966), Germaine Greer (*The Female Eunuch*, 1971) and Kate Millett (*Sexual Politics*, 1970); the last of these is generally seen as most relevant to the development of specifically literary criticism rather than cultural criticism in general.

Feminist literary critics had a wider aim than merely detecting bias in the depiction of female characters in novels. Humm suggests that their agenda was: to address the issue of a masculine literary history 'by re-examining male texts, noting their patriarchal assumptions and showing the way women in these texts are often represented according to prevailing social, cultural and ideological norms'; to address the invisibility of women writers – taking note of those who have subsequently been neglected and of women's oral culture; to offer readers new methods and fresh critical practices, focusing on techniques of signification; and to encourage their readers to act as feminists by creating new writing and reading collectives (Humm 1994: 7–8). As will be seen below, all of these aims have been explored by critics of children's literature. One of the most influential texts contributing to this process, especially in relation to books written by women (whether the implied audience is adult or younger) has been Sandra Gilbert and Susan Gubar's *The Madwoman in the Attic* (1979). This gives fresh attention within a broadly historical and cultural context to canonical texts by authors such as Jane Austen, the Brontës and George Eliot, and has fostered similar studies of a range of lesser known women writers. As well as this rereading of the canon, another influential critical work looking at disregarded female writers and their situation in a male-dominated society is Elaine Showalter's *A Literature of Their Own* (1977).

More recently, in the wake of what has been termed 'third-wave' feminism, because of its change of focus towards a greater acceptance of diversity of ethnicity and culture among women, there has been a shift from concentration on female representation towards examination of constructions of masculinity and sexuality. Consequently the discipline is today termed 'gender', rather than 'women's' studies, partly as a result of the work of Judith Butler, who 'argues that rather than being natural or innate, gender is actually a series of stylised acts and behaviours that are repeated until they give the illusion of authenticity' (Flanagan, in (ed.) Rudd 2010: 32). This emphasis on performativity, rather than innate behaviour, has given rise to studies of a variety of performances of gender, such as cross-dressing. Nevertheless, the fact that feminist scholars were the pioneers in the field should never be overlooked. As Roberta Seelinger Trites observes:

■ No organized social movement has affected children's literature as significantly as feminism has. Since the resurgence of the women's movement in the 1960s, many children's novels published in the English language have reflected the goals of the movement. Girl protagonists, for example, have often been more active and vocal than their counterparts in earlier literature. They have had more options for adventures outside the home, for forming more varied friendships, and for setting diverse goals. As a result, their narratives have had more complexity. (1997: ix) □

Prejudice: Children's books and women authors

Early work on gender and children's literature stemmed from the concern expressed by second-wave feminist cultural critics throughout the 1970s about what they perceived to be potentially harmful representations of femininity in books and other cultural texts aimed at children, in view of the growing appreciation of the formative role of early reading in the development of the self. Their view that gender is socially constructed led to a focus on the socialisation process and the role of stories in inculcating in children normative ideas about gender roles. More specifically, early studies in the field investigated the limited and limiting roles accorded to female characters in fictions aimed at pre-readers and early readers. That many children's books were written by marginalised women writers seems also to have been a factor in the lack of value attributed to them.

Much of the early work on detecting bias in books for children also had a broader basis than simply that of gender; critics who were active in the fields of race and class were also sensitive to the negative portrayal of female characters. Two widely disseminated books written from this broader perspective are Bob Dixon's *Catching Them Young I: Sex, Race and Class in Children's Fiction* (1977) and *Racism and Sexism in Children's Books* (1979) edited by Judith Stinton.[1] None of the contributors to this debate had any hesitation in subjecting the classics of children's literature to criteria which took little account of the prevailing attitudes of the period in which the books were written; these critics were understandably more concerned with how such books influenced the socialisation of children into twentieth-century society.

As indicated in Chapter Four, fairytales also came under scrutiny. Feminist critics found Bruno Bettelheim's Freudian perspective inadequate as a lens for analysis of the situation and subjectivity of the female characters, while a number of creative writers produced alternative versions of traditional tales.[2] Both Marina Warner and Jack Zipes dissented from several aspects of Bettelheim's analysis, Zipes in particular editing a collection of anti-sexist alternative tales, *Don't Bet on the Prince* (1986). This also includes a short critical discussion in which Zipes highlights this debate:

■ To talk about fairy tales today, especially feminist fairy tales, one must, in my opinion, talk about power, violence, alienation, social conditions, child-rearing and sex roles. It is no longer possible to ignore the connection between the aesthetic components of the fairy tales, whether they be old or new, and their historical function within a socialisation process which forms taste, mores, values, and habits. (1986: 2) □

Another field examined by feminist critics has been that of picture-books. Alleen Pace Nilsen (1971) analysed Caldecott Award winners, finding that females were significantly underrepresented relative to male characters, while a high proportion of those female characters who did feature as protagonists (twenty-one out of twenty-five) were depicted wearing aprons, thus being cast in traditional domestic roles at a time when almost 40% of American mothers were working outside the home. This empirical research into androcentric picturebooks could, with the benefit of hindsight, be dismissed as reductive, literally a matter of 'apron counting', but it helped to raise awareness and encouraged further evidence-gathering which, in turn, led to more inclusive publishing policies. A similar study by 'Feminists on Children's Literature', also published in 1971, extended this largely negative critique to books for a more varied age range and designated by publishers as 'especially for girls': stories involving proactive heroines, but with regressive or 'cop-out' endings, and those which, more positively, 'allow for character development beyond the stereotype' (1971: 21). A more nuanced study of forty-nine Newbery Award winning books (Powell et al. 1993) anticipated a number of strands in subsequent feminist criticism of children's literature, namely a focus on the connection between gender and genre; the presence of strategies of containment at the end of stories with strong female protagonists; and stories which subvert and even overturn stereotypical ideas about gender. Such studies have, however, encountered the criticism that they assume the child reader will simply identify with the heroine, rather than engage in resistant reading.

The school story genre, popular in both book and comic format, has traditionally exhibited a high degree of polarisation in gender roles. While much of the discussion of the boys' school genre is largely historical in focus, so that gender-related elements have seldom been examined until relatively recently,[3] critical analysis of girls' school stories has been more alert to this aspect. Rosemary Auchmuty, whose *A World of Girls* (1992) did much to enhance the status of the girls' story and who, with Joy Wotton, was general editor of the two volume *Encyclopedia of School Stories* (2000), defines the situation:

> ■ The critical literature of girls' and boys' school stories has tended to be separate ... with considerably more attention focused on the latter. This is not surprising given the association of boys' schools with the ruling class and intellectual culture ... The rise of feminist scholarship in the last three decades has prompted a number of separate studies of girls' school stories, with the initial critical condemnation ... giving way to a recognition of the books' potential to challenge patriarchal norms and empower their young readers. (in (eds) Sims and Clare 2000: viii) □

Thus gender issues were inevitably part of the context of the critical discussion. A study by Mary Cadogan and Patricia Craig (1976), while not in itself taking a feminist perspective, inspired various responses from a gender-based perspective, focusing on whether the female roles presented had a positive or negative effect on their readers self-image. In her two studies of the girls' school story,

■ Rosemary Auchmuty particularly suggests that, in offering depictions of all-female worlds with strong role models, friendship between and among women, and a range of ways of being which went far beyond conventional prescriptions of femininity, girls' school stories provided – and still provide – an escape for girls and women from the worst pressures of patriarchal life …. (Auchmuty in (eds) Sims and Clare, 2000: 29–30) □

An area strongly associated with dominating male characters, in which until well on in the twentieth century the females generally had only a subordinate role to play, is that of the adventure story. Margery Hourihan's critique of this genre begins with an acknowledgement of the importance of story and of how within Western culture the hero tale 'tell[ing] how white European men are the natural masters of the world because they are strong, brave, skilful, rational and dedicated … has dominated children's and young adult literature, passing on the traditional values to each new generation' (1997: 1–3). Hourihan attempts to uncover the meanings and attitudes presented in stories ranging from Homer's *Odyssey*, through fairytales, to *Star Wars*, using an approach based on such features as the binary oppositions (discussing what is presented as good or bad), the narrative point of view, and 'consideration of what is foregrounded, what is backgrounded and what is simply omitted', in order to determine the hierarchy of values constructed (1997: 4). Her analysis leads her, for instance, to conclude that analysis of Sendak's seemingly 'innocent' picturebook, *Where the Wild Things Are* (1963), reveals that Max 'is clearly a potential member of the patriarchy' (1997: 12), even though this is unlikely to be as evident to an adult reading it to a child as would be the paradigmatic instances of Ulysses, Aeneas or Robinson Crusoe.

The hero tale and, in its wake, the vast number of comics with heroic male characters, are blatantly addressed to a young male readership (although often enjoyed by young female readers). Parallel to the boys' comics, a considerable range of periodicals have been addressed to girls, ranging from the *Girls' Own Paper* through the many comics featuring life at girls' boarding schools to the popular magazines which from the 1960s onwards have provided teenage female readers with stories and information designed to make them feel part of their peer group and ready for all that life has to offer in terms of relationships. Many feminist scholars have worked on this considerable body of material. Kimberley Reynolds' *Girls Only: Gender and Popular Children's Fiction in Britain, 1880–1910* (1990) explores the cultural significance of the considerable expansion of popular reading matter in a period when literacy was on the increase and thus markets had widened. She shows how 'despite its concern with female welfare and the reform of legislation and attitudes which victimised women', the *Girls' Own Paper* seems to have been more designed to make women content with their role in a patriarchal society than to be prepared for any role in running such a society (1990: 150).

For much of the earlier part of the twentieth century, traditional girls' comics, with a preponderance of school stories, dominated the market, but in 1964 the advent of *Jackie* brought into the teenage domain something resembling the world of the women's magazines, with an emphasis on romance, advice about fashion, and 'solutions' to readers' problems. The danger that comics like this might encourage a conformist mind-set perturbed feminist critics such as Sue Sharpe (1976) and Angela McRobbie (1978; 1981), while Valerie Walkerdine (1984) was concerned at the stereotyped female roles that she perceived in some stories in other girls' comics such as *Bunty* and *Tracy*.[4] More recently, extensive work on comics and magazines, particularly those aimed at young adult female readers, has been undertaken by Mel Gibson. In a useful historical perspective, she traces the development of the teenage magazine, as distinct from the comic; she shows how 'the increasing dominance of the magazine … resulted in the disappearance of the girls' comics … [as they] became detached from models of girlhood in Britain through the shifting gender, age and class associations of the comic format' (in (eds) Styles and Bearne 2003: 98).

Another task undertaken by feminist critics of children's literature, encouraged by the examples of Gilbert and Gubar and of Showalter, was the discovery and rehabilitation of women writers whose work was either forgotten or had come to be perceived as too at ease with stereotypical roles. As has been noted above, analysis of some undervalued genres, such as schoolgirl fiction, was a part of this process, as also was the work of critics such as Lissa Paul (discussed below) who took a more theoretical stance. There was also a positive shift towards reclaiming the work of women writers who had been doubly marginalised – as women and as writers of low status literature for children. Subsequent to Reynolds' 1990 study, which scrutinises books by authors such as Evelyn Everett-Green (1856–1932) and L.T. Meade (1879–1914), further forays into fiction popular with girls have been made by the contributors to *Popular Children's Literature in Britain* (2008), in which Dennis Butts and Elaine Lomax look at the work of Barbara Hofland (1770–1844) and 'Hesba Stretton' (Sarah Smith 1832–1911), respectively. Both of these authors were notable in their own time, and Lomax argues that not only did Stretton 'take advantage of popular forms and themes to promote pressing social, moral and spiritual agendas', she also 'create[d] a platform … for the expression of a powerful, if sometimes contradictory, female voice' (2008: 146).[5]

A further area revealed by surveys of children's reading (see Chapter Two) is that girls seem to prefer to read cooperatively, thus creating female communities of readers. Some years previously, Nina Auerbach (1978; 1986) had researched nineteenth-century women who could be seen as subverting patriarchy by their cooperative reading, but little investigation had taken place on the cooperation between girl readers. A study by Meredith Rogers Cherland, focusing on their reading of the romance genre, throws light both on this cooperative reading and on the material enjoyed. Cherland notes how Linda Christian-Smith's study of the reading of romance fiction by girls from a range of class and ethnic backgrounds had recorded that girls were not only influenced by their reading but also read 'against the grain'. This work encouraged Cherland to examine how a number of eleven-year-old girls 'did gender' and constructed their identities in the context of both their society and their reading (1994: 14–15). She found that their desire for agency was developing, but that in some instances their reading matter suggested to them that it was better not to take risks: 'Being a "good" girl was the wisest choice' (1994: 190). She concludes that in order to understand how inequality in society is maintained, study of children's reading matter and classroom interaction is necessary; they 'are not passive consumers of cultural meanings: they can, and do, resist', and their resistance can give teachers a starting point for working toward change – a change in which the role of literacy as social practice is fundamental (1994: 212).

Feminist theory and children's literature

While the aspects identified above are clearly of considerable importance, particularly within the pedagogical area, the theoretical underpinning has been equally significant in the establishment of a feminist approach to children's literature. The predominantly practical criticism discussed above was followed by a poststructuralist shift to research into how the genres aimed at girls help to shape their self-identity and aspirations as readers. The insights of post-structuralist theorists such as Judith Butler, and the influence of the French cultural theorist Michel Foucault (1926–84), who emphasises the way in which dominant discourses constitute normative social identities, including those based on gender, language and sexuality, led to an increased awareness that gender cannot be isolated from other criteria as the sole determinant of identity, but needs to be seen in terms of a complex interplay of factors including social class, sexual orientation, ethnicity and age (an aspect particularly relevant in relation to the young reader). This in turn has led to a more explicit focus on theoretical perspectives, and in due course to work related to constructions of masculinity and alternative modes of sexuality.

Lissa Paul's 'Enigma Variations: What Feminist Theory Knows About Children's Literature' (1987) could be described as a manifesto concerning the kinship between children's literature and writing by women. Paul's rationale for 'appropriating feminist theory to children's literature' resides in the devaluation and marginalisation of both women's literature and children's literature by 'the educational and literary communities' (Paul, in Hunt (ed.) 1990: 149). She claims that images of entrapment in children's literature are matched by those discerned by feminist critics in women's literature, and illustrates how both groups have subverted these traps (such as the locked rooms of fairytales and the eponymous 'secret garden') into places of flourishing, sometimes by survival tactics involving guile (as displayed by Mary and Colin in Burnett's classic). Paul goes on to examine how feminist critics have accorded value to 'otherness' by employing the insights of a range of disciplines such as linguistics, Marxism, communication and reader-response theories, cultural anthropology, and psychoanalytic theory (1990: 155–6). What is more, she claims, is that this capacity to 'bring together a "hard body" of critical theory in a "user-friendly", often warm and funny, way is what marks feminist criticism' (1990: 156); Paul exemplifies these qualities in her own critiques of the work of a range of writers. For instance, she goes on to discuss *The Secret Garden* (1911) in more detail, showing how, at the climax of the story, when Colin proudly reveals to his father his newly found exuberant health, Mary fades into the background, having learned to be a follower not a leader, in accordance with the values of her period. This contrasts, Paul indicates, with the greater fulfilment offered by Margaret Mahy to her heroine in *The Changeover* (1984). Paul concludes, 'Story by story, the signs and plots of women's lives begin to find a rightful place, alongside the more familiar male signs, in the mind's eyes of the readers – male and female, adult and child' (1990: 163).

I have devoted attention to Paul's essay, not only because of its originality and subsequent influence, but also because, as she intended, it epitomises the wit and creativity of the best feminist criticism. Incorporating a wide knowledge both of the foremothers of feminism and of children's literature, it sets a standard for subsequent criticism. Equally distinctively personal in style, as well as being influential, is her slightly longer *Reading Otherways* (1998), which incorporates a series of questions which she suggests should be addressed by critics of children's literature and which she herself uses later in the monograph:

- – whose story is this?
  - – who is the reader?
  - – when and where was the reading produced?
  - – who is named? and who is not?
  - – who is on top?

- who gets punished? and who gets praised?
- who speaks? and who is silenced?
- who acts? and who is acted upon?
- who owns property? who is a dependant?
- who looks? and who is observed?
- who fights for honour? and who suffers?
- how are value systems determined? (1998: 16) □

On this basis Paul firstly looks again at fairytales, observing that tales created since the 1970s evince a preference for 'active' rather than 'passive' heroines, together with an awareness of how feminist theory has witnessed 'a change in the interpretation of those terms' (1998: 39). She goes on to reread Alcott, acknowledging that, rather than being seen as supporting the patriarchal order, she has a place 'as a "foremother" of feminist literature' (1998: 54). Nina Bawden's *Carrie's War* (1973), Paul finds, raises a range of 'feminist questions of speech and silence, of names and namelessness, of honour and suffering ...' (1998: 71). Paul describes what she does in *Reading Otherways* as a process of 'getting readings wrong and working out correctives' (1998: 73). It is apparent, both in what she has to say about criticism and in her own critiques of children's literature, that Paul sees the function of the feminist critic of children's literature to be one of offering readings, often of established texts, which are both challenging and provisional.

In her provocatively entitled *Waking Sleeping Beauty* (1997), Roberta Seelinger Trites also makes use of feminist theory, focusing on 'the positive values of gender' in order to reflect her belief that much of the work of exposing sexism had already been carried out. Rather than producing more in this field, she looks at areas such as the novelistic portrayal of protagonists who use their voices, whether in speech or writing, to overcome cultural repression or to enhance their sense of empowerment. She also examines narrative structures which 'express concepts of community and identity as political issues' (1997: xi). The concept of subjectivity, fundamental to which is the role of language, is another theme she explores, quoting Francis Jacques, who claims that 'subjects only develop a sense of self-identity if they are able to think of themselves ... in all three grammatical persons' (1997: 27). Trites shows how novelists such as Virginia Hamilton and Margaret Mahy create characters who 'take the subject position as a way to grow and as a way to celebrate themselves, not as a way to have power over other people by putting them in the object position' (1997: 46).[6]

Subjectivity is also the theme of Christine Wilkie-Stibbs' *The Feminine Subject in Children's Literature* (2002), which relates the theoretical work of French feminist critics, notably Cixous, Irigaray and Kristeva, on the concept of *'the feminine'* (italics original), to a number of texts by

Margaret Mahy (again!) and Gillian Cross. As Wilkie-Stibbs indicates, the concept of '*the feminine*' differs from everyday usage, referring to 'an aesthetics of corporeality ... not reducible to biological or sexual definition, neither does it preclude sexual difference. It includes women but does not exclude men'. She proposes this category 'not only as an aesthetics of the literary subject but also as a mode of literary engagement that is not gender specific nor gender determined' (2002: 1–2). The children's books discussed she sees as illustrating the quality of 'speaking the body', irrespective of the gender of the protagonists concerned, while avoiding any either/or polarity, positing instead circularity and fluidity.

Widening the field of gender: The turn to masculinity

'Hegemonic masculinity' is defined by R.W. Connell as 'the configuration of gender practice which embodies the currently accepted answer to the problem of the legitimacy of patriarchy, which guarantees (or is taken to guarantee) the dominant position of men and the subordination of women'.[7] The various period-related modes of this quality have been so prevalent and powerful throughout the centuries that it was not until feminists began to question the notion that females should automatically be in a subordinate position, in both literature and life, that mainstream criticism began to query the unstated assumptions about the male role that this implied. As noted above, discussion of books and comics directed to boys was, until recently, likely to take a historical perspective, taking account of the role of the (generally ex-public-school) boy in empire building as well as in society at large, without questioning the image of 'manhood' underpinning it. Joseph Bristow (1991) was among the first to go beyond this. He claims that narratives addressing boys, in a range which included the *Boys' Own Paper*, public school stories and adventure fiction, do in fact present various modes of the masculine, making a variety of incompatible demands on the hero figures – from moral restraint to intrepid exploration, implicitly revealing that 'characteristic male identity is something that never can be fully gained' (1991: 226). As John Stephens indicates in an important collection of essays on masculinities,[8] 'this dominant form [boys fiction] appears simultaneously to propose [to its young readers] a schema for behavior [sic] and to insist on their subordination as children, to conflate agency with hegemonic masculinity, and to disclose that, for them, such agency is illusory' (2002: ix–x).

The articles in Stephens' collection examine progress since the initial problematisation of masculinity. Both Stephens himself and some of the contributors warn of the danger of establishing a new normative masculinity which, while taking into account the necessity for a character to show some degree of awareness and sensitivity, could become just as hegemonic as the patriarchal versions which have been rejected. Stephens[9] presents 'three principal male schemata deployed in junior fiction (Old Age Boy, New Age Boy and Mommy's Boy)', claiming that 'what makes the protagonist, usually a New Age Boy, preferable to his peers is that in the course of the narrative his masculinity is defined as the attainment or disclosure of an element of self-awareness which enables him both to take responsibility for his own life and to take on significant social commitments' (2002: 38). The novels Stephens discusses, representative of the 1990s, present New Age Boy – usually 'a male child in his primary school years who is beginning to display the traits of the New Age Man' – not as 'Everyday Boy', but rather as an outsider who characteristically 'reads for pleasure and may aspire to be a writer himself', someone who displays moral rather than physical courage (2002: 44).

Perry Nodelman's article in Stephens' collection[10] draws attention to the way in which some children's stories, such as Potter's *Peter Rabbit* (1902) and Sendak's *Where the Wild Things Are* (1963), portray young male characters as indulging in a kind of acceptable naughtiness, chiming in with the notion that the young male needs to be 'civilised' to conform with society's standards. Nodelman also looks at a variety of books which are aiming to 'transcend the formulas of popular fiction ... [portraying] boys seeing through the conventional constructions of masculinity, learning to be more sensitive, or more loving or more openly imaginative or literate' (2002: 11). Kimberley Reynolds[11] offers a range of texts which 'offer visions of society in which sex and gender are facts, and difference is enjoyed, but in which all groups are equally able to participate' (2002: 113). Yet, as Nodelman points out, such books face a culture which tends to assume that boys do not read, and in which 'masculinity is constructed in ways that undermine the value of reading and thinking' (2002: 14). Among the other issues receiving attention in Stephens' collection is the portrayal of masculinity in picturebooks (Kerry Mallan, who pinpoints the impossibility of their allowing for variety in bodily form), and a scrutiny by Robyn McCallum of politics and gender in some Disney films.

Non-traditional gender identities

Cross-dressing

As indicated above, the work on gender of Judith Butler is fundamental to a good deal of the criticism discussed. In her study of cross-dressing in children's literature, Victoria Flanagan cites Butler's *Gender Trouble* in which the claim is made that 'gender is performatively constituted through the "stylized repetition of acts" that approximate rather than express a stable and fixed gender identity ([1990] 1997: 179)'. Flanagan suggests this is 'germane to the construction of female-to-male cross-dressing in children's literature, which similarly embraces the notion of gender as illusory and performative' (2011: xv). This particular variety of cross-dressing Flanagan finds to be the most frequently encountered in children's literature; not only do the heroines generally seem to perform effectively in the male role, their stories serve to 'demonstrate the limitations that normative gender categories can impose on individuals' (2011: xvi). A notable instance of this success is the story of Joan of Arc, of which there are many children's versions. Flanagan explains the achievement of such heroines as resulting from the fact that they 'are generally situated within an environment or setting which is greatly removed from contemporary consensus reality ... [and this] enables them to use cross-dressing in a metaphoric or strategic way that comments upon the constructedness of gender in the real world occupied by the readers ...' (2011: 15). Flanagan suggests, however, that stories about males cross-dressing as females often portray them as unable to perform properly because they are unable to modify their habitual gender-based behaviour; consequently their male 'biological sex is never adequately disguised ... [and their] inability to give a convincing feminine performance is often constructed in a humorous, carnivalized fashion' (2011: 50).[12] Thus the male role is in effect a step up for the female as impersonator, while the female role is a humiliation, exciting ridicule, for the male attempting it.

The protagonists within the categories considered above have chosen to 'cross-dress' for reasons which arise from the exigencies of the plot rather than because of any lack of stability in their own gender. On the basis of a number of recent texts,[13] Flanagan goes on to examine how the fictional portrayal of a further category of cross-dressers contrasts with the more traditional treatment: 'Whereas female cross-dressing has traditionally provided a serious critique of socially contrived gender categories, and male cross-dressing is commonly trivialized into a comedy routine, the transgender paradigm presents female cross-dressing in a more conservative and negative fashion. Conversely, it is the male cross-dresser within this model whose gender construction challenges gender stereotypes and seeks to redefine "masculinity" and "femininity"' (2011: 216). Flanagan claims that not all the novels she considers fully come to terms with what might be described as a 'queer' agenda in terms of a destabilisation of the whole concept of gender identity. Nevertheless, she introduces three books[14] in which the male protagonists 'defy normative gender and sexual categories, exemplified in each instance by the illicit pleasure they derive from transgressing the gender divide through cross-dressing' (2011: 251). Whether these are to be seen as genuine initiators in this area of literature remains to be determined.

Queer theory

Flanagan's discussion of transgender protagonists, noted above, might perhaps equally appropriately have been included under the broad heading of 'queer', for as Michelle Abate and Kenneth Kidd point out in the Introduction to their collection of essays, *Over the Rainbow* (2011), any agreed definition of the term 'queer' has proved elusive. Citing the pioneering work of Eve Kosofsky Sedgwick, which 'helped to produce as well as to popularize the academic study of nonheteronormative gender and sexual identities' (2011: v), they go on to trace the way in which 'queer', starting in the sixteenth century as an adjective meaning 'strange', 'unusual', and 'out of alignment', gradually became associated with 'same-sex attraction and gender-bending behavior'. As such it has a wider connotation than the more specific coupling of 'lesbian/gay' (though novels focusing on such relationships form the subject matter of one of the sections of the book), thus being inclusive of earlier fiction, such as schoolboy magazines and a number of classic children's texts, where 'homosocial and even homoerotic' elements not infrequently occur (2011: 3–4). Abate and Kidd's volume traces the previous history of LGBTQ studies of children's literature, and presents analyses of a range of children's fiction, from the classics of the children's canon to recent texts which exhibit a more overt treatment of the issues concerned. About the latter they ask whether 'queer literature for young readers [can] effect, as well as document, change' (2011: 146). In the third section, 'The emphasis shifts to narrative forms that might be said to queer literature, to complicate our notions about distinction, form, and value' (2011: 7). This culminates in a discussion of recently evolving interactive fanfiction and computer games, in which 'the line between reader and writer (or creator and gamer-player) is just as fuzzy as the lines between "straight" and queer, child and adult' (2011: 8). The editors also express their hope that queer theorists may come to appreciate the importance of children's literature (as distinct from adult literature that features child characters) in the study of 'queer' childhood.

While it is clearly impossible to provide a synopsis of all the seventeen articles that make up this volume, garnered (with the exception of Andrea Wood's piece about computer games) from a range of publications, Roberta Seelinger Trites' essay on *Little Women*[15] is worth a special mention, since it links up with references above to both Alcott and Lissa Paul. Trites looks at the range of performance displayed by Jo March, from her dramatic enactment of 'predatory masculine sexuality' early in the novel to an 'ultrafemme' flirtatious role later on – in fact playing 'roles that are defined by lesbianism, by androgyny, by homo-sociality, by homoeroticism, and even, eventually, by heterosexuality' (2011: 33–4). Jo's relationship with 'marmee' gives her the power of self-acceptance, as 'she learns from her mother that only with other women is she allowed to express fully her feelings about such taboo subjects as anger' (2011: 40). At times too she takes over her absent father's role of nurturing the family. For much of the novel she rejects the idea of the heterosexual relationship of marriage, while the strength of her bond to her sisters, notably Beth, is frequently emphasised. Trites suggests that initially Laurie too is portrayed as a sister substitute to Jo, and it is only when he begins 'to eschew his androgyny and enact his masculinity' and kisses her, that this relationship becomes threatening to Jo, because he is 'inflicting on her the inequality necessitated by the norms of Victorian heterosexuality', a role she is not prepared to adopt (2011: 48–9). Trites suggests that Jo's eventual marriage to Professor Bhaer can be seen as a form of displaced lesbianism because he is 'poor, alien, and powerless' and this in effect emasculates him (2011: 49). The fact that Alcott wrote this 'happy ending' under pressure from her publishers, Trites opines, does not make it easier for later readers to accept: 'If anything, understanding that the economics of the patriarchy drove Alcott to distort her own artistic vision for her characters makes the ending of *Little Women* even more tragic' (2011: 51). Trites' essay provides for this classic text a stimulating critique which is a paradigm of both the queer and the feminist approaches to criticism.

A useful summary of the perspective on children's literature of queer children's literature is provided by Kerry Mallan:[16] 'From a queer perspective, the most successful fiction for children makes visible the processes that seek to enforce heteronormative categories and binaries, and that foreground subjectivity as multifaceted and shifting. The most successful queer stories "queer" their readers by provoking them to query the assumptions that underpin notions of normal and abnormal identity, especially sexual identity' (in (eds) Nel and Paul 2011: 189).

Conclusion

Progress towards a broader understanding of gender in relation to children's literature, whether in terms of the characters portrayed and the outcomes of the plot, the underrated position of female authors, and more recently the realisation that masculinity cannot be seen as a monolithic category, accelerated in the latter part of the twentieth century, largely due to the work of feminist scholars who initially drew attention to factors which were implicit in so many of the books. A further range of studies is referenced by Erica Hateley (in (eds) Nel and Paul 2011: 86–92). It is inevitable that both fiction and criticism will continue to evolve rapidly in this area. Hateley concludes: 'As long as "gender" is understood to be a constituent aspect of identity of subjectivity, what and how gender "means" must continually be queried, challenged, redefined and recast. Doing so offers hope for shifting from the *OED* definition of gender as a noun, toward its definition as a verb, to "come into being", without reference to being male or female, masculine or feminine, but instead, as human' (2011: 92). Another field which has attracted a good deal of recent critical interest is that of translation studies, the subject of the next chapter.

CHAPTER NINE

Translation and Globalisation

Darja Mazi-Leskovar and Pat Pinsent

Introduction

The area of translation of children's literature seems only to have come to the attention of most English-speaking literary critics in the latter half of the twentieth century. This may arise from a combination of two factors:

- Many of what might be termed the 'foundation' texts, such as fairytales and Aesop's Fables, seem to have become part of our common heritage so that it is easy to forget their 'foreign' origins.
- The majority of the best-known early classics of children's literature (once it came to be an acknowledged genre) were written in English. Probably the only familiar texts that are not first language English are Johanna Spyri's *Heidi* (1881), Carlo Collodi's *Pinocchio* (1883), Erich Kästner's *Emil and the Detectives* (1929) and Astrid Lindgren's *Pippi Longstocking* (1945); even so it is a safe assumption that young English-speaking readers today are less aware of these than of the works of Lewis Carroll, J.M. Barrie, Kenneth Grahame and other English writers.

Perhaps because of the abundance of children's books in English, supported by the increasing dominance of English as a world language (with the result that authors from so many other parts of the world are English speaking), it is all too easy to overlook books which need to be translated in order to reach largely monoglossic English child (or adult) readers. The effect of this has been that as the importance to international understanding of knowledge of other cultures is at last appreciated, translation theorists have more often been individuals concerned with the rendering of English texts into other languages than translators into English.

One of the most influential figures in the development of understanding the importance, particularly to young readers, of knowledge of the literature of other countries was Jella Lepman, whose *A Bridge of Children's Books*, first published in German (as *Die Kinderbuchbrücke*) in 1964, recounts how, in the aftermath of the Second World War, she was instrumental in setting up the International Youth Library in Munich in 1949 as a resource for children in a country devastated by war. As she explained at the time to possible sponsors:

■ German children are practically without any books at all, once their literature from the Nazi period has been removed from circulation. ... These children carry no responsibility for this war, and that is why books for them should be the first messengers of peace. (2002: 35–6) □

Although in no sense a work of literary criticism, this book, with its vivid recreation of the post-war situation, provides a foundation for the understanding of subsequent intercultural initiatives. In 1953, with the intention of fostering the knowledge of other cultures as a disincentive to international conflict, Lepman founded the International Board on Books for Young People (IBBY), which in 1957 began publication of its international journal, *Bookbird*. This has continued to provide valuable information both about books in languages less spoken than those of Western Europe, and about the merits of available translations.

An organisation founded in 1971, with similar aims but a rather more academic emphasis, is the International Research Society for Children's Literature (IRSCL). As the entry by Joe Zornado in *The Cambridge Guide to Children's Books in English* (2001) states:

■ From the beginning the IRSCL has considered serious cultural and political questions in terms of children's literature, including gender stereotyping in texts for children, problems of translation, the history of children's literature, the application of critical theory to children's literature, and multiculturalism in children's literature. (2001: 372) □

Both these international organisations, as well as publishing journals, organise national and international conferences; the proceedings of such events have in recent years frequently included valuable critical material about translation. Gillian Lathey observes:

■ [The] third [IRSCL] symposium ... in 1976 represented a turning point: it was the first, and for many years the only, children's literature conference devoted to translation and the international exchange of children's books. (2006: 1) □

In the current chapter, in addition to the theoretical studies discussed, reference will be made to some presentations at conferences sponsored by such organisations as these.[1]

The development of an international perspective

A comparatively early study which, unlike most histories of children's literature, took into account books published throughout Europe was produced by a German children's author, Bettina Hürlimann. The translation by Brian Alderson, *Three Centuries of Children's Books in Europe* (1967), presented to English readers an informal commentary and survey of a number of books, all of which had been read by Hürlimann herself. They were categorised into genres, the bibliography being arranged on a national basis, though inevitably most extensive on German literature.[2]

This commendable attempt to transcend national boundaries reflects an increasing awareness of the importance of avoiding an insular concern with only the children's literature of one's own nation. The 1976 IRSCL conference alluded to above has been seen as the first attempt to provide a critical focus on translation. The conference proceedings[3] raise a number of issues about translation which have subsequently been subjected to critical examination and are considered below.

Zohar Shavit's *Poetics of Children's Literature* (1986) includes a chapter on translation (reproduced in (ed.) Lathey 2006), which uses her own research into translations of children's books into Hebrew as a basis for an attempt to establish patterns of translation behaviour: these, she claims, highlight some of the constraints common to children's literature generally. She suggests that two principles are common to both translation and children's literature in general, while the emphasis on one or the other differs according to the presuppositions of a particular contemporary society. These principles are 'an adjustment of the text to make it appropriate and useful to the child', as conceived by the society of the period, together with an adjustment of the text's literary and linguistic features to current social perceptions of the child's abilities. (2006: 26). The result of this is that translated children's literature is subject to constraints of an educational nature and is likely, Shavit suggests, to adapt translated texts to fit in with what is conventional and well-known in the children's literature system in the target language. She finds that 'the prominent stylistic norm in translation into Hebrew of both adult and children's literature is the preference for high literary style wherever possible' (2006: 39). Whether or not her conclusion is universally valid, Shavit's examination of translation within an ideological context has provided a stimulus for similar discussions in relation to a number of different texts and languages.

Challenges related to translation

Children's literature is heavily influenced by translation, something which is scarcely surprising since 'translations form a major part of our world literary heritage' (Jobe 2004: 912). The study of translation in the field of children's literature has been strongly affected by research into mainstream literature, by literary studies and translatology (Van Coillie and Verschueren 2006: vi). It has uncovered the fact that several challenges encountered in mainstream literature are present also in children's literature. Among them are the application to children's literature of such notions as a polysystem of languages and literatures,[4] or of the methodology of Gideon Toury and Zohar Shavit who, among others, researched how to give children's literature a proper place in the all-embracing system of literature and of literary studies. The importance of the source literature of the text to be transposed into the target language was highlighted in 1986 when Zohar Shavit applied polysystem theory to the field of children's literature.

Several other issues, raised by translation scholars, have gained importance also in children's literature and children's literature studies. Among these is the concept of the aim, elaborated by the functional linguists Hans Vermeer, Katharina Reiss and Christiane Nord; this seems to be particularly appropriate to the field since the function of the text has always been of outstanding importance where an audience of children is concerned, and most such texts are expected to have a clear purpose. Children's literature has to meet the expectations of the target readers and the context in which they are reading. Related to this is the question of the choice of translation strategies: to what degree should the text be adapted for its target readers? The application of domestication and foreignisation (see definitions below) is another great challenge. The positions and findings of Lawrence Venuti who wrote about the invisibility of translators[5] are echoed in the study of children's literature. Nonetheless, the translation of children's literature poses also specific challenges, among which are those of the translation of picturebooks and illustrated books in which words and images meet.

The issues concerning the translation of children's literature have also been multiplied by the proliferation of the new media and by market requirements. Since the electronic and audio-visual media form an important part of the range of cultural products available for children, some of the challenges related to literary translation have gained new features. For example, the book market seems to expect translations of bestsellers to be published in a relatively short time, something that was particularly apparent in the case of translations of J.K. Rowling's *Harry Potter* books.[6] However, most challenges related to the translation of books for children still derive from the very nature of children's literature and are connected with the importance it attributes to its audience.[7] Literature that is determined by its readers and by the view that society has of them is defined by the concept of childhood that 'shifts constantly from period to period, place to place, culture to culture' (Hunt 1995: ix). Translated literature for children reflects these shifts and thus the perception of childhood and the image of the child represent one of the most important challenges for translators of children's literature. As these images are determined by the views of the source culture as well as by those of the target context, they represent a constant challenge for translators. Translations are recognised as playing a particularly revealing role in the target context, since they disclose 'assumptions made by translators and other intermediaries about the competence of child readers' (O'Sullivan 2005: 91–92), and about the target culture. These challenges may seem even more difficult to contend with than those related to the speculations of Philippe Ariès in his *Centuries of Childhood* (1962) or the ideas expressed by Neil Postman in his *Disappearance of Childhood* (1982). The positions taken by these two scholars, despite facing a certain amount of criticism, had a considerable impact on the perception of childhood and of culture in general.[8] Literacy and assumptions about the reading abilities of young readers have remained in focus for scholars, teachers and translators. Since the preconditions for reading of literature include some knowledge of the world, that may contribute to an understanding of the content, and to the reader's ability to deal with 'the aesthetic and fictional construct of literature' (O'Sullivan 2005: 91–92); such prerequisites are even more significant when reading books in translation.

Literary translation targeting children follows the general standards for translation of mainstream texts: the translation has to make sense; it is expected to convey the spirit and the atmosphere of the original and to address the implied reader in a natural way. However, this does not suffice for the text to become a natural part of a target literature and to function within a new semiotic[9] space. A translation can be accepted into the target literary system only if 'the recipients are able to receive the foreign codes on the basis of their own cultural codes; that is, they must be able to relate "foreign" and "native", accepting or rejecting that which is foreign owing to understanding or non-understanding' (Nikolajeva 1996: 36). When such prerequisites do not exist, cultural references may need to be changed in order to bring the meaning closer to a future target reader. To achieve such aims, translators can resort to various translation strategies. As each of these is in a way an adaptation of the original, the term 'adaptation' is used as the umbrella concept covering them all.

Scholars of children's literature have proved that most of the challenges faced by translators of mainstream literature are present also in the translations targeting non-adult readers. Due to the specific requirements related to their age, translators aiming at children and teenagers also have to consider other issues. Among these is the challenge posed by the readers' limited intertextual experience, based primarily on the particular local or national tradition. However, this experience can be expanded by translations that have bridged the gaps between literary traditions and, thus, established new intertextual connections.[10] Hence, transposition of texts from one language into another allows literary creations that would have remained enclosed within the borders of one language or tradition to enrich the literary realms of other languages and cultures.

In the context of books[11] for children, the presence of illustration represents another specific challenge because in illustrated books and picturebooks it is not only the verbal part of the book that addresses target readers, but the entire interplay between verbal and visual texts. To achieve this aim, the visual elements, creating the artistic aspect of a literary work, may have to be adapted to the new audience. This challenge seems to be closely related to the issue of a double implied audience. Books for children may well be intended for child readers but adults are closely involved with most of them, both before and after purchase. It is adults who supervise whether or not books comply with didactic and pedagogic norms in a specific target context. Books, especially those targeting younger children, in reality address readers of all ages. Since children's literature is determined by the reader, this discrepancy between the implied source readership and the extended target audience may give rise to dilemmas, especially in relation to the image of the child, childhood and the world. Literary images, determined by the source cultural context, may contain specific cultural signs unknown in other semiotic contexts. As they potentially represent a challenge for presumed readers, translators, who are likely to have a thorough knowledge of both source and target cultures, are expected to possess the sensitivity which is the prerequisite for the 'harmonisation' of the two cultural contexts. Faced with the dilemma of balancing fidelity to the original with adaptation to the target sphere, they have been trying to solve this challenge by applying various translation strategies. Among the most complex of these are domestication and foreignisation. The former aims at adapting the original to the target readers' cultural context and their presumed experience, while the latter aims at preserving those aspects of the source culture that, despite their foreignness, do not seriously interfere with the understanding of the text by presumed readers. These two translation strategies have been in focus ever since research into translation studies began to stress the role of the target reader. Their application, especially in the case of retranslations, may be seen as a mirror, reflecting the bridging of the gaps between cultures and traditions.

Translation of children's literature presents several additional challenges. The central issue concerning translation of literature for non-adult readers has however already been resolved: scholars now agree that the translation of literary masterpieces of children's literature demands as much skill and artistry from translators as does the translation of quality literature aiming at adults. This recognition has transformed the perception of children's literature and of the role translators play in the field. Translators are seen as 'Creators of Translated Books' (Pinsent 2006: 6) and as mediators. Gillian Lathey puts the 'invisible storytellers' of children's literature in the limelight in her study *The Role of Translators in Children's Literature* (2010). The acknowledgement of their role in the overall artistic creation of a literary text in translation has been given due tribute at least from the middle of the twentieth century, notably with the introduction of special national and international awards for the translation of children's literature. From 1981 the Astrid Lindgren Translation Prize, sponsored by the International Federation of Translators (FIT) and by the Astrid Lindgren Fund, has been a sign of the recognition of the importance of the translation of children's literature and a significant challenge for translators worldwide. Within the international children's literature community, the nomination of outstanding translations as IBBY Honour Books may be also viewed as a challenge fostering the best translation practices.

Another positive change in the area of translation seems to be a heightened awareness of the importance of the promotion of literary expression in various languages worldwide. Considering the established division of cultures and languages into central or great–impact cultures and non-central ones,[12] it seems vital to stress that books for children, regardless of the region where they originate or the language in which they are written, are invaluable for humanity globally. The same is true of translations. They have an intrinsic value irrespective of the source language from which they are transposed.

Research has disclosed that translations move within the so-called 'translation flows' connecting various literatures, languages and cultures. The established paradigm of central and non–central languages,[13] that is, of peripheral and semi-central, is based on the frequency of referencing to a particular linguistic and cultural context. In accordance with this concept, books from central world cultures, especially those using languages of the Western Hemisphere, tend to be better represented in worldwide book markets than publications written in peripheral languages. Taking into account the status that the English language occupies in the polysystemic[14] global system and the position of literatures written in English, the Batchelder (1966) and the Marsh (1996) Awards for the translation of books into English may be seen as providing major challenges for translators worldwide. The centrality of literary systems using English represents another challenge for translators transposing literature from various non-central languages. Once literary texts are translated into English, they become more easily accessible for the ever growing audiences reading English. Additionally, they are also considered as potential intermediaries for translations into other languages, as exchanges between non-central literatures often occur via the mediation of English translations.

Adaptation

The process of translating texts for children displays several specific characteristics, among which is the pronounced frequency of adaptation. The relationship between translation, the mere change of the language of the text, and adaptation, the various additional changes made to comply with the aims of a specific text, has been discussed by various scholars. Their views, however, often collide. The very term 'adaptation' appears extremely polyvalent, as illustrated by Riitta Oittinen in *Translating for Children* (2000). Oittinen highlights various meanings ascribed to this concept and asks if it means 'a version, an imitation, an abridgement or a copy' and whether it refers to form or content (2000: 77). The scholar concludes that 'how we see adaptation depends on how we see translation' (2000: 77). Such a position sounds absolutely logical, especially because the perception of the status of the original and consequently of the adaptation differs significantly among scholars. Some take a negative stand on any kind of adaptations, while others admit them under certain conditions, and some, such as Oittinen herself, believe that adaptations are positive phenomena. According to these scholars, the discussion of translation cannot avoid the issue of adaptation since 'as long as there has been literature, there have been adaptations' (2000: 76). Despite admitting that in the area of literary translation we tend to divide texts into translations and texts that have been transformed and adapted on the basis of literal equivalence (2000: 76), Oittinen claims that 'adaptations have validity as works of literature' (2000: 160). Shavit (1986) and Klingberg (1986) express a radically opposed view, giving translations a higher status than adaptations because they believe that the original has its intrinsic value due to its mere existence, while translation is always dated, as it is conditioned by several factors that change according to the place and time of translation and the personality of the translator. For Shavit and Klingberg, adapting is a sign of disrespect to children and a symptom of nonappreciation of children's literature and of the author's rights, as indicated by Oittinen when discussing different attitudes to adaptations (2000: 93). Christiane Nord has researched the notion of functional translatology[15] and bases her translation-oriented text analysis on the view that adaptation practices in children's literature move on a scale from 'extreme fidelity to extreme liberty' (Nord 1991: 9). In the present context, the term 'adaptation' is only applied within the framework of children's literature, without considering issues in relationship to other media representations, including those based on literary texts.

In the context of translation of children's literature, there are various perceptions about literary elements which may be anticipated to seem foreign and strange to the target reader. The search for otherness in order to assimilate and appropriate it to the target culture, or just in order to add variety to what is already familiar in the target literary tradition, was called 'cultural context adaptation' by Klingberg (1986), and 'domestication' by Venuti (1995). Both scholars are critical of this translation strategy and favour foreignisation over it. They believe that the specific elements of the source text should be kept as much as possible in the translation. However, strategies used in translations of books for children appear much more varied than could be presumed on the basis of a simple dichotomy between foreignisation and domestication. My cross-textual analysis of translations of several American and English children's books into Slovenian has disclosed that, within the same target text, various translation strategies may be present. Mona Baker's research in the field of mainstream literature proves the same. It appears that such 'oscillation serves a purpose in the real world' (2010: 115).

Besides foreignising and domestication, Emer O'Sullivan, in her study *Comparative Children's Literature* (2005), also suggests the concept of 'neutralizing' to refer to translations in which 'concrete foreign aspects' are 'toned down' (2005: 98). They are neither omitted nor replaced with target-culture specific elements, as would have been the case with domestication; nor are they given a position that highlights their foreignness.

The concepts of domestication and foreignisation have been discussed from various points of view by several scholars. According to Venuti, the function of a translated text is to disrupt dominant values and patterns in the target context, something which is possible since 'translation is inherently violent because it necessarily involves reconstituting the foreign text in accordance with values, beliefs and representations that pre-exist in the target language' (2010: 65). He believes that the translator has 'the choice concerning the degree and direction of the violence' (2010: 65); in effect this is a choice between domestication and foreignisation. In 'Cultural Politics: Regimes of Domestication in English', Venuti moreover supposes that the translation becomes inscribed in 'target canons and taboos, its codes and ideologies' (2010: 68). The question arises as to under what conditions such inscriptions may have any impact on the target culture since it has been proven by the reality in the post-communist countries that due to the presence of censorship and self-censorship[16] this is only seldom the case. Even translations in which the ideas and messages did not support the prevalent target culture orientation as such could not have any important impact on the presumed audience because the importance ascribed to translations 'is not always based on the intrinsic literary value of the texts concerned'. It is more often the result of the 'concentration of power' at various levels, for example, 'on the level of the publishing houses' (Ghesquière 2006: 20), something which relates to political correctness.

Venuti considers 'domesticating' as a phenomenon strictly connected with issues of time, society, norms and power. Oittinen additionally highlights the ideological and ethical aspects of adaptation. In her article 'No Innocent Act: On the Ethics of Translating for Children' (2006), Oittinen draws attention to the so called 'positive' and negative manipulation of the text. Even though the words 'positive manipulation' might appear to create a contradiction in terms, it was also discussed by André Lefevere in *Translation, Rewriting and the Manipulation of Literary Fame* (1992). The 'negative manipulation' denotes procedures of rewriting texts in order to manipulate children's and adults' minds (Oittinen 2006: 40). The aim of such adaptation is to exercise coercion and to promote bias. The negative impact of such ideologically manipulated texts not only reveals the socio-political context of a certain period but also exerts a negative impact on national culture, an impact which may not be confined to children's literature. Censorship may thus thrust upon young readers a distorted picture of the original text, of the author and the source literature over a much longer period. This has been the case in Slovenia, where even well after 1991,[17] ideologically manipulated translations have not disappeared from bookshops and library shelves but continue to be uncritically reprinted, as proven by various studies by Slovenian researchers, among them Pokorn's *Post-Socialist Translation Practices, Ideological Struggle in Children's Literature* (2012). Pokorn reveals that translations purged of all references to Christianity are still circulating today. The damage that ideological censorship, based on totalitarian practices, produced in readers and in the entire cultural sphere, has been revealed also by other authors from the former Eastern bloc, among them the Czech-born author and illustrator Peter Sis.[18] In his article 'My Life with Censorship' (*Bookbird*, 2009, No.3), he condemns the practice of manipulation required by the Czech authorities in the field of original writing and illustration. Though this type of manipulation has subsequently been openly condemned in pluralistic societies, vigilance has to be exercised against any other excesses motivated by undemocratic extra-literary causes and purposes. It appears that in a democratic context it should suffice to pay due attention to the concept of loyalty, which is identified as fidelity to the author, the source text and target readers. When these aspects are in harmonious balance, negative manipulation is scarcely possible.

Fluency is another concept related to the manipulation of the text. It was introduced by Venuti who believed that when domestication is too pronounced, it can be misleading because it is 'capable not only of executing the ethnocentric violence of domestication, but also of concealing this violence by producing the illusionistic effect of transparency'.[19] Venuti believes that fluency may result in readers being unaware of the translator's interpretation of the text, or of the domestication factor, and therefore he introduces the concept of 'abusive fidelity' (2010: 75). However, translations as a whole may abuse the trust and confidence of children and young people, who cannot be expected to be aware of misleading translations. This is even more so when the translator's or editor's commentaries in Prefaces, Forewords or other commentaries lead the readers astray. This was not uncommon in children's literature during the communist and socialist period of Yugoslavia.[20] Therefore what appears to be problematic is not so much the choice of a mere translation strategy but the policy of restraining individuals from receiving the information that is a constituent part of the original. Such mutilation of the source text can be seen as preparing the grounds for the creation of a distorted picture of the source culture with the aim of creating prejudice. It mirrors the ideological purposes of translation practices and the censorial tendencies of the target culture.[21]

Historical perspectives concerning translation practices reveal that attitudes towards domestication and foreignisation have been changing in various literatures as well as in different historical periods. According to Gillian Lathey (2010), English translations of books published in the nineteenth century were accompanied by various notes and commentaries to prepare readers for confrontation with texts from other cultural contexts. Slovenian translations from the same period offered similar introductions in translations of texts coming from Great Britain and the USA. In the twentieth century, translations of English and American books targeting older children have shown that both of these source cultures gradually lost the stigma of complete foreignness. In the last decades of the twentieth century, the tendency to replace domestication by foreignisation became quite pronounced. Books in translation kept certain elements typical of the source culture text. Van Coillie and Verschuen, the editors of *Children's Literature in Translation* (2010), also reveal some changes in the traditional approach to translation. In their Preface they observe that, if in the past domestication seemed to be favoured in order to assure a sufficient degree of empathy with target readers, an opposite trend has become apparent since 1980. Today, 'more and more translators, out of respect for the original text and because they want to bring children into contact with other cultures, choose to retain a degree of 'foreignness' in their translation' (Van Coillie and Verschuen 2006: vi–viii). Considering the multicultural aspects of contemporary societies and the presence of various cultures in other media which address children, this seems to be a logical development. Likewise, each translation should be clearly labelled either as a translation of the entire text or as an adaptation, at least as far as the nature of the textual transposition from the source literature into the target context is concerned.

A special feature of children's literature is the adaptation of prose texts originally written for adults. A few of those which have even entered the canon of children's literature were originally highly political, since the aim of the authors was to exert a specific influence on the perceptions of the source readership. Despite such political background, texts like *Robinson Crusoe* (1719) by Daniel Defoe, *Gulliver's Travels* (1726) by Jonathan Swift, and *Uncle Tom's Cabin* (1882) by Harriet Beecher Stowe, have been appropriated by children. Zohar Shavit studied the alterations that are common to such adaptations of mainstream texts. She concluded that there are a few common constraints which should assure that texts are adapted in order to be 'appropriate and useful to the child' in accordance with the values of each targeted society. The plot, character and language are adjusted to the 'child's level of comprehension and his or her reading abilities' (1981: 172). This includes the exclusion of unsuitable scenes, particularly of those touching on taboos. Shavit gives examples of translations of books in which those sections of the text which touch on taboos are avoided. In *Gulliver's Travels* only the first two parts have entered children's literature because they contain no scenes regarded as unsuitable for a young target audience, as for example those related to bodily functions or to the love affairs of the main hero, something which is also true of Slovenian translations of this text. In Mark Twain's *The Adventures of Tom Sawyer* (1876), the scene presenting the whitewashing of the fence seems to be a locus of adaptation in some translations. Tom's engaging of children for the work he himself should have done and his arranging even to be paid for his 'generosity' in enabling them to have this 'pleasure' is not always accompanied with the satire that is rooted in the original scene. The reason is that satire and irony are thought to be inappropriate for children. Among Slovenian translations we can, nevertheless, find a translation[22] which includes Twain's social criticism, his ironic commentary on the 'sacred' values of work and pleasure. The same is true of the scene in which Tom ironises how aunt Polly uses her glasses. She is represented in a way that deprives her of some of her (already weakened) authority. It appears that the inclusion of overt or indirect criticism of society and of the world of the adults depends on the age-group of implied readers.[23] Shavit explains that the basic principle in the translation of books for children is that the scenes which do not contribute to the development of the plot can be deleted as their deletion does not jeopardise the understanding of the novel. In children's literature, the plot is generally regarded as the most important literary element. Even though such alterations, which are really adaptations, are rooted in the periods when children's literature was seen primarily as an educational tool, nowadays they remain a constituent part of its literary canon.

Whatever the translation strategy applied, scholars indicate that translations are expected to fulfil the aim appropriate to their new cultural context. The discussion of adaptation thus covers additions, deletions, abridgements, simplifications, explanations and other translation procedures that result from the application of domestication, neutralisation or foreignisation approaches. Moreover, it includes the study of the purpose which the originals have in the source culture and that of the aim attributed to translated texts in the target culture. Since, according to Hans Vermeer and Katharina Reiss,[24] their purpose may be attained only when translations are coherent, particular attention is paid to coherence on the intertextual and intratextual levels. The former refers to the relationship between the source text and the target one, each being taken as an independent literary entity; the latter refers to the relationship between various parts of the same text, either the original or the translation. Coherence as a linguistic concept, enabling understanding of any text, is of prime importance in the analysis of originals and translations of books for children. However, its importance extends also to the cultural aspect of a text, as it is related to the purpose ascribed to the original in the source culture and to the translation in the target cultural context.

The discussion of adaptation, accordingly, covers not only translation strategies expressed through additions, deletions, abridgements, harmonisations, explications and implications, all of which can be linked to domestication, foreignisation and neutralisation, but also includes the study of intertextual and intratextual aspects, both of which are related to the set purpose of the translation.

National and world children's literature in translation

Children's literatures that have appeared as the cultural expressions of the distinctiveness of individual nations can, by analogy with mainstream literature, be seen as parts of 'world children's literature'. Being a part of a huge whole, a national literature can win international recognition only by conserving and steadily developing its specific cultural distinctions. However, its national features 'can only be defined in opposition to other national literatures and to world literature' (O'Sullivan 2009: 4; Nikolajeva 1996: 20). The first to draw attention to the importance of international comparison in this field of literary creativity for children was Paul Hazard, 'a comparatist who turned to children's literature', as O'Sullivan says of this key figure of children's literature research.[25] In his seminal book *Les livres, les enfants et les hommes* (1932), translated into English as *Books, Children and Men* (1944), Hazard calls attention to the influence of cultural features in the creation of literature targeting children. He recognises national distinctions in children's literature, and highlights differences originating in opposing views of the child.[26] As he sees it, these are the main reasons why children's literature in the USA and in the Nordic countries differs from texts created for children in Latin countries. According to him, not only does the national perception of childhood have a significant impact on children's literature, but also children's literature plays a considerable part in the construction of a specific cultural or national identity (O'Sullivan 2005: 6).[27] Hazard's belief in this reciprocal influence has survived the test of time, and the period from the 1950s onwards saw the start of a growing interest in 'the world of children's literature'.[28]

Interest in national and international features of children's literature and in translation was revived both by the creation of the International Board on Books for Young People (IBBY) in 1953 and by academic research, strongly promoted also by the IRSCL, the International Research Society for Children's Literature, founded in 1970. Emer O'Sullivan cites Klaus Doderer's *Lexikon der Kinder- und Jugendliteratur* (1973: 84)[29] as 'the first comprehensive and truly international reference book on the subject' (O'Sullivan 2005: 11). The internationalisation of children's literature pushed translation and research into the limelight and scholars like Klingberg recognised 'that methods of comparative literary studies should be employed in research on children's literature' (O'Sullivan 2005: 10). Thus, similarly to the mainstream national literatures which are seen as a constituent part of the national literary, cultural and educational system, children's literatures that have developed within the boundaries of a particular nation are mirrors of national and cultural identity. Their specific traits, however, are subject to change, and accordingly, national features of a particular literature also depend on alterations of cultural distinctiveness. These changes are due not only to the instability of national identity, one of the most fundamental of our collective identities, but also to the possibility of differences in perception of a specific children's literature system. Lathey mentions various ways of envisaging the term 'national' in relation to 'children's literature'. She quotes Nikolajeva who defines it as a geographical rather than a linguistic concept (in ed. Lathey 2006).

O'Sullivan, on the other hand, claims in her discussion of the comparative historiography of children's literature, that 'the normative and restrictive category of "national literature" like other such identity constructs, has lost ground today to concepts of hybrid identities and literatures'(O'Sullivan 2005: 46). She quotes José Lambert who suggests characterising literatures by using geographical, that is, territorial determinants like 'literature in Italy', instead of the traditional term 'Italian literature'. O'Sullivan explains that the new categories would 'naturally include translations, as well as all literature by migrants and literatures of the diaspora' (O'Sullivan 2005: 46). The new diction would thus bring radical changes in conceptions of literatures where all these literary productions were not yet considered to be constituent parts of particular national children's literatures. It can be speculated that in other literatures, in which translations of works of intrinsic literary value already have the deserved status, as in Dutch, Flemish, Finnish[30] and Slovenian children's literature, it would not produce major changes.

Geographical determinants seem to gain new importance, particularly in the instances of different national literatures sharing the same language, and in the case of authors who belong to different nationalities but write in the same location. In a text written in English, for example, the description of the locale, the representation of landscape may help decisively to uncover those specific features that characterise the setting as English, Canadian or Australian. It is the geographical reality that contributes the distinctive elements of Englishness, Canadianness or Australianness to a literary text. Additionally, typical spaces and specific mythic spaces that have been given special importance in the national history or tradition also appear significant in the shaping of cultural and national identity in literature since their 'poetics of space' becomes a constituent element of the identity of a specific literary work. It tends to be expected that such an identity is also easily identifiable by readers from the 'outside', on the international scale.

Children's literature related to a certain nation or region is also defined by specific historical experiences and national memories, by myths and the multifaceted cultural heritage. The intertwining features of the diverse aspects of national and/or regional identity create a unique picture that gives a special mark to literary texts, especially those targeting children. However, even though the image of 'the presence of the past'[31] in children's literature may appear unique, it is nevertheless a section of the larger picture that shares at least some features with bordering regions, neighbouring peoples and nations. Consequently, it may be expected that children's literature that derives from the regions marked by intercultural encounters will display some common features. These are thus transcultural and transnational. Their place in the world of children's literature seems particularly pertinent.

International exchange of texts for children

When claiming that it is hardly possible to imagine a children's literature without mentioning translations, we normally evoke the situation we are familiar with in the West, where the books traditionally referred to are the classics, considered as 'the canon'. These have been written for the readers of a specific language and culture, but are enjoyed today by readers of various languages and traditions. They have entered each target culture under specific circumstances and have all been 'emancipated' from the original source text and survived in their new cultural context. In *The Role of Translators in Children's Literature* (2010) Lathey outlines the typical features of this process in England. She comments on the reception of texts for children that constitute the core of the canon in most Western literary traditions.[32] In the same study, she comments on the international exchange of books for children in the twentieth century, with the stress on the English and the US book markets. Both offer a relatively small share of translated children's literature. In Slovenian children's literature, translations traditionally form an important part of the corpus of books available on the markets. According to the reports of experts in children's literature in the Low Countries[33] and in Finland, translations have been important also for children's literature in these countries.[34] International book markets and book fairs furthermore show that a similar situation characterises several other national children's literatures. They all try to launch their best books on the global market; however, according to the polysystem theory, their success depends to a great extent on the position of the source language in the international language system.

The research into transnational cultural exchange, elaborated by Gideon Toury and Itamar Even-Zohar, demonstrated in the 1990s that the more important (central) a language is internationally, the greater is its importance in the international translation system. More recent studies by Johan Heilbron ('Towards a sociology of translation: book translations as a cultural world system', 2010) and Pascale Casanova only confirm these findings.[35] In her article 'Consecration and Accumulation of Literary Capital: Translation as unequal exchange' (2010), Casanova analyses the source and the target language/literature/culture in terms of their possession of power and influence on the world market. She divides languages, literatures and cultures into two main groups: the dominated and the dominating. As English is considered as the prime dominating language, the same status belongs to (children's) literature written in Great Britain and the USA. Heilbron, on the other hand, ranks languages, literatures and cultures into central, semi-central and peripheral. Central translation systems include English, French, German, Spanish and Russian (Heilbron 2010: 309). They have the largest share 'in the total number of translated books worldwide' (Baker 2010: 304). However, as the number of translations from and into English tends to be steadily increasing, the English translation system is classified as 'hyper-central' (Heilbron 2010: 310). This exceptional status is identified as the main reason for the high percentage of children's books translated from English and the smaller percentage of translations of children's books from other languages into English. According to Heilbron, the demarcation line between peripheral languages, traditionally labelled as 'minority languages', and the semi-central languages,[36] ranked between the central and peripheral languages, is somewhat unclear and unstable. It depends on various socio-historic factors. Conversely, translation statistics reveal that, as a rule, translations from a non-central language into another non-core language pass via a central language that functions as an intermediary or vehicular language (Baker 2010: 304).

The history of translations proves that the position of languages is not fixed and that in different parts of the world various foreign languages have played the role of the intermediary language. In the case of Slovenian literature,[37] due to historical causes, German used to be the intermediary language till the end of the First World War. Since the German translations of world bestsellers were available among Slovenians[38] living in the Austrian Monarchy, translations into Slovenian followed in a relatively short time. Thus, the first two translations of the American classic *Uncle Tom's Cabin* (1852), by Harriet Beecher Stowe, which were transposed from the German translation, were already published in 1853.[39] The following decades witnessed a gradual cultural reorientation: the number of mediating languages increased even though direct translations testified to an increasing ability to enter into direct contact with a number of core, semi-central and peripheral literatures. Nevertheless, mediating languages, particularly English and French, have remained essential when translating texts from African and Asian languages.

The last decade of the twentieth century was particularly important for children's literature since it witnessed a notable wave of translations of books that had received the Andersen Award. Thus, with the democratisation process in the whole cultural sphere, the translation of children's literature gained momentum and enriched Slovenian children's literature with works that will presumably contribute to the creation of a modern canon uniting children's literatures.

Retranslation of literary texts for children

The tradition of retranslating books for children is a long-standing one, particularly in the case of books belonging to the canon. Whenever the temporal, social or cultural background of a book appears to bear the mark of being outdated, the literary text seems to call for reconsideration. The contrastive analysis of the original and the target text can focus on the macro and micro levels and each analysis may uncover various features related to translation. The comparison focusing on the macro level scrutinises also the paratext: the front and back covers, the title and the chapter headings, the notes and illustrations. When these no longer correspond to the demands of the market, especially with regard to design, they are expected to undergo all necessary changes. On the other hand, scholars pay particular attention to the effect that the story produces on the micro level. Traditionally, the focus of the examination is whether the target text produces a similar effect to that of the source text. Scholars claim that the choice of translation strategy should not affect the content and that the effect of the piece of literature should remain the same as in the original (Belen Gonzalez Cascallana 2006: 101).

In the case of illustrated books and picturebooks, the relationship between illustrations and the text is also closely examined to determine whether it remains as observed in the source text or one element is given additional weight. The history of translation of children's books shows that the features on the macro level have undergone radical changes. The most revolutionary was the introduction of the name of translators on the title page, which occurred at various stages in different countries. This public recognition of the persons who recreate texts was the first acknowledgement of the people who enable books for children to travel from source cultures to various target cultures.

On the micro level, the changes arising from the encounters between the source and target culture were a major cause of retranslations of books for children. In the case of Slovenian translations of books written in English, the translation of the children's novel *Little Lord Fauntleroy*, by Frances Hodgson Burnett, offers a good example of the literary rapprochement of two languages and three cultures. The first translation (1909), entitled *Mali lord* (literally *Little Lord*) is strongly domesticated as it was translated at the time when English and American cultures were little known to Slovenian readers. The second translation, entitled *Mali Lord Fauntleroy* (1925), testifies to the diminishing gap between Slovenian culture and English and American cultures. The introduction of the name of the main character in the title itself was an announcement that the readers were expected to read the text as coming from a different cultural context. This combination of domestication and foreignisation strategies has given rise to changes of personal and geographical names. Later editions retain the original names, thus sticking to the foreignisation strategy.

Retranslations may differ also with reference to introductions, footnotes and commentaries. Changing cultural contexts raise the expectation of new intertextual references, so that the existing translations have to be re-examined and emended. The Slovenian translations of *Uncle Tom's Cabin*, one of the international classics, offer a telling example of such development. The first two translations from 1853 had Introductions which explained basic concepts related to the American multicultural reality. It can be supposed that without the accompanying texts the novel could not be understood by the then average reader. In 1934, a new translation, by Olga Grahor,[40] had a fairly detailed introduction which contained explanations of terms related to American history and general social culture. The exhaustive presentation of the interracial situation is a proof that the target readers already had some previous knowledge of the source culture. The retranslation of 1973,[41] which is an adaptation of the 1953 translation, only testifies to the role of censorship at the time of communism and socialism. This translation was required in order to 'clear' the text of all reference to Christianity. Having undergone such mutilation, the book in Slovenian was radically distorted as it was precisely the positive role of the Christian religion in the fight against racism that was of primary importance to Beecher Stowe. This translation remains on the market even today, despite the fact that it does not correspond to the principles of loyal translation practices. Beecher Stowe's novel has to wait for a retranslation that has already been granted to several other children's classics. These retranslations, including *Heidi* by Johanna Spyri and the classic fairytales by Andersen and the Brothers Grimm, are thus new alternatives to the ideologically prejudiced translations. Their presence on the Slovenian market testifies to the positive change in the area of translation for children. The new trend is unbiased, fair to the author and the reader. It is expected to create a new children's literature landscape that will enable new readings of entire literary works aiming at children and young people.

Translations into English

In a children's book culture dominated by best-selling novels by English language authors on one side or other of the Atlantic, it is easy to forget the importance in earlier periods of material translated from other languages. Lathey observes that 'The earliest history of children's literature in English is dominated by translations' (2010: 15). While Aesop's

Fables was not the first of these, it was perhaps the most influential: Seth Lerer asserts that 'No author has been so intimately associated with children's literature as Aesop' (2008: 35), while, as he also acknowledges, 'The history of the fable is ... the history of its translation' (2008: 42). William Caxton's translation of Aesop (1484)[42] was one of the earliest printed books in English. Subsequent translations have caused Aesop to be a major influence on literature written in English for children; the popularity of such stories was enhanced by the presence of didactic messages which made them more likely to be endorsed by adults. These stories were not alone, however: as Lathey indicates, romances, such as those from the Spanish and the Portuguese, were also frequently enjoyed by readers younger than those normally thought of as their primary audience. Disseminated in chapbook form from the late seventeenth century onwards, they enabled those children who were literate (predominately boys in the first instance) to become familiar with a wide range of stories. From the beginning of the eighteenth century, translated texts also included versions of tales from *The Arabian Nights;* the complex history of the translation of these latter into English also evidences the way in which material which might be thought unsuitable for the young was censored and abridged by translators (Lathey 2006: 43–48). Better known to later readers are the early eighteenth-century translations of the fairytales of Mme d'Aulnoy and Charles Perrault, both first published in French in 1697.

So familiar have subsequent generations become with tales such as 'Red Riding Hood' and 'Cinderella' that it often surprises readers to learn that the original audience envisaged by d'Aulnoy and Perrault was adult, though this was not the case for another popular French storyteller, Mme le Prince de Beaumont, who inserted 'Beauty and the Beast' into the teaching material (1756) which she produced on the model of Sarah Fielding's *The Governess* (1749). There were also a number of folk tales of native origin, notably featuring Jack the Giant-Killer, while several English writers, such as Sarah Trimmer, were stimulated by the popularity of such tales to produce other fiction. The major impact of 'nursery' tales on English children, however, derives from the translation of the Grimm brothers' *Kinder und Hausmärchen* from 1823 onwards, followed soon afterwards by Hans Christian Andersen's fairytales. To attempt either to summarise the complex history of the translation of these tales, or the merits of various English versions, would not be appropriate here;[43] what is intended, rather, is to recall how fundamental translation has been to subsequent English children's literature, including the creation of original fantasy, from *Alice* (1865) onwards. One significant aspect highlighted by Lathey is worth mention – the preponderance of female translators. While 'many women found translation to be a satisfying and challenging intellectual occupation conducted in the private domestic arena when public academic and professional activity was closed to them' (Lathey 2010: 95), it could be argued that there is some correlation between the low status then given to women and the invisibility generally accorded to translators.[44] These early translations also raise questions which have been touched upon in Section 9.3, concerning the balance between fidelity to the original and accessibility to the target audience.

Lathey goes on to document how various later texts, including those by Collodi, Spyri and Kästner, reached English-speaking readers, and to chart the gradual recognition of translators' work, with the institution in 1968 of the American Mildred Batchelder Award for translation for children, and its British counterpart, the Marsh Award, in 1996. As well as being a historical survey, Lathey's book tackles such issues as the effect on the role of translators of global marketing, and of re-translation; she also gives space to the voices of two prestigious translators into English, Anthea Bell and Sarah Adams Ardizzone.

Translations of English children's literature

Among the most conspicuous contemporary translations of English language texts into other languages are those of the 'Harry Potter' books by J.K. Rowling. Because of their international high profile, there was inevitably pressure on foreign publishers to produce versions accessible to their own reading public. Thus translators not only had to deal with the usual challenge of finding appropriate ways of expressing fresh material, which in this case involved idiosyncratic names and original varieties of magic, but also to work at speed so that the translated version could be available to consumers eager to be abreast of the latest events in the saga.

In order to analyse such translations, scholars need a good understanding of both English as the source language and the specific target language(s) involved. Nancy Jentsch (2002) looks at versions of Harry Potter in French, German and Spanish and discusses some of the problems the translators confronted: translating the English 'you' into languages that offer alternatives according to the relationship between speaker and addressee; coping with colloquial language and grammatical gender; and creating linguistically acceptable proper names. Jentsch's study[45] reveals for instance that the French version makes the greatest changes in Rowling's choice of names, while the other languages remain fairly close to the original – a situation consonant with French translation practice generally.[46] Another critic, Martá Minier, explores the Hungarian translation of Rowling's books, in the process of demonstrating that the translator, Boldizsár Tóth, 'neither unquestionably domesticates, nor foreignises the text' (2006: 119), since he both 'respects the "otherness" of the original [and manages to enable] Harry Potter in Hungarian ... [to] carry British, Hungarian and Western connotations almost coterminously' (in (ed.) Pinsent 2006: 132).

Interesting questions about translation are raised by several other articles in this 2006 collection, such as those by Elena Xeni, Darja Mazi-Leskovar and Margharita Ippolito.[47] Xeni discusses the problems posed by a humorous text, Sue Townsend's *The Secret Diary of Adrian Mole, Aged 13 ¾* (1982). A piece of doggerel verse by the eponymous character proved particularly challenging: Xeni chose to keep the same rhyme scheme, which she saw as integral to the humour. Mazi-Leskovar writes about her research into Slovenian translations of American classics, looking especially at four versions of *Uncle Tom's Cabin;* two are from 1853, very close in time to the original publication of Harriet Beecher Stowe's novel (1852), while two others are from the 1930s. She also discusses a 1954 re-publication with inserted editorial material and illustrations which carry strong ideological messages from the communist period. Margharita Ippolito compares the work of two translators of Beatrix Potter into Italian; she finds that, despite the fact that both date from the 1980s, they make different assumptions about how closely the translator should render terms from a different culture. Nevertheless, she claims that both evidence the publisher's assumption that it is important for Italian children to encounter 'the language and culture of the English-speaking world' (2006: 115).

Visual texts, translation and global culture

To a greater extent than in works for adults, children's books often feature the visual, whether as a dominant element or as a supplement to the verbal text, and several of the pieces selected by Lathey in her *Reader* (2006) focus on this topic. Riitta Oittinen draws attention to the importance of the translator of a children's book ensuring that the text and illustrations fit as well in the translated version as in the original, and of taking note of such other visual elements as covers, endpapers and typeface (2006: 94).[48] Emer O'Sullivan points out, 'Picture books present a special challenge to the translator, as the presence and interaction of two media make the process more complex' (2006: 114). This has become increasingly so as the text and the pictures in many modern picturebooks have an ironic relationship which is not easily conveyed in a language other than the original one. Sometimes, as O'Sullivan indicates, 'gaps in the source text may be filled by translators in the target text' (2006: 114).

A critic who has given a good deal of attention to the issue of translated picturebooks is Mieke Desmet, whose work features in several collections. In the Lathey *Reader*, Desmet focuses on the special problems faced by the translator of a richly allusive series of texts, Janet and Allan Ahlberg's *The Jolly Postman* books (1986–95; Dutch translations 1987–96), and observes how Ernst van Altena uses strategies such as 'literal translation, substitution, compensation (or addition), and very occasionally deletion' (2006: 128) to cope with cultural differences, literary style, vocabulary and rhyme, and to allow readers to encounter at least some of the intertextual aspects that are so fundamental to the attraction of these books. A wider cultural gap between source and target texts is confronted in Desmet's article in the IBBY collection, where she looks at translations of Babette Cole and Anthony Browne into Chinese. Among other things, she finds that the Chinese text makes explicit some of the deductions that an English-speaking audience is expected to derive from the pictures. Translation, as well as building bridges, may sometimes, almost involuntarily, undermine some of its own ideals; only a detailed analysis will reveal the fallacy of 'the transparency of translation' (2006: 199).

It is evident that the translation of picturebooks brings to the fore problems of cultural redaction that may be less evident when written text alone is considered. Some of the analyses of these, such as Clare Bradford's exploration of indigenous Australian visual narratives for children (2003), more properly belong in the chapter concerned with post-colonialism. More specific to the current topic is the work of Penni Cotton and the European Picture Book Collection; the latest version, an EU funded Comenius project, 'makes more than 60 picture books from all 27 EU member states, and the ethnic, linguistic and religious groups within them, available to educators, librarians, students and scholars', with the purpose of intercultural dialogue.[49] Cotton outlines the early stages of this project in *Picture Books sans Frontières* (2000), and has written a number of articles detailing its inauguration and development. Intrinsic to the project is the breaking down of barriers of all kinds; Cotton (2004: 59) describes how the choices of picturebooks for the collection are made, focusing in this instance on a text particularly germane to this process because of its emphasis on the acceptance of difference, *The Land of Corners* (Ulitzka and Gepp 1993).

The legacy of initiatives such as that of Jella Lepman discussed above is to be seen in the wider dissemination of children's literature, where necessary in translation, throughout the world. It has now become common for conferences and collections of articles to avoid confining their attention to books published in English, and thus to facilitate a cross-cultural perspective. Collections such as those edited by Roderick McGillis (2003), Jan de Maeyer et al (2005) and Justyna

Deszcz-Tryhubczak and Marek Oziewicz (2006) present material from a variety of languages and cultures, while resources such as the CHILDE (Children's Historical Literature Disseminated Throughout Europe) Culture 2000 Project, managed by Mike Ryan and Esther Gregory, provides information and digitised material related to a number of collections throughout Europe.[50]

While a variety of challenges remain, and there are still many obstacles, both at the level of translation and that of culture, to the understanding of literature from other countries, there is no doubt that the importance of the objectives of idealists such as Lepman are now recognised throughout the world. The proliferation of non-book material, together with contemporary means of communication and entertainment, poses its own problems, but the increase in understanding at least at the level of children's literature shows that progress can be made. The following chapter highlights the way in which similar developments have occurred in relation to literature dealing with topics such as 'racism' and post-colonialism.

CHAPTER TEN

Recognising the Culturally Invisible

Introduction

This chapter focuses on how, from the second half of the twentieth century onwards, there has been an increased awareness in both literature and criticism of the many groups of people who, if they have figured at all in previous mainstream culture, have seldom been given a voice. Roderick McGillis, in a collection of articles focusing mostly on post-colonialism, talks of the beginnings of the process of 'hear[ing] the voice of the other, the people more written about than writing, more spoken about than speaking', and of the gradual awareness of 'a desire for recognition on the part of people who have been either invisible or unfairly constructed or both'. McGillis also associates such 'culturally invisible or diminished' groups with women and children as being 'powerless to take part in the conversations of cultural and other forms of political activity' (2000: xxi). In the current chapter, however, feminism will not be considered, since it features in Chapter Eight; instead, as well as discussion of issues related to multiculturalism or associated with colonialism and its aftermath, attention will be given to an area only recently emerging from critical neglect, that of children's literature about disability.

The initial focus is on the anti-racist, multicultural response to some familiar children's fiction, followed by a more explicitly post-colonial emphasis, including some attention to the special case of Irish children's literature, and culminating in the newer field of disability studies.

Problems of definition

In discussing critical works, it is not always easy to disentangle various issues. Discourse concerning equality issues in particular has often been rendered opaque by the failure of participants to agree on the meaning of the terms, partly because of a general lack of consistency in usage, and partly because writers themselves are strongly involved with how matters of personal identity impinge on such definitions. The interrelationship between some of the areas concerned can also be problematic. As McGillis claims: 'Both the postcolonial and neocolonial endeavour are, in part, a reaction to what we now refer to as multicultural societies' (2000: xxiv). The current form of such societies, notably that in Britain, largely results from the subsequent settlement in the 'mother' country by the descendants of those who were originally colonised. It is a useful preliminary therefore to look at the way in which some of these terms have been used.

Ethnicity, race and racism

In a recent collection of short essays confronting some current matters of contention, *Keywords for Children's Literature* (2011), edited by Philip Nel and Lissa Paul, Katherine Capshaw Smith traces the complex history of the term 'race' from its sixteenth-century origins to its having become, on the one hand, a site for cultural and largely inaccurate biologically based prejudice in a variety of well-known children's texts, and, on the other, a convenient term for marginalised communities who are expressing their self-articulation. She finishes with a caution: 'As sensitivity to individuals of mixed backgrounds increases, any simplistic use of "race" as a critical category dissolves' (2011: 193). Perhaps in an attempt to avoid any such usage, Clare Bradford, in a short entry in the 'Names and Terms' section of *The Routledge Companion to Children's Literature*, edited by David Rudd, states her preference for 'ethnicity' rather than the 'discredited' word 'race', though she asserts that even the term 'ethnicity' is subject to a lack of clarity of definition, particularly for the diasporic groups to be found in so much of today's world: 'For [them] formulations of ethnicity incorporate three components: a current location, the homeland from which the group comes and the transnational networks which connect people of a shared ethnicity' (2010: 171). In her longer essay in the same work, Bradford suggests that some attempts to contest racialised hierarchies, rather than effecting dialogue between them, in fact fall back on the very categorisation and stratification between opposed groups which they are seeking to displace (2010: 42).

Whatever the practical merits or demerits of the term 'race', at least in the English-speaking world, it would be difficult to supplant its derivative, 'racism'. In 'Race, Ethnicity and Postcolonialism',[1] Clare Bradford quotes Graham Huggan[2] on the connections between the two terms:

■ Race is a phantom theory, founded on the imagined existence of genetically 'deficient' human descent groupings; racism, by contrast, is an empirically verifiable *practice* [italics original], based on an attribution of ineradicable differences that justifies the exploitation, exclusions [sic] or elimination of the people assigned to these 'inferior' groups. (2010: 40) □

Equality legislation, together with the guidelines which have resulted from it, has attempted to counteract prejudice based on skin colour and physical attributes, both in everyday life and in literature, especially that written for children.[3] In many instances this process has led to the formation of ambivalent attitudes towards previously popular, even ostensibly anti-racist, texts.

Multiculturalism

Despite the origin of this term in a well-intentioned endeavour to eschew national prejudice, and its association with attempts to 'represent cultural differences to young readers' (Debra Dudek, in (eds) Nel and Paul 2011: 155), it has frequently been criticised both by those who view it as devaluing majority culture and by minority groups who see in it a palliative gesture preventing a proper depiction of their own cultural mores. Dudek dismisses the criticism that books seeking to reflect cultural diversity may sacrifice literary qualities, giving examples of fiction that combines literary and artistic merit. She observes, however, that minority communities, especially those indigenous in territories originally colonised, are too often represented in text and illustration by 'white' authors.

In a short article called 'Multiculturalism' (2010), John Stephens presents the finding that the extent to which the predominant factor in multiculturalism is ethnicity or colour varies between countries according to their history. He goes on to pose the question as to how far the 'authentic' values of minority communities can be depicted adequately in the context of what he terms the 'assimilationist' tendencies of countries such as the US and France. He comments on the preponderance in recent years of citizenship tests for immigrants, speculating as to whether this could engender 'renewed social hostility towards otherness', whereas 'transculturalism, as a reciprocal sharing between two cultures' could well be an alternative policy which lends itself to the production of literary texts 'foregrounding the experience of "minority" as opposed to "dominant" groups' (in (ed.) Rudd 2010: 212–3).

Colonialism, post-colonialism and neo-colonialism

One of the clearest presentations of this cluster of terms is the Introduction to Roderick McGillis's collection, *Voices of the Other* (2000). Locating the first term in the history of imperialistic European countries, he states:

■ Colonialism is ... the term we use for an activity among peoples that involves one group assuming priority and authority over another group ... [It] is not only a political and economic activity, but it also affects cultures, and it assumes a certain mind-set: a colonial mentality. The colonial mentality assumes that the colonizer presents a more advanced state of civilization than the colonized does, and therefore that the colonizer has a right to assume a position of dominance. (2000: xxii) □

While the colonial mind-set was most evident in Victorian adventure stories, McGillis notes that some critics have seen it still being maintained in such twentieth-century stories as the 'Babar' books. He goes on:

■ Post-colonialism in literature refers to a self-consciousness on the part of emerging peoples of a history, a culture, and an identity separate from and just as important as those of the imperial 'masters'. (2000: xxiii) □

The response of post-colonial writers may on the one hand be an attempt to maintain a Eurocentric position even while trying to establish a distinctive identity, or on the other, particularly among those with roots in the indigenous population, an attempt to resist Eurocentric dominance, focusing on issues of race and culture. This response may in turn be met with neo-colonialism, 'a renewed drive on the part of the dominant social and cultural forces to maintain their positions of privilege' (2000: xxiv). McGillis lists popular culture (such as Disney) among such neo-colonial reactions.

In relation to literary criticism, however, the term post-colonialism tends to be applied to all forms of response to colonisation; Clare Bradford emphasises:

■ Postcolonialism ... does not refer to a period 'post' (i.e. after) colonialism and does not mean that colonialism is over and done with. In their seminal work, Bill Ashcroft et al (1989, p.2)[4] announce that they use the term 'postcolonial' to cover all the culture affected by the imperial process from colonization to the present day. (in (ed.) Rudd 2010: 229–30) □

Peter Barry suggests that a main characteristic of post-colonialist criticism is its rejection of the assumption that all literature can be judged by a 'universal' standard, regardless of its regional and other aspects (1995: 191–2).

The seminal text in the field of post-colonial studies is Edward Said's *Orientalism* (1978),[5] which was followed fifteen years later by his *Culture and Imperialism* (1993). Despite the ostensible focus on the East implied by the title of the earlier book, Said's analysis of the relationship between coloniser and colonised has been applied more widely and has given rise to many subsequent studies not confined to the Orient; in addition, in his later work, Said himself amplifies his own arguments 'to describe a more general pattern of relationships between the metropolitan West and its overseas territories'(1993: xi). Said's basic contention is that Western perceptions of subjugated cultures are frequently constructed in terms of a power relationship that views them as antithetical to Western cultures and is often founded on a discourse which itself is based on little more than 'travellers' tales', a corpus of material that has coloured much subsequent writing. He expands on this in his later book, not only to include other parts of the world, but also to illustrate his thesis by reference to narrative fiction, notably novels by Joseph Conrad and Jane Austen. In the Introduction to the later study, he observes how European writing constantly emphasises:

■ the disturbingly familiar ideas about flogging or death or extended punishment being required when 'they' misbehaved or become rebellious, because 'they' mainly understood force or violence best; 'they' were not like us, and for that reason deserved to be ruled. (1993: xi–xii) □

While Said presents a broad perspective based on the history and culture of both the West and the colonised nations, Bill Ashcroft, Gareth Griffiths and Helen Tiffin (1989; 2nd ed 2002) explicitly focus on post-colonial literary responses to colonisation. Basing their analysis on writing by people living in nations originally colonised by Britain, they examine the 'stages of development', from texts produced by 'a literary elite whose primary identification is with the colonizing power' (2002: 5), through a large body of work by 'natives' with the support of the authorities, towards the development of truly independent literatures. They see as an important factor in this process the creation of local varieties of English appropriate to the expression of the former colonies' own distinctive brands of culture. Ashcroft et al. claim that:

■ The process of cultural decolonization has involved a radical dismantling of the European codes and a post-colonial subversion and appropriation of the dominant European discourses. (2002: 220) □

This process may, they suggest, involve a wholly different set of canonical texts, as well as a rereading of the existing ones (2002: 221–22).

Said's consideration of literature is largely but not exclusively devoted to British authors whose novels directly or indirectly depict the effects of empire, while the authors of *The Empire Writes Back* (1989) focus on the literatures of former colonial nations; neither of them gives more than incidental attention to works written, or in due course presented to, children.[6] One of the most notable post-colonial critics of children's literature is Clare Bradford, whose work will be discussed below.

Rereading the classics

Many of the classics of children's literature, written in a period when British imperialism and the resultant colonisation were taken as a norm, pose problems both for scholars and for classroom teachers who want to familiarise their pupils with these canonical texts. Both groups recognise, however, that the writers internalised the imperial mind-set to the extent that even though such books are not explicitly about the subjugation of other races, their unconscious ideology implicitly assumes the superiority of the British. Even fiction writers whose characters never leave British shores fail to question the morality of wealth which results from colonial possessions or the desirability of training young British men for empire-related ventures overseas. As Peter Hunt and Karen Sands (in (ed.) McGillis) comment: 'At its peak, imperialism affected every type of literature, from hymns to children's magazines, and every class in society' (2000: 43). A detailed account of some of the books in which this aspect is revealed is to be found in the work of Daphne Kutzer (2000), who focuses on children's literature from the late nineteenth to the mid-twentieth century; her analysis suggests that implicit assumptions about white superiority are likely to be more influential on children's opinions than the more blatant colonialism of writers such as Marryat and Ballantyne. Defining imperialism as the 'promotion of the racial superiority of white Europeans, and especially Englishmen, over darker-skinned non-Europeans' (2000: xvii), she analyses the work of a range of earlier writers before focusing on the work of Kipling and his successors. She suggests that:

■ the themes that pervade all his fiction, themes of invasion, of the importance of hierarchy … of the dangers and necessities of empire, of the interplay between colonizer and colonized, of the need for creative insubordination, are themes that are woven throughout much of the writing for children in the early years of the twentieth century. They become more muted, but no less present, in children's books well into the twentieth century. (2000: 45) □

Looking at the two most popular women novelists for children of the late nineteenth and early twentieth century, Kutzer claims that

■ Burnett's heroines are much more Victorian than Nesbit's and the entire tone of Nesbit's work is more modern, yet both writers demonstrate the way tropes of empire and nationalism are part of even the most domestic fiction of the era. (2000: 76) □

Both Burnett and Nesbit unquestioningly accept the empire as a good thing and a source of wealth; foreigners may be useful servants but are potentially dangerous if not well supervised. Other writers whose work is subjected to Kutzer's analysis include A.A. Milne, Hugh Lofting and Arthur Ransome, together with some significant post-war authors. On the basis of this analysis, she claims:

■ If children's fiction is one way of acculturating children into an acceptable ideology, then classic children's texts from the Boer War to World War II suggest to children that British imperial rule over countries is a good thing, for both Britain and for imperial outposts. (2000: 138) □

Another English language classic, this time from Australia, Ethel Turner's *Seven Little Australians* (1894), is subjected to analysis by Clare Bradford; she observes the 'significant omission' from the 1900 edition of an indigenous Australian story featuring in the first edition. Bradford suggests that this omission 'works to silence [the] contradiction around the existence of indigenous culture, the illegitimacy of the colony's beginnings, and its "sorrowful history" of displacement and genocide' (in (ed.) McGillis 2000: 104–7). Thus, in the context of a former colony, as distinct from the British mainland, post-colonial issues become more explicit; the implications of this and the related topic of the work of indigenous writers are considered by Bradford throughout her extensive critical analyses, notably in her wide-ranging study, *Unsettling Narratives* (2007), which explores both settler and indigenous literature in Canada, New Zealand and the United States as well as Australia.

In its exposé of the imperialist assumptions of a great deal of classic children's fiction, Kutzer's book, while more limited in focus than Bradford's work, is of particular value to those who otherwise might not detect all the nuances which combine to exert a continuing influence on young readers. Kutzer does not, however, take on board the question of whether, given their flaws, such texts should remain available to young readers. Any attempts at censorship on the grounds that they foster an imperialistic mind-set would of course be futile, given the inevitability of children encountering the material in one form or another: film, play, computer game, etc. What is perhaps most important is that those who are responsible for children's intellectual formation should be aware of the implicit messages contained in such texts. It could be claimed (cf. Pinsent 1997, chs. 2 and 3) that the most important task is that of familiarising children with the ways in which ideology is conveyed and making them aware of the presuppositions of the periods in which such books were written.

Race and modern British children's fiction

The impetus towards the recognition that much children's fiction reflects outworn attitudes towards race and culture only took off in Britain during the last quarter of the twentieth century. The words of the Bullock Report, *A Language for Life* (1975) proved highly influential:

> ■ No child should be expected to cast off the language and culture of the home as he [sic] crosses the school threshold, nor to live and act as though school and home represent two totally separate and different cultures which have to be kept firmly apart. (1975: 286)[7] □

In the wake of Bullock, a number of books with an educational focus were published which provided a critique of children's fiction on the basis of race and culture; attention was directed both towards some of the classics mentioned in the previous section, and to more recent books which attempted to provide a corrective to the unsatisfactory attitudes now detected in these canonical texts. In his two books entitled *Catching Them Young* (1978a and b) and his later *Now Read On* (1982), Bob Dixon took on a range of controversial issues – sex, class and political ideas – as well as race. Other writers in this field include Judith Stinton (1979), David Milner (1983), Gillian Klein (1985) and the prolific children's novelist, Bob Leeson, whose *Reading and Righting* (1985) provides a rapid survey of earlier children's fiction, together with an extensive bibliography of 'progressive books for young readers' compiled by another activist in the field, Rosemary Stones. All these works could be described as polemical rather than literary critical.[8] However, *Through Whose Eyes* (1992), a slightly later book by another important writer of children's fiction, Beverley Naidoo, presents not only a useful review of how literature colours racial attitudes among young readers, but also information about a research project she conducted. Located at a secondary school in a predominantly white area, it presented students with books reflecting different attitudes towards race and racism. Naidoo found that the project succeeded in raising the pupils' awareness of the issues concerned, and established the need for a culturally diverse English curriculum, but that a great deal of the effect of such measures depended on the attitudes of teachers.

It seems apparent that messages about anti-racism and cultural differences are most effective if conveyed incidentally rather than in a blatantly didactic manner. Pinsent (1993: 103–106) argues for the use of folk story and fantasy, in addition to texts which take a realist perspective, as a means of showing how differences are integral to society. Additionally, intertextual use of well-established story paradigms, such as the romance, can be effective in attracting reader's sympathies to characters whose relationships cross the 'racial' divide (cf. Pinsent in (ed.) Reynolds 2005: 194–196).

Post-colonial criticism and the literature of subjugated communities

The collection edited by McGillis (2000) includes studies both of post-colonial theory and of the portrayal of indigenous people and the emergence of their authentic voices. Among these, the transition from settler society to multiculturalism in Australian children's fiction is traced by John Stephens, while Jean Stringam and Dieter Petzold present different aspects of the Canadian experience. Kenyan and Nigerian fiction also receive mention.

The question of how far it is possible for readers from majority groups to understand the perspective of dominated cultures is a particular focus of Bradford's work. In *Reading Race: Aboriginality in Australian Children's Literature* (2001), she provides a chronological survey both of the portrayal of indigenous characters in books by 'white' authors, and of the development of Aboriginal literature as such. Given the distinctiveness of Aboriginal art, a particularly rich area is that of visual narrative; one of Bradford's most interesting contributions in this area is her paper 'Aboriginal Visual Narratives for Children: A Politics of Place' which was given at a Cambridge conference in 2000 entitled 'Reading Pictures'.[9] She begins by emphasising the limitations experienced by critics nurtured in a Western literary tradition because of their inability to read such texts in the same way as those brought up in the indigenous tradition. Setting her discussion of contemporary picturebooks into the context of the first published work for children by an Aboriginal artist,[10] she shows how recent artists of the same origin have incorporated their own cultural and narrative traditions into their work, and have thus engaged 'with Western forms and practices in order to interrogate the assumptions and ideologies of the dominant culture' (2003: 76).

A cautionary note about the use of post-colonial criticism is, however, supplied by Victor Ramraj (in (ed.) McGillis) who reminds readers that this approach only focuses on one part of a multifaceted experience:

> ■ To look at these societies only through colonial lenses is, in a way, to see the colonized exclusively in terms of Caliban, ignoring another important, but different sort of colonized on Prospero's island – Ariel ... In functioning basically as a corrective of one master narrative [postcolonialism] has itself become a master narrative that ignores the many other narratives of the complex and varied lives lived in colonies and former colonies. (2000: 264) □

Irish children's literature

Because of its proximity to England, the political, economic and cultural history of Ireland has been so intertwined with that of its larger neighbour that colonialism in Ireland is part of a complex colonial/neo-colonial/post-colonial context unlike any other part of what used to be the British Empire. In view too of the frequency of shift of residence between the two countries, deciding on the 'Irishness' of authors is also often problematic. For instance, Maria Edgeworth (1767–1849), one of the most influential pioneers of writing aimed at a young audience, with *The Parent's Assistant* (1796) and *Early Lessons* (1801), was Anglo-Irish. Valerie Coghlan observes: 'Little of Edgeworth's writing for children bears any particular relation to Ireland. An exception to this is *Orlandino* (1848) which is an interesting reflection of Ireland at that time' (in (ed.) V. Watson 2001: 231).[11] Another instance of ambiguity, this time involving not only national allegiance but also audience, is the case of Jonathan Swift's *Gulliver's Travels* (1726), written while he was living in Dublin. Despite its enormous influence on subsequent English children's literature and a considerable number of versions adapted for young readers, it was certainly never intended for a child audience.[12]

The literatures of what are now two distinct nations are difficult to disentangle,[13] and the history of both adult and children's literature, and thus of literary criticism, has to be viewed as shared, at least until the foundation of the Irish Free State in 1922. As Valerie Coghlan and Keith O'Sullivan observe, 'Most Irish adults over the age of thirty-five grew up reading books that were written and published primarily for British and American children' (2011: 1). Nevertheless, by the end of the twentieth century, a corpus of children's literature written by people born and/or living in Ireland, and making Irish life a theme in their writing, had begun to emerge. As a consequence, criticism of Irish children's literature, itself also largely recent in date, tends to concentrate on books published from about 1980 onwards. The Irish Society for the Study of Children's Literature holds regular conferences and research seminars on Irish and international children's literature, and has published several volumes based on conference papers.

Valerie Coghlan and Keith O'Sullivan state that their edited collection, *Irish Children's Literature and Culture: New Perspectives on Contemporary Writing* (2011), 'critically engages with major forms, genres, themes and preoccupations ... [and also examines] the literary, political, and societal influences' on this literature (2011: 1). Issues resulting from the smallness of the Irish children's book market are addressed by international scholars Emer O'Sullivan and Sandra Beckett, while Ciara Ni Bhroin looks at the continuing global popularity of Irish myth and legend. Other studies consider current issues related to television and film, but the editors reflect that 'the essays in this volume show that present-day Irish writing for young people remains heavily indebted to the past ... [both] mythical and historical' (2011: 5). Nor does it tackle all facets of contemporary life: in a study of Irish Young Fiction, Pádraic Whyte comments that in spite of a number of treatments of issues such as sexuality, abortion and teen pregnancy, there is a paucity in this fiction of lesbian and gay characters (2011: 72–3).

The subject matter of another volume devoted to Irish children's literature and published in the same year, Pádraic Whyte's *Irish Childhood: Children's Fiction and Irish History*, is consequently very apposite. One theme explored here by Whyte is 'the construction of the child character as a metonym for the Irish nation' (2011: xvii). He describes his book as 'a close textual analysis of specific novels and films that engage with aspects of twentieth-century Irish history', reflecting his belief that a case-study approach is preferable to 'sweeping surveys' (2011: xviii). An important theoretical context is the 'revisionist debate, which challenged ... homogenous accounts of the past' (2011: xxvii). He goes on to claim that his study 'reveals many of the intricacies of cultural debates in ...[contemporary] Ireland ... Issues of "local" and "global" perspectives of the nation and the production of internal and external representations of Irish identity are to the fore of these discussions' (2011: xxx). In view of Ireland's chequered colonial and post-colonial history, this finding is not unexpected.

Disabled people

Critical discussion of the portrayal of disability in books for children only came to the fore in the latter years of the twentieth century. As Kathy Saunders states:

> ■ In comparison to analysis of race and gender bias, an ongoing debate on the impact of disability images in children's material, informed by an analysis of disability in contemporary society, has been slow to develop in the fields of both children's literature and disability studies. (2004: 1) □

Prior to comparatively recent times, it was all too easy for non-disabled readers to believe in the title character's near-miraculous recovery from debilitating paralysis in Susan Coolidge's *What Katy Did* (1872), or to accept the way in which disabled people tended to be portrayed either as 'saints', such as Cousin Helen in the same book, or as villains, like Blind Pew in Stevenson's *Treasure Island* (1883).[14] On the basis of an analysis of a range of texts, Lois Keith suggests that, more than a century after these classics were published, stereotypical views about disability are still to be found in children's literature; additionally, she notes the continued prevalence of the metaphorical use of the inability to walk as an image for powerlessness (2001: 249).

One of the first critics to venture into this area was John Quicke (1985), whose study of a range of twentieth-century children's fiction was intended to promote understanding by parents and teachers, and to facilitate children's acceptance of disabled young people, particularly in a family or school context. At the time when he was writing, Quicke found that many books intended to facilitate awareness of disability were of poor quality, and in some instances those designed to increase the readiness of young people to accept people with a disability seemed to be guilty of displaying other forms of prejudice, or of adopting too negative an approach (1985, ch. 2).

Inevitably any critical work which focuses on specific children's books is limited by those which are available at the time when the critique is written; general principles have to be derived from scrutiny of a range of books which are quite likely not to remain in print for long and thus be unavailable to later readers. Some critics attempt, however, to work towards a more general approach by grouping texts into categories, in the hope that trends will emerge. A collection of essays about twentieth-century fiction, edited by Helen Aveling (2009),[15] attempts to achieve a broader perspective by grouping the papers under the headings 'Stereotypes', 'Role Models' and 'Inclusion and Segregation'. Particularly interesting in the last of these categories is Rebecca Butler's

examination of the fictional portrayal of relationships between a disabled child and a sibling; she concludes that the texts she has examined
support her hypothesis that 'disability makes the sibling relationship
more intense, more complex and, most significantly, more ambivalent' (2009: 332). Butler has also completed a study of the responses of
young readers, both disabled and otherwise, to a range of books featuring disabled characters.[16] In particular, she found that group discussions
of such texts often revealed insightful reading, especially if the group
included children both with and without disabilities.

The situation in relation to this branch of literature is rendered
more complex by the variety of possible disabilities, and the changes
in the terminology acceptable in the description of people who are suffering from them (such as recent avoidance of terms such as 'cripples'
or 'handicapped'). Some of the complexities in dealing with the topic
are indicated in a chapter partly devoted to it in Pinsent (1997, ch. 8),
which goes on to discuss the ways in which some recent books have
dealt with the subject more effectively than was often the case in the
past, sometimes through the medium of picturebook or fantasy.

Critical perspectives today are informed by a consciousness that a
significant aspect of disability is the way in which society disables people
by a lack of provision of the kind of support that would enable eve-
rybody to function to their full potential. Helen Aveling contrasts the
Medical Model of disability, which places the emphasis on what people
cannot do, with the Social Model:

■ The Social Model ... perceives the individual holistically rather than labe-
ling [sic] them with medical terms ... Society disables people ... when a
person is excluded because of their access needs from something that
other people in society take for granted. For example, using the Social
Model, a wheelchair user who is unable to use a bus or enter the cinema
is disabled because the bus does not have a lowered floor and the cinema
a ramp, not because of their impairment. (2009: 14) □

The paper by Saunders quoted above makes an attempt to discern which
of these two models has been predominant in some selected children's
books, particularly Anne Fine's *The Granny Project* (1983). Saunders suggests that this book foregrounds the way in which an approach based
on social needs is a more effective way to cope with the problems posed
to a family confronted by the onset of Alzheimer's disease in the grand-
mother. Fine's book also raises a related issue which has received little
attention in critical discussion of children's books, that of the portrayal
in children's fiction of elderly characters. Numerous elderly people,
especially grandmothers, are of course to be found in fairytales, where
their depiction is often polarised between, on the one hand, weak and

dependent victims, and, on the other, malevolent witches and the like. While studies of fairytales, such as Marina Warner's *From the Beast to the Blonde*, give some attention to this question, the extent to which this use of stereotypes has influenced later fictional portrayals has not been widely explored.[17]

Conclusion

It has only been possible here to look at some of the groups that were until recently 'silenced' in both children's literature and its criticism – more attention, for instance, needs to be paid to the depiction of minority religious groups. It is to be hoped that the principles which can be derived from a perusal of texts confronting other equality issues can give lines for such enquiry. It has, however, been argued that the most significant silenced group in the area of children's literature is that of the children themselves. In a challenging article, Perry Nodelman interjects this perspective into the debate, comparing the way in which both child psychology and children's literature can be seen as reducing children to a similar status to that of the 'orientals' who are the theme of Said's thesis. In assuming children's inherent inferiority and in effect 'female-ness', together with the other qualities analogous to those which Said sees as being attributed by Western writers to the 'subject races', those authorities who claim to speak for children – because they are silenced by adult society – do at least need to be aware of what they are doing:

■ We critics of children's literature ... [need] to stop forgetting or ignoring or denying that all children's literature is as inherently imperialist as all human discourse tends to be. (1992a: 34) □

Thus Nodelman is in effect throwing down the gauntlet to all critics of children's literature to read Said's work with a consciousness of their own imperialist tendencies. It remains debatable, however, whether the subject of the next chapter, young adult (YA) fiction, in view of the fact that it is often also read by 'genuine' adults, is complicit in such 'imperialism'!

CHAPTER ELEVEN

The Limits of Childhood: Young Adult and Crossover Fiction

Clare Walsh

Introduction

U.C. Knoepflmacher and Mitzi Myers (1997: vii) argue that all works of fiction written for young readers by adults are inherently dialogic because they 'create a colloquy between past and present selves'. This chapter will, however, be confined to a review of critical approaches to fiction for young adults (YAs) which has been perceived by gatekeepers to have challenged the limits of acceptability in terms of subject matter and style (Beckett (ed.) 1999; Trites 2000), and/or which has attracted an adult readership (Falconer 2009). While Rachel Falconer suggests that cross-reading (defined by her as adults reading books aimed at young readers) is a relatively new phenomenon which emerged in the decade leading up to the millennium, recent anthologies of essays that focus on the work of pioneering writers of YA fiction from the mid-twentieth century onwards, most notably that of the controversial American writer Robert Cormier (Gavin (ed.) 2012), lend support to the view that YA fiction has from its inception blurred boundaries in terms of readership, subject matter and style.

The origins and development of YA fiction

According to Roberta Seelinger Trites (2000: 9), 'Literature specifically written for and marketed to adolescents came into its own in America when World War II changed the country's economy nearly forty years after the work of G. Stanley Hall[1] had called attention to adolescence as a psychological phenomenon.' The emergence of adolescents as autonomous consumers thus created a market for literature that reflected their perceived concerns and invited them to question dominant adult values. Blurred boundaries regarding intended readership are, however, evident in the fact that J.D. Salinger's *Catcher in the Rye* (1951), which has come to be seen by many literary historians as *the* seminal YA novel,[2] was not written *for* adolescent readers, but came to be appropriated *by* them. Indeed, this novel encapsulates two of the characteristic aspects of early YA fiction: the presence of a disaffected first person adolescent narrator (in this instance, Holden Caulfield), and the portrayal of the majority of adults as weak and ineffectual (Holden's term for them is 'phonies'). Its unflinching treatment of the themes of premature death and grief, and above all its subversive attitude towards adult authority, led to the claim made as late as 1978 by a Washington school board, that the novel was part of 'an overall communist plot'.[3]

S.E. Hinton was seventeen when *The Outsiders* (1967) was published, an early instance of a teenager writing a controversial novel for her peers. With its graphic depiction of class-based gang warfare narrated from the point of view of a young adolescent male protagonist, Hinton's gender-crossing novel is said to have initiated a tradition of 'New Realism' (Heaney 2005) in YA fiction. As one of the first novels for YAs to tackle the then taboo subject of teenage sexuality, Judy Blume's *Forever* (1975) continued this tradition. A flavour of the negative criticism the novel attracted is evident in Michele Landsberg's rhetorical question: 'How is it possible to devote an entire novel to teenage love without conveying one tremor of rapture, joy, delight, intensity, sadness, dread, anxiety or tenderness? Blume's "love" is all fumbling and bra hooks, semen and birth control pamphlets' (1988: 192). While the latter comment does not do justice to the novel's ironic tone and refreshingly non-punitive portrayal of a sexually active teen heroine, it reflects an anxiety shared by many critics that such issues-led books for YAs are in danger of sliding from imaginative fiction into mere social didacticism. Yet Nicholas Tucker comes close to the mark when he says of the controversy generated by Blume's novel:

■ there is ... a deeper rejection of the whole concept of childhood as a time for intense sexual curiosity ... It remains a side ... of childhood that we do not much want to think about, and children's writers who meet such interests at least half-way have to accept the aggressive critical consequences. (1994: 180) □

All three of the aforementioned books were subject to censorship as potentially harmful to the sensibilities of YA readers (West 1996), but none more so than Cormier's *The Chocolate War* (1974), one of the most banned books in the USA for any age group (Beckman 2008).

YA new realism and postmodern aesthetics

Peter Hunt (2001: 51) has described Robert Cormier (1925–2000) as 'in the top ten writers who are essential reading for an understanding of the development of children's literature in the twentieth century'. Yet Cormier's first and best-known novel, *The Chocolate War* (1974), was initially written with an adult readership in mind until his publisher shrewdly recognised its potential appeal to YAs. In an early critique, the liberal humanist critic Fred Inglis judged the pessimistic closure of this novel as having transgressed an unwritten rule that, however bleak the events portrayed in the course of a work of fiction aimed at young readers, they should ultimately be left with a sense of hope:

■ Hero-victim and reader are left with the pains and the clichés of concussion. The crude lesson is threefold: that all institutions systematise violence; that violence upholds power without reason; that individuals cannot hope to change these facts. These are the sentimentalities of disenchantment. (1981: 226) □

Inglis' potent phrase 'the sentimentalities of disenchantment' points to the danger of equating literary 'realism' with unrelenting bleakness. In a subsequent critical essay, Perry Nodelman (1992b) likewise suggests that part of the appeal of *The Chocolate War* can be explained precisely by the fact that Cormier panders to the narcissistic pleasure adolescent readers are likely to take in the atmosphere of paranoia that pervades the novel. This seems paradoxical given the use of the narrative device of shifting focalisation employed throughout, which ought to provide multiple viewpoints on the events depicted. Robyn McCallum argues that this, in turn, can be explained by the fact that the novel is a monologic text masquerading as a polyphonic one: 'There is on the one hand a sameness in the world view these characters represent and on the other hand an inability on the part of the characters to engage with and enter into dialogue with each other' (1999: 32). Indeed, in their shared disdain for their parents' lives and their voyeuristic attitude to the opposite sex, the novel's cast of thirteen adolescent focalising characters sound suspiciously like Holden Caulfield.[4]

Despite these negative criticisms, a recent anthology of essays on Cormier's work edited by Adrienne Gavin (2012) pays tribute to the long and varied contribution the author has made, especially in terms of the ambition of the themes he explores in his writing and the complexity of his narrative style, both of which have undoubtedly helped to elevate the literary status of this relatively young and seemingly ephemeral genre. For instance, Gavin suggests that Cormier is unusual amongst writers for YAs in tackling contemporaneous political themes which remain topical:

■ He was … influenced by the period in which he began writing his teen fiction: a time of terrorist attacks and hijackings, the Watergate scandal, the Vietnam War, questioning of political authority and systems, and the collapse of old cultural norms. (2012: 7) □

The essay by Pat Pinsent (2012: 48–63), which explores the influence of Graham Greene on Cormier's work, foregrounds his sustained use of Catholic-inflected religious iconography in order to probe the nature of human evil and counters the charge of nihilism by arguing that many of his novels hold out the possibility of redeeming grace. Holly Blackford's queer reading of *The Chocolate War* and its sequel, *Beyond the Chocolate War* (1985), opens up an alternative perspective on these novels based upon an implicit analogy between Trinity school and the repressive homophobic ideology of the Hitler Youth movement (2012: 96–112). In the final essay in the collection Dimitrios Politis (2012: 145–159) applies Wolfgang Iser's Theory Of Aesthetic Response to argue that the experimental narrative techniques Cormier employs encourage active and potentially resistant, rather than passive, readers. This accords with the view of a number of critics that Cormier was one of the first YA novelists to employ postmodern techniques in terms of both form and content.[5]

The most comprehensive and theoretically informed study of YA fiction to date is by Roberta Seelinger Trites (2000) who adopts a Foucauldian approach in her analysis of the workings of power in a wide range of novels by American and British writers. She argues that their writing should be viewed as an outgrowth of postmodernism on the grounds that they share an impulse to interrogate the social and discursive constructions of the identities of their adolescent protagonists. This, in turn, creates what she terms a paradox of authority:

■ characters created by adult writers test the limits of their power within the context of multiple institutions for the benefit of adolescent readers who supposedly gain some benefit from experiencing this dynamic vicariously. (2000: 97) □

Thus Trites stresses the complex negotiations these young protagonists make with repressive institutional power structures, including the family, church, government and school, claiming that it is the 'recognition that institutions are bigger and more powerful than individuals' (2000: 97) that sets YA fiction apart from fiction aimed at younger readers. Her overall thesis is that a power/repression dynamic lies at the heart of YA fiction, but, following Foucault,[6] she emphasises that power can be productive, as well as repressive, in that the oppositional identities it creates are attractive to teenage readers. This, she suggests, accounts for the predominance of rebel-heroes in many YA novels. Furthermore, she notes that in 'Anglophone cultures separation from parents is a prerequisite for growth' (2000: 55). Nevertheless, she claims earlier that YA novels '*indoctrinate* adolescents into a measure of acceptance' (2000: 27, my italics), a determinist view that appears to be at odds with the poststructuralist stance that she adopts elsewhere.

Trites' argument is at its strongest when she discusses the discursive construction of sexuality and death in Chapters Four and Five respectively. She argues persuasively that sexuality is both a site of power *and* repression in many YA novels in that it is portrayed as 'a rite of passage into adulthood' (2000: 84), but also as a problem in need of regulation. She cites with approval Aidan Chambers' metafictive novel *Breaktime* (1978) as a rare instance of a text in which both the heterosexual protagonists are 'empowered by their sexuality' (2000: 97). She contrasts this with his equally metafictive novel *Dance on My Grave* (1982) which centres on a homosexual relationship and which she views as 'more repressive than liberating' (2000: 105). This judgment, however, ignores the fact that the novel is only incidentally about sexuality, and is primarily about coming to terms with the death of a lover. In fact, Chambers' depiction of gender as performative and of (bi)sexuality as radically contingent in this novel anticipates the work of the poststructuralist feminist theorist Judith Butler in her influential book *Gender Trouble* (1990).[7]

In Chapter Five, Trites attempts to account for the preoccupation with death in the YA novels she analyses, something that at first seems surprising given the remoteness of death and dying to the majority of adolescents. She identifies three recurring patterns in the way death is represented: it occurs on stage; it is often violent and untimely; and it leads to a tragic loss of innocence (2000: 120). She contrasts this unflinching treatment of death as 'a threat, a finality' with the cyclical imagery associated with death in texts for younger readers (2000: 118). Trites concludes by advocating the need to employ poststructuralist methodologies when analysing YA fiction in order to foreground the kind of contradictory subject positions she claims these novels offer their young readers (2000: 144).

Cross-writing

The collection of essays on cross-writing edited by Sandra Beckett (1999) grew out of the International Research Society for Children's Literature

(IRSCL) Congress in 1995. She argues persuasively that cross-writing needs to be seen as an international phenomenon.[8] Thus a strength of the collection is that it comprises essays by fourteen scholars from eight different countries discussing the work of contemporary authors writing in a wide range of sub-genres. In the Introduction, Beckett makes the contentious claim that: 'More and more books illustrate the limitations of audience age as a defining category and refuse to be confined by any such arbitrary boundary constraints' (1999: xviii). Yet the first essay, by Helma van Lierop-Debrauwer (1999: 3–12), implies that *authors*, unlike books, continue to be categorised in terms of the average age of their primary readership. She discusses three kinds of what she refers to as 'border crossing': writers such as Roald Dahl who begin as writers for adults and then become successful children's writers; writers for children, such as Russell Hoban, who shift to writing for adults, but find it more difficult to be taken seriously in this role; and 'polygraphs', such as A.A. Milne, who write for both audiences (1999: 4). Lierop-Debrauwer goes on to argue that such boundary blurring should be welcomed as a means of emancipating children's and YA literature from its inferior status relative to literary fiction for adults. This explains Zohar Shavit's observation (1999: 89) that many children's authors claim to adopt an 'open' address in a thinly disguised attempt to sidestep the lowly status that continues to be accorded to writing for children and YAs. It would appear, then, that for all their arbitrariness, the boundary constraints referred to by Beckett remain peculiarly persistent.

This view is challenged by the French author Michel Tournier, whose cross-writing is the subject of Beckett's own essay. He claims that the quality of adult fiction should be measured by the accessibility to child readers of its style, thereby inverting the traditional status hierarchy referred to above by Lierop-Debrauwer and Shavit. For instance, Tournier regards his own abridged version of his adult novel *Friday* (1967), written in 1971 and subsequently published in 1977 under a children's imprint, as the superior version: 'The first *Vendredi* is the first draft, the second is the good copy' (1999: 39). What is interesting is that Tournier bases this judgement on aesthetic criteria, viewing the novel published for children as 'purer, less cluttered and more chiselled' (1999: 40) than the original adult novel. Yet, as Beckett observes, even Tournier had to admit that his adult novel *The Erl-King* (1970), about Nazi Germany, was too sombre in subject matter to be re-written in a form that was suitable for children (1999: 40).

This calls into question the thesis put forward by Maria Nikolajeva (1999: 63–80) that no meaningful boundary exists any more between books written for adults and children. In order to support her claim, she undertakes a close reading of three novels. The first of these (*Skriket fra jungelen – A cry from the jungle*, 1989, by Norwegian Andersen Medal winner Tormod Haugen) was ostensibly published for a child reader-ship, although I would suggest the implied addressee is, in fact, a YA. One was for a dual audience (*Northern Lights*, 1995, by British author Philip Pullman), and one for an adult readership (*Frøken Smilas fornemmelse for sne* – *Miss Smilla's Feeling for Snow*, 1992, by the Danish author Peter Høeg). All of them explore the theme of adult exploitation of children for dubious scientific purposes. By comparing their respective treatment of plot, setting, characterisation, narrative perspective, temporality and genre, Nikolajeva concludes that there are few discernible differences between them. What this comparative analysis does indicate is the increasingly permeable boundary between fiction for adults and YAs, rather than between fiction for *children* and adults, although the age at which children attain the status of young adulthood will, no doubt, remain a source of critical debate.[9]

Chapters Eight and Nine of Nikolajeva's book provide case studies of repressive cultural contexts, Russia during the Soviet era and the American South in the late nineteenth century respectively, in which fictions for children functioned as innocent 'screens' (1999: 130) for political and social satire. These would seem to constitute examples of what Barbara Wall (1991) refers to as 'double address' texts in that only the knowing adult reader is likely to have realised their full allegorical meaning. Even more challenging is the urge many Holocaust survivors have experienced to bear witness to the terrible events they lived through for a post-memory generation of young readers. In her essay, Adrienne Kertzer (1999: 167–182) argues that Isabella Leitner's sanitising for a child readership of the more traumatic aspects of her Holocaust memoir, although well-meaning, strips it of its moral force. According to Kertzer, the protectionist maternal narrative stance Leitner adopts paradoxically leads her to suppress the memory of her own mother's voice expressing her faith in the future without which 'there is no lesson; survival makes no sense' (1999: 169). Kertzer acknowledges the dilemma of communicating the events of the Holocaust to young readers: 'If we tell our children what we know, do we run the risk of burdening them too, making them inheritors of our nightmares?' (1999: 171). Yet she suggests that this needs to be balanced against the danger of erasing 'the anger, fury and grief of the daughter-survivor' (1999: 172). The Afterword to Leitner's book attempts to historicise the Holocaust for young readers (1999: 179), but Kertzer views this as too little, too late.

John Stephens (1999: 183–198) begins his essay by defending a clear demarcation between fiction aimed at pre-teen readers on the one hand, and adults on the other, with reference to the work of a number of Australian authors who write for both audiences. However, he then goes on to locate young adult fiction midway along a continuum between the two on the basis of 'a bundle of narrative elements'

(1999: 184). Such fiction is, he argues, more likely than fiction aimed at adult readers to take the form of a quest for an essential selfhood but, unlike in fiction for younger readers, the attainment of this goal is likely to be severely constrained by hostile social and institutional forces (1999: 194–195). He relates this quest narrative to three inter-related concerns: a search for a place/purpose in the physical and social world; a move from solipsism to intersubjectivity; and a quest for the other, often realised through the trope of romantic love (1999: 195). Stephens' approach offers a useful antidote to the tendency amongst some critics to homogenise early, middle and late adolescent readers. By contrast, the final essay in the collection, by Lissa Paul (1999: 239–254), welcomes the blurring, rather than refining, of age-related boundaries. She anticipates the advent of what she terms 'a new aesthetic of cultural clashes' (1999: 241) which relies less on a reader's age and more on her/ his experiential knowledge and when children and YAs begin 'writing and talking back' (1999: 249).

Cross-reading

Rachel Falconer defines the phenomenon of cross-reading as one in which adults choose to read books for children 'not (or not only) for a child's sake, but for her- or himself' (2009: 7). She dates the genesis of this practice very precisely to the publication by Bloomsbury in 1998 of the first *adult* edition of *Harry Potter and the Philosopher's Stone* (2009: 1). Her aim is to investigate why this turn to children's fiction by adult readers should have coincided with the approach of the millennium. She challenges the negative view promulgated by the tabloid press that it should be seen as symptomatic of a more general culture of dumbing down, in this instance reflected in the emergence of the pejorative term 'kiddult' to refer to irresponsible adults who allegedly refuse to grow up (2009: 3). Instead, she interprets cross-reading as a testament to the increasing sophistication of contemporary writing for children and YAs, due, in other words, to a scaling up in quality, rather than a dumbing down.

Nor does Falconer accept the idea that cross-reading should be dis-missed as a mere market-driven ploy by publishers to maximise the sale of books in what is undoubtedly an over-crowded marketplace in which books have to compete with an increasingly wide range of multimedia texts. To counter this view, she quotes Philip Pullman's suggestion that adult readers have sought refuge in children's books in order to escape from 'artistic posturing' (2009: 5) by writers of postmodern fiction. More positively, Pullman claims that adult readers find in children's fiction the pleasures of 'pure story', combined with the kind of ambitious themes that are rarely explored in contemporary literary fiction for adults due to its tone of sustained irony. Falconer also rejects the idea that 'cross-over' fiction heralds the end of children's fiction, instead welcoming it as a bridging device with the potential to foster inter-generational understanding (2009: 29). This contrasts with Deborah Thacker's more jaundiced view that it is one more manifestation of the colonisation by adults of children's culture (cited in Falconer 2009: 31).

In her analysis of the appeal of the Harry Potter septology to adult readers, Falconer draws a distinction between the first three books, which she claims are informed by an aesthetics of 'lightness', and the final four books, which are much darker in tone and which are infused by an obsession with mortality, marking a shift in tone from the playful to the pessimistic (2009: 71). By contrast, she argues that Pullman's *His Dark Materials* trilogy adopts a dual address from the outset which encourages a postmodern scepticism about theocratic absolutism (2009: 73); this, however, he achieves by inviting adult readers to share the child's imaginative capacity to think 'as if', thus 'releas[ing] them from entrenched attitudes and modes of being' (2009: 85–6). Somewhat surprisingly, Falconer downplays the dense intertextuality of the trilogy which seems likely to be a rich source of pleasure for knowing adult readers; instead she stresses that the ecocritical theme introduced in the second book, *The Subtle Knife* (1997), offers a timely wake-up call to child and adult readers alike (2009: 94).

The discussion of Mark Haddon's novel *The Curious Incident of the Dog in the Night-Time* (2003) in this context is rendered somewhat problematic by the fact that the author has made clear in interviews that he wrote the book with an implied adult readership in mind in an attempt to escape from the 'ghetto' of writing for children.[10] Nonetheless, Falconer's observations about the 'split perspective' (2009: 101) that occurs when an adult is required to see the world through the eyes of a young first-person narrator with Asperger's remain pertinent. She describes this as a three-stage process which involves shrinking the world to a child's point of view; perceiving it as enlarged; and then accepting the critical force of the curious child's gaze as it is turned on to the world of adults (2009: 111). Like *Curious Incident*, Geraldine McCaughrean's YA novel *The White Darkness* (2005) constitutes a kind of metafictive comment on the whole process of adults writing novels for young readers. It involves an intergenerational pairing of narrators, but the voice of the adult, the nineteenth-century polar explorer Titus Oates, is a projection of the imagination of the fourteen-year-old contemporary protagonist Sym Wates, thereby stressing the 'fluidity of temporal perspective' (2009: 122). The journey to the Antarctic that Sym and Titus undergo is a gruelling one involving extremes of physical suffering, betrayal and death; this leads Falconer to pose an interesting question about why adult readers should 'choose to experience abjection from the point of view of a child or teenager' (2009: 114). Her response is the convincing one that perceptions are heightened when filtered through the perspective of 'a young, more naïve witness' (2009: 117), rendering them both revelatory and liberating, as well as morally abhorrent and sublimely terrifying.

Falconer's penultimate chapter focuses on David Almond's YA novel *Clay* (2005) which, Falconer points out, is reminiscent of Haddon's novel in that it combines a spare style with complex themes (2009: 132), but which is similar to McCaughrean's in that it uses a magic realist mode to plumb the depths of adolescent psychic abjection. She argues that, like Pullman's trilogy, *Clay* involves a quest for latent spirituality in a post-religious age and thus figures the transition from childhood to adolescence as an Edenic Fall (2009: 140). Yet, unlike Pullman's co-protagonists Lyra and Will, Davie and Stephen in *Clay* go on an apparently regressive psychic journey back to early childhood which serves to debunk the myth of childhood innocence (2009: 152). Falconer's final essay examines C.S. Lewis's *The Silver Chair* (1953) as a case study of the increasingly prevalent phenomenon of adults re-reading their childhood selves through books. She suggests that such temporal achronology can lead to 'a kind of advance retrospection' (2009: 168). Thus she interprets Lewis's novel as a work of metafiction which justifies the re-reading of children's literature by adults (2009: 178). This leads her to argue, somewhat counterintuitively, that Prince Rilian is the subject of the novel whose role it is to act as a surrogate for the adult reader, a reader who is initially enchanted, but who ultimately becomes free (2009: 188). Falconer concludes that the re-reading of classic works of children's fiction by adults, while it may be literally backward-looking, is often potentially redemptive, rather than reactionary.

Transgressing boundaries in contemporary young adult fiction

The work of the contemporary British writer Melvin Burgess crystallises many of the issues touched upon throughout this chapter. He has openly acknowledged his debt to Robert Cormier and seems to relish his own notoriety as an author who is prepared to push back the boundaries of acceptability in his work for both children and YAs. By exploring taboo areas of experience, including drug culture, incest, violence, swearing, sexuality and sexual abuse, amongst others, his writing has undoubtedly contributed to what Neil Postman (1994: 125) refers to as the 'adultification' of children's literature and culture. Yet a recent anthology of essays in the New Casebook series edited by Alison Waller (2013) evaluates his work in largely positive terms. While Waller (2013: 6) detects a somewhat uneasy blend of sentimentality and social realism in *Nicholas Dane* (2009), a novel which graphically depicts the physical and sexual abuse of its eponymous hero/victim in a children's home in Britain in the 1980s, she points out that it was based on actual interviews Burgess conducted with child abuse victims (2013: 8). This leads him to describe it as a work of 'found fiction' (2013: 12; 191), a generic category that Waller accepts somewhat uncritically, despite the fact that it is at best misleading, and at worst mystifying. While, as Waller suggests (2013: 8), Burgess's aim to give a voice to the socially marginalised is a laudable one, the idea that he simply 'found', rather than elicited and then actively shaped, these stories can give them a somewhat spurious veneer of authenticity and can make it difficult to argue that the novel's treatment of violence may be voyeuristic or even gratuitous.

Two essays in the collection defend Burgess's novel *Doing It* (2003) against author Anne Fine's criticism that it is 'filth' fit only for a prurient adult readership (*Guardian*, 29 March 2003). In a thought-provoking essay, Chris Richards suggests that both Fine and Burgess are guilty of 'a kind of gender essentialism', Fine in relation to a homogenising view of young female readers' likely reaction to the novel, and Burgess in his:

■ representation of a monolithic, undifferentiated view of such male culture, projecting into the construction of the male characters and the relations between them one kind of white, lower middle-class, heterosexual and homosocial conviviality. (2013: 32) □

Both Richards and Michelle Gill (2013: 50) argue persuasively that the novel should be viewed as comic rather than erotic, with the male protagonists, for all their predatory rhetoric, being 'handled' by the girls and with the tone throughout being 'playful, humorous, non-judgemental'. Two other essays take as their focus Burgess' highly metafictive novel *Sara's Face* (2006) which explores the topical theme of contemporary celebrity culture. Joel Gwynne (2013: 64) stresses that the position of the eponymous (anti-)heroine is an ambivalent one from the outset. Drawing on Anita Harris' (2004) terms, Gwynne argues that it remains unclear whether Sara is a 'can do' girl, or an 'at risk' girl (2013: 65). Likewise, Kay Samball (2013: 87) suggests that there are textual clues that Sara 'may be performing victimhood'. Like the legendary rock star, Jonathan Heat, she uses 'excess, bad taste and offensiveness as tricks to gain publicity' (2013: 88). It could be argued that Burgess is making a sly comment here about his own status as an author-celebrity who invites media speculation about just how far he will be prepared to go in challenging the limits of YA fiction. The controversial nature of his work is calculated to appeal to his target YA readers, especially since books their parents do not want them to read (the advertising slogan for *Lady*) are likely to be relatively rare.

Perhaps because of the ambivalent tone of his writing, his tendency to employ multiple first-person narrators and the open-endedness of the closure of many of his novels, Burgess's writing evokes very different responses from critics. For instance, *Lady: My Life as a Bitch* (2001) has been hailed as 'comic allegory about adolescent sexuality' (Reynolds 2007: 114), and condemned as a punitive moral fable which 'literalises [the central protagonist's] selfish and promiscuous nature' (Walsh 2004: 144–5). Likewise, the ending of the novel has been interpreted variously as nihilistic (McGillis 2009: 268), and as moralistic and life-affirming (Hollindale 2013: 150). This raises the question of whether Burgess has abdicated his responsibility to guide the responses of his young readers, or whether he credits them with the ability to make up their own minds about the ethical issues his novels address. McCallum and Stephens (2013: 113) endorse the latter view, arguing that his dystopian novel *Bloodtide* (1999) 'constructs ethical dilemmas which prompt readers to posit solutions other than those reached in the text'. The fact that Burgess' work gives rise to very different critical readings is in itself a testament to the moral and stylistic complexity of his writing.

Conclusion

Given the word 'adult' in YA fiction, it is perhaps not surprising that the boundary between it and fiction aimed at, and read by, adults is a permeable one. It seems likely that many young readers pass over this in-between stage and, like Roald Dahl's Matilda, go straight from children's fiction to reading fiction for adults. Indeed, as discussed above, a number of the books now regarded as classics of YA fiction were initially written with an adult readership in mind. A more recent phenomenon is the movement in the opposite direction, with adults increasingly being drawn to books aimed at young readers, including books written by successful young writers (Falconer 2009: 36). This would seem to be due in part to the enhanced quality of such fiction in terms of its narrative complexity, its exploration of serious themes, and its intertextual allusions to a wide range of stories, from Norse myths, through biblical epics, to urban folktales. It is somewhat ironic, however, that, just as adults have sought refuge in YA fiction, many writers of literary fiction for this age group have embraced postmodern modes of storytelling. No doubt many adult readers experience illicit pleasure when venturing into the stormy world of adolescence and literary affect[11] can be heightened by confronting existential problems through the fresh but probing perspective of the adolescent gaze. Transmedia adaptations have further opened up the audience for such texts. In truth, there appear to be few limits to the themes that can be explored in YA fiction, especially since censorship is difficult to countenance in the Internet age. It may not be long before texts written for children and YAs comprise so many cultural reference points to new technologies that they will be almost entirely opaque to less technologically aware adults. It is at this point that YA fiction can truly be said to have come of age. Not surprisingly, literature for young adults frequently alludes to technological aspects of the contemporary world, one of the areas discussed in the following chapter.

CHAPTER TWELVE

Other Areas of Children's Literature Criticism

Introduction

In this final chapter, some consideration will be given to areas which have so far been given little or no attention: the adaptation of written text to other media, new and old, together with the link this process has with the commodification of children's literature; the interrelated aspects of science and technology, together with the increasing involvement of young people in the process of production of literature; and religion, spirituality and ecocriticism, a grouping which embraces concern, perhaps most deeply felt by young people, about the future of our planet.

Transmedia adaptation and commodification

While the adaptation of children's books for the theatre and subsequently for the cinema is far from being a new phenomenon, the increasing involvement of large-scale commercial interests, together with the existence of a variety of multi-media outlets, has transformed the situation in recent years. As David Buchbinder[1] observes, the main issue in the past was often whether the adaptation was 'an accurate re-presentation of the original', whereas more recent adaptation theory examines wider issues, notably including the question of the reason for the production of the adaptation. Buchbinder quotes Linda Hutcheon (2006) who regards 'adaptation as a form of repetition without replication' and asserts that the resultant, inevitable changes involve 'modifications in the political valence and even meanings of stories' (Hutcheon 2006: xvi, cited by Buchbinder 2011: 130). This implies that:

■ It would be a better strategy ... if the adaptation of an originary text into whatever medium were considered first on the merit of what it is out to do *as a text in its own right* rather than being viewed simply as always already a poor imitation of a better original. (Buchbinder 2011: 136, italics original)[2] □

Similarly, in a discussion of adaptations of the work of J.K. Rowling[3] for film and videogame, Andrew Burn[4] asks:

■ What happens when a print narrative is transformed into a film (a relatively familiar phenomenon) and then into a computer game (a less well-understood process)? And how do child audiences, readers, spectators, players, actually engage with these texts? ... This field has been dogged by a tendency to privilege the literary source, though more recent work has perceived the dialogue between literature and film as a two-way process, in which both media produce new works characterised by their distinctive formal and aesthetic properties, and in which influence may flow in both directions. (2006: 228) □

Making use of the work of Walter Ong (1982/2002), Burn analyses the responses of a number of children aged twelve or thirteen to a specific scene from *Harry Potter and the Chamber of Secrets* in book (1998), film (2002) and game (2002) format, claiming that Rowling's written style uses many of the conventions of oral narrative – recollection, reworking, redundancy – and that these lend themselves to both a filmic and a computer game format. He illustrates these aspects, used by the oral storyteller to ensure memorability, by reference to the way in which the hero (in this instance Harry) possesses some stereotypical character qualities, and how his problems are externalised rather than psychologised, while the narrator becomes closely associated with him as a means of immersing the audience in the story (2006: 231). Burn concludes that an appreciation of the educative potential of the various media involved demands that 'we ... expand our conceptions of literacy to embrace films and games and ... expand our notion of popular media to include literature' (2006: 247).

Another analysis of the adaptation of the Harry Potter novels to film is made by Suman Gupta (2003),[5] who focuses on the paradox that the very nature of cinema is that it uses image and sound to create the illusion of reality, even when, as in this instance, the subject matter is fantasy. He shows how, for instance, a sense of continuity is established through such means as the use of repeated musical themes, dark environments and colour contrasts in costume (2003: 146). Observing how the special effects also add to what he terms 'the collusion between producer and consumer', he concludes that the films achieve 'the audio-visual realization of magic (sic) world as virtually real *in* our world' (2003: 149 and 150; italics original).

In an analysis of the popularity of the Harry Potter books, Stacy Gillis[6] cites a number of unfavourable criticisms of Rowling's writing, including Zipes' critique of its commodification, in which he observes how the rise of 'corporate conglomerates controlling the mass media' have been among the external forces which have caused the Harry Potter books and others to be 'driven by commodity consumption that at the same time sets the parameters of reading and aesthetic taste'(Zipes 2001: 172, quoted by Gillis 2008: 303).[7]

Gillis explores how:

■ the cross-media manifestations of the intertext that is the Potter brand – books (both in the series and spin-offs), toys, games (board, card, computer and so on), websites, clothing, and of course the movies – foregrounds [sic] Harry Potter as a global brand. (2008: 303) □

She claims that part of the reason for the success of the 'brand' is that, by the use of such aspects as the uncanny and the Gothic, 'adult desires are embedded within these texts'. Hence, she argues, 'children's literature criticism ... must reach out to other disciplines and explore those histories, theories and intertextualities which can deepen our understanding of how children's literature functions' (2008: 315).

The existence of a wide range of other variants of trans-media adaptations, such as the transformation of the Asterix strip cartoons into a screen format and the screen versions of a number of well-known picturebooks,[8] support the contention that it has now become insufficient for critics to confine themselves to the printed format when discussing texts which have transcended the boundaries between media. In her analysis of '*His Dark Materials* in performance' (2006),[9] Kimberley Reynolds uses a term derived from the German critic, Hans Heino Ewers, 'multimedia system offers' (abbreviated to MSOs); these have considerably increased in numbers in recent years: 'A fully evolved MSO chain will include print-based versions of a text as well as, audio and film/TV versions, computer games, web sites, associated merchandise, and in some cases even possible music' (2006: 187). Reynolds comments on the extent to which 'the mass media currently draws [sic] on children's fiction for core material' (2006: 190). She cites the National Theatre's adaptation for the stage of Pullman's *His Dark Materials* trilogy[10] as an instance of:

■ striking a fine balance between heritage and mass media, infusing each with the insights and energy of the other ... [to] which adaptors – whatever their medium – of the future can look when transforming children's texts into performances that in turn open new worlds for readers, viewers and players. (2006: 204) □

Literature and the 'real' world of today

The engagement of literature, perhaps more especially children's literature, with the world 'out there' has often been problematic. Yet the interpenetration of science and technology not only with the subject matter of books but also with how they are produced and read, together with the increasingly blurred boundary between fact and fiction, has become more marked with developments from the late twentieth century onwards.

It is perhaps apposite to begin with the question of whether non-fiction books can be seen as part of the corpus of children's literature, since there is ample evidence that many young people avidly read both fact and fiction for what they can learn from them about the world. As Farah Mendlesohn observes, those who claim that anyone who 'argue[s] for didactic, information-dense novels for children' is ignorant about children's literature, are 'invalidating the reading experience of an entire set of children ... who read for informational, not emotional satisfaction, and might have been hard put to it to remember either the plot or the characters, but for whom the *information* was a source of desire and empowerment' (2009: 52, italics original). As Perry Nodelman observes, non-fiction is one of the areas often omitted from children's literature criticism,[11] despite surveys of young people's reading providing evidence of its appeal, especially to boys.[12] *A Guide to Children's Reference Books and Multimedia Material* (1998), edited by Susan Hancock, provides, in addition to its extensive survey of publications, a certain amount of historical background relevant to this neglected topic.[13]

That teachers and librarians are increasingly aware of the importance of recognising quality in the area of non-fiction is apparent from the establishment in 2012 by the School Library Association of an Information Book Award in three age categories, voted for by children themselves. In this the SLA were emulating the American National Council of Teachers of English which in 1989 had inaugurated the Orbis Pictus prize for promoting excellence in non-fiction.[14]

The not unrelated area of the criticism of historical fiction has also received minimal attention in recent years, despite the reading of such literature being, as Mendlesohn indicates, 'a route [to academic degrees] common to many historians' (2009: 1). In a collection of essays on this subject, *Historical Fiction for Children*[15] (2001), the editors, Fiona Collins and Jeremy Ridgman, indicate how their own interest in the topic had been to some extent prompted by 'an awareness that the genre has been neglected in recent decades' (2001: v). They go on to consider the responsibility of the historical novelist to maintain a balance between historical truth and the need to engage young readers, a concern explored in their first section, which discusses a wide range of largely twentieth-century texts by writers such as Peter Dickinson, Joan Aiken and Leon Garfield. This is followed by insights supplied by a number of practitioners of the craft, including reprinted articles by Philip Pullman and Rosemary Sutcliff. There is also a section focusing on the educational use of historical fiction.

Mendlesohn's stated interest in the area means that while her extensive critical study (2009) of science fiction for young people does not provide a critique as such of information texts for young people, it does take account of the way in which many young readers use this genre as a means to inform themselves about science and technology. As well as a critical examination of over 500 books published since 1950, she includes the results of a survey answered by over 900 adult readers concerning their personal recollections of reading science fiction both as children and as adults. She contends that the science fiction offered to young readers in the latter part of the twentieth century differs from the adult form in lacking the basis in scientific knowledge that many of these young readers are craving, and seldom has as a theme the attractiveness of careers in science. The relative paucity of scientific information such novels provide reflects the feeling entertained by many critics with a literary background that books for young people should not be too information-dense – a situation which, as Mendlesohn points out, contrasts with the intrinsic popularity of factual science writing for young people (2009: 64).

Noga Applebaum's chapter in Reynolds' *Modern Children's Literature*, 'Electronic Texts and Adolescent Agency: Computers and the Internet in Contemporary Children's Fiction' (2005: 250–263), expresses her conviction that contemporary electronic media will engender considerable changes in the way that children's fiction is structured. In a later monograph (2010), she justifies her focus on the portrayal of technology in science fiction, citing Adam Roberts' contention that 'a piece of futuristic, extrapolated technology' is often the concept or invention that identifies a story as belonging to this genre (2010: 3). Thus science fiction has often been a means for 'exploring contemporary dilemmas within the context of scientific and technological discoveries' (2010: 3). While not scrutinising so wide a range of texts as does Mendlesohn, she devotes chapters to the relationship between technology and nature, and to the implications of the considerable number of texts which use the theme of cloning. Additionally, she focuses on the influence of modern technology on narrative structure, as a result of digital formats which impinge on that of the traditional book. Without analysing electronic games as such, she looks at how the implied audience for science fiction books is already well versed in such alternative narrative structures. A similar development is also signalled in Kerry Mallan's analysis of technoscience and critical theory in relation to children's fiction.[16] She suggests that the reciprocal relationship of science and fiction fostered by both science fiction and new media can 'open up new theoretical space to explore questions about life, death, and all that matters' (2011: 166).

To a certain extent, both Applebaum and Mallan leave the question of the forms such future initiatives might take somewhat indefinite; Kimberley Reynolds takes up the challenge of providing greater definition at the end of *Radical Children's Literature* (2007). Having deplored the fact that a number of recent children's books tend to demonise technological developments, thus reflecting their authors' 'anxieties about interactions between children and new technologies', she goes on to state: 'I have yet to find a children's book that unreservedly celebrates such things as the way cyberspace makes it possible to transcend the self and operate outside the economic and practical restrictions of reality' (2007: 170). Perhaps more significant is the role she anticipates young people taking in relation to the production of their own fiction. She quotes Eliza Dresang[17] who comments on how 'digital age readers are remaking the texts they have by transferring reading skills from one form of literacy to another in what she [Dresang] refers to as a text's '"connectivity"... they are using their transliteracy to convert traditional texts into a proto-transliterature' (2007: 178). In her 'Conclusion: The Foundations of Future Fictions', Reynolds goes on to talk about how young people are now producing their own fiction, particularly 'in response to narratives already in circulation', whether on page or screen (2007: 180). This, as she observes, means that readers can no longer have the pleasure of knowing how a book will end but will have rather the alternative experience of 'knowing fictions featuring favourite characters will be available indefinitely' (2007: 183). She concludes: 'It is through the experiments of those who are serving their literary apprenticeships online that the next round of narrative innovation is likely to occur' (2007: 184). As they move between different varieties of narrative and/or media, such readers/writers are best equipped to create new and unfamiliar types of story.

Religion, spirituality and ecocriticism

Among the earliest books written for or adopted by children, moralistic and religiously didactic works took a prominent place. From Bunyan's *Pilgrim's Progress* to such nineteenth-century exemplars as Mary Martha

Sherwood's *The History of the Fairchild Family* (1818), Hesba Stretton's *Jessica's First Prayer* (1867) and the numerous edifying pamphlets published by the Religious Tract Society, such texts have received critical attention largely in histories of children's literature.[18] Subsequently, in parallel with decreasing church congregations, religiously motivated children's literature (other than that for a niche market such as Sunday Schools) and its concomitant criticism became less prominent. More recently, however, there has been something of a revival in critical studies looking at literature with a religious perspective, a movement impelled by the foregrounding of religious issues within society at large. Some of this criticism has focused on overtly pro- or anti-Christian literature, as manifested particularly in the polarisation of the attitudes towards religion in the children's fiction of C.S. Lewis and Philip Pullman.[19] At the same time there is an increasing realisation of the need to take into account the place in Britain of non-Christian religions, notably Islam but also to a certain extent Judaism.

Before examining some of this material, it is apposite to bear in mind a question raised by Suman Gupta, specifically in relation to the Harry Potter books but more generally applying to literary criticism which starts from a religious perspective. While indicating that he has no problem with criticism which investigates the social and political aspects of religious adherence, Gupta, as someone 'entirely unreligious' (2003: 69), feels excluded from the critical debate propagated by those who start from the assumption that their own religious stance is shared with their readers.[20] In particular, Gupta finds abhorrent the arguments of critics such as Richard Abanes (*Harry Potter and the Bible*, 2001), who sees Rowling's books as based on an occult world view, though Gupta finds it possible to engage with criticism (such as Elizabeth Schafer's *Exploring Harry Potter*, 2000) which investigates the symbolic meanings both of the literary work and of the Bible itself (Gupta 2003: 74). It is therefore worth emphasising that all the criticism referred to here investigates the social, political, historical and literary contexts of the literature discussed.

The papers given at a conference held in Belgium in May 2002, with the title 'Religion, Children's Literature and Modernity in Western Europe 1750–2000', are representative of the Christian aspect of religious criticism. In a plenary address,[21] Peter Hunt contrasted the dominance of 'religiously-driven, primarily Evangelical literature' in 1800 with the twenty-first-century position in which religion is often sidelined or treated with hostility. He argued:

> ■ firstly that religion of all kinds has been virtually silenced in mainstream children's literature, and this has left both a philosophical and sociological void, perhaps uneasily filled by myth and fantasy. Secondly, religion has actually taken on strong negative connotations .... (2005: 205) □

In the face of this situation, he demonstrates how religion has not, in fact, gone away, but 'is still central to our needs and our culture's view of our children's needs': the debate about the work of Pullman, and the attacks on the alleged 'occult' aspects of Rowling's Harry Potter series, show that 'religion is at the heart of the children's book debate and children's books are at the heart of a religious debate' (2005: 305).

The other papers in the same collection, while inevitably focusing on Christianity, certainly broaden the debate by looking at a Europe-wide range of locations. Rita Ghesquière argues that, far from religion being a taboo subject, there are many instances of religious themes being hidden within contemporary European children's literature. Other aspects given attention in this collection include systems of inspection of religious literature applied in various countries, together with diverse approaches to publishing and distribution.

Some subsequent critical attention related to broadly Christian perspectives has examined the treatment of religion not only by Pullman and Rowling but also by a range of other children's authors.[22] It has, however, become increasingly evident that confining attention to Christianity is far too narrow within today's multicultural society. The other Abrahamic faiths have inevitably been to the fore in this process.

Perhaps inevitably, a good deal of children's literature in which the perspective is Jewish tends to feature the Holocaust; this in itself has attracted a certain amount of criticism, both positive and negative[23] (Chapter Eleven discussed Adrienne Kertzer's objections to Isabella Leitner's Holocaust memoir for a child readership). While Gillian Lathey's study of autobiographical writings set during the period of Hitler's power (1999) is not restricted to books featuring Jewish characters, they inevitably provide the main focus. Pat Pinsent's brief survey, 'Jewishness and children's literature' (2000), goes back to Grimm and Dickens to provide a context for more recent treatments of the topic, and concludes that while contemporary non-Jewish children's authors have a tendency to be mainly concerned with warning their readership against anti-semitism:

> ■ those who have been brought up in the Jewish community evidence the vigour of its continuing traditions ... [and are more likely to] take Jewishness as a norm ... and succeed in making such characters distinctive by means of their personalities, rather than by their racial or religious origins. (2000: 328) □

A much more detailed treatment of this theme is to be found in Madelyn Travis's *Jews and Jewishness in British Children's Literature* (2013). While admitting the necessity of books about the Holocaust, Travis regrets the paucity of British children's books about Jewish characters within other contexts, since 'in the absence of a range of genres, Jews will be seen only in terms of past trauma and not as people with a rich cultural heritage who have played an active part in British society and continue to do so'.[24] In the conclusion to her book, Travis suggests that the literary preoccupation with Jews in earlier British fiction – to an extent out of proportion to their numbers in Victorian society – reflects a tension about their incorporation into a largely monocultural Christian country. More recently, and especially since the Second World War, their inclusion in children's books could be seen as part of the general endeavour to represent minorities; in the case of Jews this has been shown not only in fiction set in contemporary Britain but also in revisionist accounts of historical situations. Travis argues that some of the debate concerning the position of Jews in contemporary society is really part of the larger debate about British national identity, and thus it could be seen also to apply to other groups, notably Muslims. As in all portrayals of minority groups, this creates the paradox of attempting to balance the imposition of a liberal refusal even to acknowledge difference with a valuing of the differences that do exist.[25]

In recent years a number of children's books written in English have dealt with the complex issue of the situation of Muslim characters living in Western society. While such books have inevitably had mixed reviews, perhaps one of the most useful approaches to criticism from a literary point of view is that by Canadian children's author Rukhsana Khan. A useful source for her ideas is the talk she gave in 2008 to the World Congress of the International Board for Books for Young people (IBBY) in Denmark.[26] After a brief survey of Canadian attitudes to Muslim immigrants and a note about the irritant effect of culturally insensitivity, Khan turns her attention to the strategies that might be adopted by authors to raise awareness of 'normal' characters belonging to minority communities. Even the deliberate rejection of stereotypes, she suggests, may have an element of propaganda about it, something which young readers are quick to detect. She emphasises, 'There has to be a legitimate story you're trying to tell. The book has to be entertaining on some level. Behind the story, by all means, you can dispel stereotypes and enlighten, but such issues have to arise organically and not be superimposed as an author's agenda, no matter how well intentioned'.[27]

In addition to critical material directly related to a specific religious confession, increasingly there have appeared works of criticism with a more general spiritual or ethical perspective, as illustrated by the titles of two collections of critical articles: *Towards or Back to Human Values? Spiritual and Moral Dimensions of Contemporary Fantasy* (edited by Justyna Deszcz-Tryhubczak and Marek Oziewicz 2006); and *Ethics and Children's Literature* (edited by Claudia Mills 2014). Both of these collections embrace a wide range of perspectives, the earlier one including a sub-section entitled 'Fantasy as asserting interconnectedness of all life, stressing the need for cooperation, and fostering environmental awareness'. Articles included raise the issue of ecocriticism, a subject increasingly featured in books addressed to young readers, whose generation is likely to be faced in due course with the problems caused by today's adults and earlier inhabitants of our planet. A collection of articles explicitly relating to this theme and resulting from the 2008 IBBY conference, entitled *Deep into Nature: Ecology, Environment and Children's Literature* (edited by Jennifer Harding, Elizabeth Thiel and Alison Waller 2009), includes discussion of ecological aspects of contemporary and earlier children's literature set in places ranging from Britain to Lapland, Thailand and Australia. Several papers discuss the function of children's literature in ecological education, while David Whitley, in 'The Natural World in Disney Animation', contrasts the relatively straightforward ideology of conservation propounded in *Bambi* (1942) with the complexity engendered in *Finding Nemo* (2003), claiming that the later film 'deals in, but does not try to resolve, many of the ambivalent feelings we have about what is involved in the domestication of wild animals' (2009: 276). A few papers in the IBBY collection touch on some of the theoretical issues raised by the ecological movement in relation to children's literature; notable among these is William Gray's exploration: '"Out of the Everything into Here": Romanticism, Ecocriticism and Children's Literature'. While referring to fairytale and the work of Novalis, Macdonald and Tolkien, among others, Gray also makes extensive use of the work of Kate Rigby[28] to support his contention that, however much the enchantment of 'faery' seems to imply a breaking out from this world, fantasy literature, in the end, involves a renewed understanding and appreciation of it, consonant with the concept of 'panentheism [rather than 'pantheism'] … the belief or doctrine that God is greater than the universe and includes and interpenetrates it' (2009: 132). Without infringing on the domain of theology as such, Gray cites with approbation Rigby's contention that 'some form of "panentheism" is a necessary corrective to the tendency of the Romantic imagination to dissolve itself either into some fantasy of nature or into some phantasm of God (or Absolute Subject), both of which turn out in the end merely to be the poet's self writ large' (2009: 134). Thus, finally, the experience of the fantasy world is not an escape from this world but a return 'to work on *this earth*' (2009: 137, italics original). In another paper, Melanie Newman examines whether it is possible to take an ecological stance in children's literature without undue anthropomorphism, and concludes that the sense of being at one with the environment could engender the kind of writing which would engage child readers with 'deep' ecology: 'When storytelling is such a feature of our past, it surely has a role to play in finding our way through the crisis of the present and some part in imagining a future in which the health of our environment and our relationship with it can be restored' (2009: 184).

The role of children's literature in engendering an ecological perspective is a subject upon which the distinguished critic Peter Hollindale wrote in 'The Darkening of the Green', a piece published in *Signal* as long ago as 1990; more recently it has been reprinted in *The Hidden Teacher* (2011), where it can be read alongside his later re-engagement with the topic. In the earlier paper, Hollindale, who describes his own views on the subject as 'the very darkest green' (2011: 79), recounts how his early reading of books which showed that non-human life had value in its own right made him aware of the dangers to the environment, even before 'the heterodoxy of 1950 became the orthodoxy of 1990' (2011: 87). An extended discussion of Lucy Boston's *A Stranger at Green Knowe* (1961) preludes his final contention that 'dark green' literature may be a means of teaching children about their responsibility for the planet and thus of engendering hope for it. He revisits this final point in his later paper, 'Hope against Hope', in which his critiques of Robert O'Brien's *Z for Zachariah* (1975) and Peter Dickinson's *Eva* (1988) foreground fiction which makes accessible to young readers the issues involved concerning the future welfare of the planet. He concludes by outlining some of these issues and conjectures:

■ The more children grow up alert to these questions and determined to improve on the human performance, the better our chances are. And stories are very important. They take us across the bridge from the thinkable, where we are, to the imaginable, where we need to be. (2011: 110) □

In the same year, 2011, Geraldine Massey and Clare Bradford published what they describe as an 'overview [which] demonstrates the paradigmatic shifts which have characterized the development of ecocriticism' (in (eds) Mallan and Bradford 2011: 109). Presenting two alternative views of this evolution, one recounting various stages of the process, the other distinguishing between 'first wave' (for instance, biographical and regional studies, the reinterpretation of literary works from an environmental perspective) and 'second wave' (such as ecofeminism and the profound effect of humanity on the environment), they claim that both of these represent a move from 'formalist approaches, with their emphasis on studying the text in isolation' towards a greater awareness of the cultural forces behind the production of a text (2011: 111). They contend, however, that many recent environmental texts are over-preoccupied with the effects on an implied Western readership, ignoring the fact that 'environmental degradation is far more likely to negatively affect Third World than First World populations' (2011: 118). Such tensions in fact characterise the whole field of environmental science itself, while portrayals within children's books of the global situation, perhaps inevitably, avoid the pessimism of some environmentalists, thus, however, weakening the message given. They conclude: 'The passions and fears which inform discussions of environmental futures have shaped the development of ecocriticism as a scholarly field, and are inextricably woven into environmental texts for children' (2011: 125).

The fields of religious criticism and eco-criticism, together with the others discussed above, seem likely to be extensively developed in the future. Other fields currently subject to increased critical interest are highlighted in the Conclusion.

Conclusion: Future Trends

Just as children's literature itself is no longer disparaged as 'kiddie lit', whose only adult readers were thought to be teachers and parents of young children, contemporary criticism of this literature has come of age and is no longer marginalised as merely an optional addition to 'proper' literary criticism. The processes by which this has been achieved have been outlined in the preceding chapters, tracing the development from, on the one hand, a predominantly nostalgic eulogising of the texts enjoyed by adult book-lovers when they were children, and, on the other, the pedagogical emphasis of educationalists. Much of the early academic focus was either historical or author-based. By contrast, at this stage of the twenty-first century, it is apparent that all the areas explored by current literary theory are very germane to recent children's literature, perhaps particularly those relating to gender and to the nexus of translation, globalisation and the position of minority cultures. Some critics, such as Nodelman, have accused current critical theorists who write about children's literature of losing sight of 'the child' – an entity which was itself called into question by theoretical critics such as Jacqueline Rose and Karín Lesnik-Oberstein. Certain names have stood out in the process of children's literature criticism's growth towards maturity – for instance Peter Hunt, Jack Zipes, John Stephens, Kimberley Reynolds, Maria Nikolajeva, and, because of the considerable influence of his relatively slim output in the field, Peter Hollindale.

Inevitably, this relatively brief survey of the contemporary situation in children's literature criticism has been dominated by Anglophone sources. Other than in Chapter Nine, on translation and globalisation, the focus has been on the work of English-speaking scholars, rather than the substantial contribution made by those from other parts of Europe.

It is impossible to determine the future directions of children's literature criticism. One area that emerges is the need for future criticism to take account of adaptation of texts not only to screen or other media forms but also to language and culture contexts never envisaged by the original authors. Another increasing area is that related to book production and 'book history', marking the return to a bibliographical tradition, notably in the work of Matthew Grenby. This could perhaps be seen as a reaction against the unduly theoretical emphasis of some scholars, but conversely, theoretical approaches are still widely practised, as evidenced by the sub-title of Mallan and Bradford's 2011 collection, *Engaging with Theory*.

Other current developments in criticism are taking account of the increasing importance to young readers of digital texts, including picturebooks – a topic discussed by Margaret Mackey in the second edition 2015 of Arizpe and Styles' *Children Reading Pictures*. The increasing attention given to the way in which young people interact with text, frequently in digital format, links with work related to the increasing amount of research on their cognitive processes, an introduction to which can be found in Maria Nikolajeva's essay, 'Voicing Identity' in the 2014 edition of *Modern Literary Criticism* (edited by Catherine Butler and Kimberley Reynolds).

Another area that seems likely to be fertile is that of 'schema poetics'. Clare Walsh outlines its development from 'the work of A[rtificial] I[ntelligence]' theorists, who 'posit the existence of interpretative scripts or *schemas* which individuals store in background memory to make sense of events in the world' (2004: 107, italics original). This means that in any situation, humans have expectations, formed both by life and literature, of the likely features to be encountered. Walsh uses this in an analysis of Mark Haddon's *The Curious Incident of the Dog in the Night-Time* (2003), a book popular with both adult and younger readers, arguing that within the unfamiliar situation portrayed in this original text, different interpretations may result from the different schemas developed by different age groups. Literary texts will often disrupt schemas and thus lead to both cognitive change and an affective response. John Stephens also uses the schema framework in an essay that has already been discussed (see Chapter Eight) on the various masculine schemata presented in boys' fiction (2002: 44). He amplifies on the potential of this approach in a paper in Mallan and Bradford's collection. He suggests that the combination of reader response theory with 'representations of social reality' that the use of the concept of schema involves means that such theories are likely to be particularly congenial to the discipline of children's literature, in which reader response theory has proved to be of lasting applicability. In his paper he defines schemas (or schemata) as 'knowledge structures, or patterns, which provide the framework for understanding', thus shaping our knowledge of objects, situations, genres and ideologies (2011: 13–14). They are static networks of our memories, activated as we encounter new experiences whether of life or literature. The more dynamic 'scripts', formed as a result of having heard or read countless stories, mean that causal links can often be omitted as they will be supplied by the person encountering the story. Stephens explores a range of culturally diverse picturebooks to illustrate how novel elements interplay with, for instance, the 'normal childhood schema' to transform and widen readers' perceptions 'of relationships between selfhood and otherness' (2011: 34).

It is perhaps appropriate that Mallan and Bradford's book also includes the above-mentioned paper on ecocriticism by the editors, for it seems evident that both children's books featuring environmental issues, and the criticism of such texts, will be of particular significance in future years. This preoccupation also relates to current work on space/ place theory, a further development of the work on the chronotope which has featured in recent studies by Maria Nikolajeva. Additionally, perhaps in response to increasing anxiety about the future of the planet, many recent books for young adults create dystopias, something explored in recent studies such as Richard Shakeshaft's essay in *Modern Children's Literature* (Butler and Reynolds 2015: 234–250).

Given the sparseness of children's literature criticism prior to the 1980s, the considerable amount of scholarly work since then is impressive. It is also worth note that an impressive amount of research in the area is currently being carried out by PhD and Master's students in an increasingly large number of academic institutions. It is inevitable that new critical works are constantly appearing, so that the current survey can do no more than indicate the landmarks at this moment in time. I hope, however, that some of the principles suggested and the comments on the texts considered will provide a basis for judgement concerning the relevance and value of future additions to the now increasingly substantial corpus of children's literature criticism.

Notes

INTRODUCTION

1. Grenby & Reynolds (eds, 2011), Mickenberg & Vallone (eds, 2011), Philip & Paul (eds, 2011), Rudd (ed., 2010), and Wolf, Coats, Enciso & Jenkins (eds, 2011).
2. Nikolajeva defines the 'chronotope' as 'the indivisible unity of time and space' in a work of literature (1996: 121).
3. Published in *Signal* in 1991 and republished in *The Hidden Teacher*, 2011.
4. Reproduced in (ed.) Hunt (1991: 57–70)

1 BEGINNINGS

1. As satirised in the title of L.C. Knights' famous essay, 'How Many Children Had Lady Macbeth?' (1933).
2. Indeed, whether or not Green's approach be judged excessively nostalgic, his desire to establish the 'most important' writers reflects something of a Leavisite desire to establish a hierarchy of talent.
3. In the light of subsequent events, it is somewhat ironic that Inglis highly praises the (undoubtedly meritorious) children's novels of William Mayne (who was later convicted of paedophilia) as possessing the positive moral qualities associated with great literature; he sees Mayne's writings as 'a touchstone of the seriousness and creativeness we expect to find in great literature ... Mayne's simplicity and modesty embody ... a way of living well' (p.15).
4. Interestingly, Leavis himself initially downgraded Dickens by not regarding his work as part of 'The Great Tradition', but by 1970 (well before Inglis's book), when F.R. and Q.D. Leavis' *Dickens the Novelist* was published, he had granted recognition to the major Victorian writer!
5. The pedagogical aspect will be considered in Chapter Two, which deals with child-centred approaches.
6. As indicated by Rosemary Auchmuty in *The Encyclopedia of Girls' School Stories* (2001: 20).
7. As indicated in Victor Watson, *The Cambridge Guide to Children's Books in English* (2001: 714–5).
8. As indicated by Frank Eyres's *British Children's Books in the Twentieth Century* (1952), a slim volume published for the British Council's *Arts in Britain* series, and Kathleen Lines's *Four to Fourteen* (CUP, 2nd edn 1956) published for the National Book League.
9. The third edition, edited by Brian Alderson and published in 1982, is discussed below.
10. A phenomenon which has, if anything, become more marked in the years since 1990.
11. Division of subject matter into genres had, however, been a means of structuring the material in the histories of children's literature named above.
12. Later writers such as Lois Kuznets (1994) and Tess Cosslett (2006) provide a more academic perspective on children's literature with animal characters, either 'real' or toys.
13. This statement by Cadogan and Craig ignores the fact that Sarah Fielding's *The Governess* (1749) could be claimed to be the first book set within a girls' school, tiny though 'the little female academy' is, with its nine pupils.

14. As suggested by Karen Patricia Smith in a review (*Children's Literature Association Quarterly*, 13(1), spring 1988, p.40).

2 CHILD READERS

1. As suggested in the Introduction, it could be claimed that there is a further group – Theory people; representatives of this category are, however, relatively thin on the ground until the late twentieth century.
2. Their collection was originally prepared for publication in 1974, in the run-up to the Bullock Report, *A Language for Life*, which devotes a salient chapter (1975: 124–138) to the role of literature, not only in relation to the development of children's language, but also as having value in its own right.
3. Books which are explicitly created as guides for the teacher are not discussed here, though it should be noted that in many instances (in line with the policy adopted in the Bullock Report, mentioned above) they base their recommendations on a well-supported appreciation of the literary and educational needs of the young reader.
4. Harding's article on 'The Role of the Onlooker' (*Scrutiny*, vol. 6, 1937) formed the basis for a good deal of the early study of children's responses to literature, notably in his chairmanship of the Dartmouth conference, reported on in *The Cool Web* (1977: 379–392).
5. An interesting illustration of this phenomenon can be seen in the examples provided on 'Mr Hoye's IB English website' (http://mrhoyesibwebsite.com/Critical%20Theory/Reading%20Against%20The%20Grain/Resistant%20Readings.htm, accessed 4th February 2014).
6. See also Chapter Three.
7. Meek's important role in the then current debate about children learning to read with 'real books' rather than with reading schemes is indicative of the fundamental importance of children's literature to a number of educationalists, several of whom were located at the London University Institute of Education.
8. For instance, Robert Protherough, *Developing Response to Fiction* (1983); Donald Fry, *Children Talk about Books: Seeing Themselves as Readers* (1985); Patrick Dias and Michael Hayhoe, *Developing Response to Poetry* (1988); Michael Hayhoe and Stephen Parker, *Reading and Response* (1990) (which includes a paper on response by Meek) and Charles Sarland, *Young People Reading: Culture and Response* (1991).
9. A point which could be related to the concept of 'resistant reading' mentioned above.
10. See Chapter Three for fuller discussion of this work.
11. This is a shorter, interim, version of the full report which came out later.
12. Undertaken by the Children's Literature Research Centre at what was then the Roehampton Institute (now Roehampton University), under the direction of Professor Kimberly Reynolds.
13. http://www.literacytrust.org.uk/assets/0001/4543/Young_people_s_reading_FINAL_REPORT.pdf accessed 5th February 2014.
14. *Bookbird*, 47(3), July 2009, pp.57–8.
15. *Ways with Words: Language, Life and Work in Communities and Classrooms* (Cambridge University Press, 1983).
16. *Private Practices: Girls Reading Fiction and Constructing Identity* (Taylor and Francis, 1994).
17. *Through Whose Eyes? Exploring Racism: Reader, Text and Context* (Trentham Books, 1992).
18. www.open.ac.uk/Arts/reading, accessed 4th February 2014.
19. More recent work on multimedia adaptation is discussed in Chapter Twelve.
20. The important aspect of books borrowed from friends is more difficult to quantify but is displayed in the Roehampton 1996 survey cited above (note 12).

3 NARRATIVE AND CHILDREN'S LITERATURE

1. An alternative attempt to provide clarity on the subject is offered by Maria Nikolajeva: 'As a working definition we must ... accept children's literature as literature written, published, marketed and treated by specialists with children as its primary target' (1997: 9). Though slightly wider, this is in effect much the same as Townsend's.
2. The approach to the question of definition of children's literature taken by Peter Hollindale (1997) is discussed later in this chapter.
3. See David Lodge (1981) *Working with Structuralism*, Chapter 2, for a succinct classification of the various types of analysis offered by the theorists alluded to above.
4. *Narrative Fiction: Contemporary Poetics*, London: Methuen, 1983: 2, italics original.
5. *Story and Discourse: Narrative Structure in Fiction and Film*, Ithaca: Cornell University Press: 1978: 151.
6. A term brought into prominence by Wayne Booth in *The Rhetoric of Fiction*, Chicago: University of Chicago Press, 1961; 1973.
7. See Chapter 2, 'Child Readers'.
8. Tracing the various versions of the title of this classic text is not relevant here so I shall confine myself to the title by which it is most generally known. See Chapter 7 for further discussion of *Peter Pan*.
9. There seems to me little doubt that both Barrie's narrator and his adult narratee are to be regarded as male.
10. Some consideration is given later in this chapter to the effect of oral narrative, with reference to the work of Walter Ong.
11. There is considerable debate as to whether Bakhtin (1895–1975) is responsible only for those works published under his name or also, as was subsequently claimed, those attributed to fellow Russians Pavel Medvedev and Valentin Voloshinov. See Pam Morris (ed.) *The Backhtin Reader*, London: Edward Arnold, 1994, pp.1–4 for an account of the scholarly dispute on the subject. Here it is convenient to refer to all these writings as authored by Bakhtin himself.
12. Hollindale's 'Ideology and the Children's Book' was first published in *Signal* (January 1988). In 1991 it was reprinted by the Thimble Press as a pamphlet, reprinted in 1994. Subsequently it has appeared in print again (with minor alterations) as one of six essays in *The Hidden Teacher: Ideology and Children's Reading* (2011). I shall be using the most recent version here, but it is worth noting that Stephens' discussion of ideology (1992: Chapter 1) gives a prominent place to material from the earlier edition (pp. 9–11).
13. Quoting J.B. Thompson, *Ideology and Modern Culture: Critical and Social Theory in the Era of Mass Communication*, Cambridge: Polity Press, 1990: 62.
14. By M. Baynton, London: Sainsbury Walker 1988.
15. Mood, Theme and Rheme, and Transitivity.

4 FAIRYTALES

1. Usage differs between 'fairy tales' and 'fairytales'; the latter will be used here except when quoting from other texts.
2. Following Zipes (2000: xv), the term 'fairytale' is generally used in this chapter to refer to what he describes as the 'literary' fairytale, rather than the oral folktale, though the boundary between these is inevitably blurred, given the oral origins of many fairytales.
3. See Zipes (2000: 1).
4. An excerpt from their work is included in (ed.) Maria Tatar (1999: 373–378).
5. Excerpts from translations of Propp's *Theory and History of Folklore* (1984) and *The Morphology of the Folk Tale* (1988) are included in (ed.) Tatar (1999: 378–387).
6. Its original title was *An Introduction to the Interpretation of Fairytales*, but it has been re-published (1982, 1987, 1996, etc.) under the shorter title.

7. http://marie-louisevonfranz.com/b/ifl/.
8. See note 7.
9. Two texts which discuss children's literature, including fairytales, from a developmental perspective while focusing on pedagogical considerations are Elizabeth Cook's *The Ordinary and the Fabulous: An Introduction to Myths, Legends and Fairy Tales for Teachers and Storytellers* (1969) and Peggy Heeks' *Choosing and Using Books in the First School* (1981).
10. It also lends a greater degree of authority to his translation of the Grimms' tales (1987) and his later study of the brothers' lives and works (1988).
11. Interview with John Smelcer, *Ragazine* Sept–Oct 2014, 10(5), http://ragazine.cc/2012/10/Zipes-interview, accessed 15th October 2014.
12. See note 11.
13. 'Peasants tell Tales: The Meaning of Mother Goose', in *The Great Cat Massacre* New York, 1984, reproduced in (ed.) Tatar, (1999: 280–291).
14. Neil Philip brings together variants of this story from all over the world, in a collection in which he resolutely avoids theorising, *The Cinderella Story: The Origins and Variations of the Story Known as 'Cinderella'* (London: Penguin, 1989).
15. Even before the work of some of the theorists, there were a number of collections of new anti-sexist stories freely adapted from traditional tales, for instance, Catherine Storr, *Clever Polly and the Stupid Wolf* (1966); Jay Williams, *The Practical Princess and other Liberating Fairy Tales* (1978); Robert Munsch and Michael Martchenko, *The Paperbag Princess* (1980); and Babette Cole, *Princess Smartypants* (1986).
16. Excerpts from both of these are to be found in (ed.) Tatar (1999), pp.291–308.
17. To be found both as a chapter in *FairyTale as Myth, Myth as Fairy Tale* (Kentucky UP 1994) and reproduced in (ed.) Tatar (1999: 332–32) from (eds) Bell et al., *From Mouse to Mermaid: The Politics of Film, Gender and Culture* (Bloomington: Indiana UP 1995)
18. See note 11.

5 FANTASY

1. The notion that literature should offer moral guidance to the young seems curiously dated, though I suspect it is still implicit in the minds of some authors. Certainly a good deal of nineteenth-century literature that blatantly attempted to give moral guidance was in a realist rather than a fantasy mode, though notable exceptions to this include the work of Charles Kingsley.
2. In a series entitled 'In their own words: British Novelists', programme 3, 'Nothing Sacred, 1970–1990', available from the Open University, see www.ouworldwide.com/tv-buyer.asp.
3. See Chapter Four.
4. Charles Kingsley, George MacDonald, J.R.R. Tolkien (*Lord of the Rings*), C.S. Lewis (*Perelandra* trilogy), and Mervyn Peake.
5. Manlove has written extensively on fantasy, and has also compiled an encyclopaedic reference book for the student of children's literature, *From Alice to Harry Potter: Children's Fantasy in England* (2003).
6. As various as Edmund Spenser's *The Faerie Queene* (1590–1609), Samuel Johnson's *Rasselas* (1759), Mary Shelley's *Frankenstein* (1818), Franz Kafka's *Metamorphosis* (1912) and George Orwell's *Animal Farm* (1945), to name but a few.
7. Notably in the work of Scott, Dickens and the Brontës.
8. I have omitted here the examples he gives of each variety as it is more convenient to discuss some of the leading exemplars below.
9. Thus Tolkien's work could scarcely be dismissed as lacking either relationship with the real world or moral guidance.

10. There is, however, an abundance of material looking at Tolkien and his work primarily from a religious but non-literary perspective – see http://tolkienandchristianity.blogspot.co.uk for a list.

11. By no means all of the fiction of these writers, however, is relevant to the current section.

12. Originally given at a conference in Bournemouth in 1952 and reprinted in *Only Connect*, Egoff et al. (eds) (1969: 80).

13. Such as *Count Karlstein* (1982); *The Firework Maker's Daughter* (1995); *Clockwork* (1996); *I was a Rat* (1999); and *The Scarecrow and his Servant* (2004).

14. Both these authors have also written a wide range of other children's books which do not come into the category being discussed in this section.

15. *The Owl Service* (1967) and *Red Shift* (1973) belong to the next subsection, while *The Stone Book* Quartet (1976–9) is better classified as historical fiction. Garner's most recent novel, *Boneland* (2012), is described on the bookjacket as 'a novel for adults, concluding a trilogy that was begun for children'. Praise from Philip Pullman – 'this was worth waiting for' –is also to be found on the jacket.

16. Oxford was also, rather later, Philip Pullman's alma mater. The spirit of Lewis Carroll seems still to be impelling Oxford-educated writers towards children's fantasy.

17. Butler's discussion, mentioned above, devotes attention to the full range of the fiction of these two writers.

18. Notably Robert Cormier and Peter Dickinson.

19. Together with such by-products as *Fantastic Beasts and Where to Find Them* (2001); *Quidditch Through the Ages* (2001); and *The Tales of Beadle the Bard* (2007/8).

20. Like several other studies of her novels, its cover bears the disclaimer, 'Not authorised or approved by J.K. Rowling', an unusual feature in a work of criticism.

21. Gray (2009: 185–9) devotes a Postscript to the reasons why he does not include the Harry Potter saga in the fantasy tradition of Tolkien, Lewis and Pullman – partly for reasons of space, partly because, in spite of its use of myth, its strongest links are to the school story.

22. Such as articles by Roslyn Weaver and Marion Rana in the *Journal of Children's Literature Studies*, 8(1), March 2011.

23. There are of course many other anthropomorphic characters in popular children's books ranging from Wilbert Awdry's railway engine tales to more recent texts depicting cars in a similar humanoid role.

24. P.A. Ganea, Canfield C.F., Simons-Ghafari K, Chou T, 'Do cavies talk?: The effect of anthropomorphic books on children's knowledge about animals' in *Frontiers in Psychology* (DOI:10.3389/fpsyg.2014/00283, reported on website http://blogs.scientificamerican.com/thoughtfulanimal/2014/03/27/animals-who-wear-clothes-and-talk-actually-impede-learning) accessed 8th April 2014.

25. Not everyone agrees that such an effect is to be deplored: Maija-Liisa Harju in (eds) Deszcz-Tryhubczal and Oziewicz, (2006: 181) asserts that 'We must ... look to the animal fantasy to support and encourage a personalistic world view that considers all life to be equal, connected and purposeful'.

26. Collected in *Time Everlasting* (ed.) Pinsent (2007).

6   VISUAL TEXTS

1. It must of course be acknowledged that the distinction drawn above is by no means rigid, and different sections of the same text may be judged as being on opposite sides of this divide.

2. Many of the aspects highlighted by critics whose work is discussed below are equally relevant to wordless picturebooks, where the narrative structure and characterisation are maintained by the details in the pictures and by their sequence.

3. Usage varies between 'picture book', 'picture-book' and 'picturebook; I propose to use the last of these except where a different usage occurs in quotations. William Moebius, in the entry on 'Picture Books' in Nel and Paul (eds) (2011: 169–173) gives some attention to the rationale behind the different modes of referring to such texts.

4. Reasons for their popularity with adults are given in a short piece by Rick Walton: 'Adults can enjoy picture books as much as children do' (http:www.writersdigest.com/editor-blog/guide-to-literary-agents/picture-books-are-not-just-for-children, accessed 13th August 2014). Walton supplies ten reasons why this is the case, such as their use of more sophisticated language than early reading books for children; the fact that they tend to be shared, leading to bonding between adult and child; and their potential for developing visual intelligence by means of the interaction between text and picture.

5. The work of these two picturebook artists seems also to have been a formative influence on the understanding of the genre by the critic Brian Alderson, who was involved in exhibitions of the work of both of them, and in writing the catalogue, *Looking at Picture Books*, for an exhibition by the National Book League (later the Book Trust) in 1973.

6. 'A Picture Equals How Many Words? Narrative Theory and Picture Books for Children', *Lion and Unicorn* 7/8, 1963/4, 20–33.

7. Excerpts from both of these are to be found in (ed.) Peter Hunt (1990).

8. Such as Sonia Landes, 'Picture Books as Literature', *ChLA Quarterly* 10.2, Summer 1985, 51–4.

9. The importance of Sendak's oeuvre to Nodelman's argument is revealed in the index by the fact that there are more than twice as many references to his work as to any other artist or topic, other than picturebooks as such.

10. Such as Quentin Blake, Raymond Briggs, Anthony Browne, John Burningham, Michael Foreman, Pat Hutchins, David McKee and countless others.

11. Pat Hutchins' *Rosie's Walk* (1969); John Burningham's *Mr Gumpy's Outing* (1970), *Come Away from the Water, Shirley* (1977) and *Granpa* (1984); Janet and Allan Ahlberg's *The Jolly Postman* (1986); and Shirley Hughes' *Chips and Jessie* (1988).

12. In (ed.) Pinsent (1993).

13. See also her résumé of the development of picture books from 1945 onwards in (eds) Reynolds and Tucker (1998).

14. E.g. books by Ezra Jack Keats, Charles Keeping, David McKee, Michael Foreman.

15. Their section on culture includes an article by Clare Bradford about Aboriginal visual narratives, mentioned in Chapter Ten of the current book.

16. Such as *When the Wind Blows* (1982) and *Ethel and Ernest* (1998).

17. *Chips and Jessie* (1985).

18. See http://scottmccloud.com/2.print/1-uc/, accessed 9th September 2014.

7 POETRY AND DRAMA

1. Together with Donald Hall's *The Oxford Book of Children's Verse in America* (1985).

2. For instance, Legouis and Cazamian's *History of English Literature* (first published 1926/7) treats the work of Lear and Carroll in a single sentence, but makes no reference to their young audience (1971: 1159).

3. Styles has subsequently participated in a project with the University of the West Indies; as a part of this she has collaborated with Professor Beverly Bryan in editing *Teaching Caribbean Poetry* (London: Routledge, 2013).

4. The Opies produced several other (unannotated) collections of nursery rhymes, notably *The Oxford Nursery Rhyme Book* (1955) and *The Puffin Book of Nursery Rhymes* (1963).

5. Their unannotated collection of such rhymes, *I saw Esau: Traditional Rhymes of Youth* (1947), was later reissued as *I saw Esau: The Schoolchild's Pocket Book* (1992), illustrated by Maurice Sendak.

6. In *Children and Their Books: A Celebration of the Work of Iona and Peter Opie* (1989), edited by Gillian Avery and Julia Briggs, Clive Hurst presents reflections on their work in 'Selections from the Accession Diaries of Peter Opie' (pp.19–42).

7. An early Protestant example is Edmund Graile's *Little Timothy, His Lesson* (1611), which presents near-doggerel versions of bible stories.

8. It occurs, for instance, in anthologies as far apart in date as *The Children's Omnibus* (1932), edited by Sylvia Lynd, and Neil Philip's *The New Oxford Book of Children's Verse* (1996).

9. 'Simple Surfaces: Christina Rossetti's work for children' in (ed.) David A. Kent, *The Achievement of Christina Rossetti* (1987).

10. As if to reinforce McGillis's point about the amount of critical attention *Goblin Market* has received, an earlier chapter, by D.M.R. Bentley, in the same collection is also devoted to the poem, and discussion of it forms a significant element of Jan Marsh's *Christina Rossetti: A Literary Biography* (1994).

11. http://textualities.net/david-fergus/a-,ajpr-minor-poet/, accessed 27th February 2014.

12. Marion Hodge, 'The sane, the mad, the good, the bad: T.S. Eliot's *Old Possum's Book of Practical Cats*', in *Children's Literature in Education,* vol. 7, 1974.

13. Ted Hughes, 'Myth and Education' in G. Fox et al.(eds), *Writers, Critics and Children* (1976, pp.77–94).

14. Michael Lockwood, 'Ted Hughes: The Development of a Children's Poet' in *Children's Literature in Education* vol.40, issue 4, pp.296–305, December 2009.

15. Causley is quoted in Styles as saying that he does not concern himself about his audience (1998: 248).

16. In (eds) Styles, Joy and Whitney, *Poetry and Childhood* (2010, pp.1–15).

17. *It Doesn't Have to Rhyme: Children and Poetry,* (eds) Jennifer Harding and Bridget Carrington, 2012. This collection of papers from the conference also includes the text of another talk by Rosen, 'Why write poetry for children: challenges, choices opportunities and possibilities' (pp.28–46).

18. It is notable that very little twentieth-century poetry for children makes reference to the most important historical events of the period, such as the two world wars.

19. See www.thimblepress.co.uk/poetry.htm and www.claas-kazzer.de/signal/poetryaward.html for further details.

20. *Signal 100,* 2003.

21. Fortunately for the future of children's poetry in the English language, the Centre for Language (later Literacy) in Primary Education (CLPE) instigated in 2003 its own award for the best poetry collection. This was judged on similar terms to that of the *Signal* poetry award, and accompanied each year by a booklet discussing the work of the winner and the thought processes of the judges. Another prestigious journal in the United States, *The Lion and the Unicorn,* founded a similar award in 2005. See www.clpe.org.uk/page/67.

22. Hollindale cites Roger Lancelyn Green's *Fifty Years of 'Peter Pan'* to note that its 'only significant predecessor as children's theatre ... [was] *Bluebell in Fairyland* by Seymour Hicks' (1986: 216).

8   GENDER STUDIES AND QUEER THEORY

1. For further information on educational material designed to promote the reading of literature from an 'equality' standpoint, see Pinsent (1997), Chapter 1.

2. See Pinsent 1997: 79–81 for descriptions of some of the books concerned.

3. Attention to the range of masculinities implied had to wait a little later for attention – see Stephens (ed.) (2002), while the homoerotic elements frequently underlying relationships between characters are examined in Claudia Nelson, 'David and Jonathan – and Saul – revisited: Homodomestic Patterns in British Boys Magazine Fiction, 1880–1915' in M. Abate and K. Kidd (eds), 2011: 32.

4. Sue Sharpe (1976) *Just Like a Girl: How Girls Learn to be Women*, Harmondsworth: Penguin; Angela McRobbie and Mica Nava (eds) (1984) *Gender and Generation*, London: Macmillan. A lengthy discussion of what he sees as the fallacies in these approaches is to be found in Martin Barker (1989) *Comics: Ideology, Power and the Critics*, Manchester: Manchester University Press.

5. Another relevant study rehabilitating female authors is Elizabeth Thiel's *The Fantasy of Family: Nineteenth-Century Children's Literature and the Myth of the Domestic Ideal* (Routledge, 2008) which shows how what Thiel describes as 'transnormative' families, comprising a variety of structures other than that of the traditional two parents, are to be found in the work of a number of women writers including 'Brenda' (Mrs G Castle-Smith) and A.L.O.E. (A Lady of England, Charlotte Tucker, 1821–93).

6. Given the earlier mentioned tendency for those active in the rooting out of inequality in society to have a perspective that embraces race and class as well as gender, it is worth noting that Trites ranks highly such black writers of children's literature as Virginia Hamilton and Mildred Taylor.

7. R.W. Connell, in *Masculinities* (1995: 77, quoted by John Stephens, 2002: ix).

8. The volume in a series on children's literature and culture of which the general editor is Jack Zipes.

9. In '"A Page just waiting to be written on": Masculinity Schemata and the Dynamics of Subjective Agency in Junior Fiction' (2002: 38–54).

10. 'Making boys appear: the masculinity of children's fiction' (2002: 1–14).

11. 'Come Lads and Ladettes: Gendering Bodies and Gendering Behaviours' (2002: 96–115).

12. Examples of the humorous effect of the male being unable to perform effectively as a female are to be found in texts as various as Mark Twain's *Huckleberry Finn* (1884), Kenneth Grahame's *The Wind in the Willows* (1908) and Anne Fine's *Bill's New Frock* (1989).

13. Such as Peter Pohl's *Johnny my Friend* (1985; female living as a male) and Aidan Chambers' *Postcards from No Man's Land* (1999; male living as a female).

14. Peter Wells, *Boy Overboard* (1997); Shyam Selvadurai, *Funny Boy* (1994); and Irini Savvides, *Sky Legs* (2003).

15. 'Queer Performances: Lesbian Politics in *Little Women*', in (eds) Abate and Kidd, 2011: 33–58).

16. In (eds) Nel and Paul (2011: 189).

9   TRANSLATION AND GLOBALISATION

1. The following subsections were contributed by Darja Mazi-Leskovar: 'Challenges related to translation', 'Adaptation', 'National and world children's literature in translation', 'International exchange of texts for children' and 'Retranslation of literary texts for children'. The rest of the subsections are by Pat Pinsent ('Introduction', 'The development of an international perspective', 'Translations into English', 'Translations of English literature' and 'Visual texts, translation and global culture').

2. See review by Mary Abe in the *Children's Literature Association Quarterly*, 3(4), Winter 1971, pp.7–8. http//.muse.jhu.edu/journals/chq/summary/v003/3.4.Abe.html, accessed 21st May 2014.

3. Edited by Göte Klingberg et al. (1978).

4. Introduced in 1970 by Itamar Even-Zohar.

5. Venuti, Lawrence (1995) *The Translator's Invisibility*. London and New York: Routledge.

6. The first two Harry Potter books were published in Slovenian in two years: *Harry Potter and the Sorcerer's Stone* (1997) in 1999, *Harry Potter and the Chamber of Secrets* (1998) in 2000. The following novels were in the Slovenian market in a year or even less: *Prisoner of Azkaban* (1999) in 2000; *Harry Potter and the Goblet of Fire* (2000) in 2001; *Harry Potter and the Order of the Phoenix* (2003) in 2003; *Harry Potter and the Half-Blood Prince* (July 2005) in 2006. The final novel, *Harry Potter and the Deathly Hallows* (July 2007), was published as soon as February 2008.

7. Children's literature traditionally targets an audience ranging from infancy to adulthood, despite the even more pronounced distinction between teenage or young adult fiction and children's literature addressing younger readers. Whatever the division, this literature addresses the period of life when development and growth take place at all levels of personality. Its complexity involves steady changes, including the change of interests which is inevitably reflected also in the search for appropriate reading matter. Authors are constantly challenged to meet the demands of such a variety of prospective book readers.

8. Ariès triggered the discussion of childhood as a sociological category, while Postman claimed that the disappearance of childhood is connected with the advent of audio-visual media (particularly TV) which have blurred the difference between the world of adults and children which, according to his speculation, had been established by the book.

9. As translation methods or strategies deal with meaning, semiotic terms appear most appropriate in such a context.

10. Desmet claims that a text can survive in translation even 'through the intertextual and intervisual references, which are sometimes unknown in the target culture' (Desmet, 2001).

11. In the present context, the term *book* is used to indicate any form of printed publication targeting a child reader.

12. This is only one of the existing paradigms which illustrate the difference in the 'importance' of languages/literatures/cultures globally.

13. According to the theory of languages of José Lambert, 1991, 'In Quest of Literary World Maps' in Harald Kittel, and Frank P Armin (eds), *Interculturality and the Historical Study of Literary Translations*, Berlin: Erich Schmidt, (133 –144), languages and cultures are divided into central (used by important numbers of speakers) and peripheral ones. The term 'non-central' is used in this context to refer both to peripheral and semi-central systems.

14. According to the concept of literary polysystems, each literary polysystem includes all texts – in original and in translation – which enter a certain literary corpus. A literary text thus becomes a part of the broader social and cultural context. All texts enter into dynamic relationships and thus have an impact on the whole system (as commented in various contributions in *Critical Readings in Translation Studies* (Baker, ed.), e.g. in Maria Tymoczko (2010), 'Ideology and the Position of the Translator: In What Sense is a Translator "In Between"?').

15. Functional translatology seems to be important for this context since it analyses how translations are constructed and how they operate as target texts.

16. See: Kocijančič Pokorn, *Post-socialist Translation Practices: Ideological Struggle in Children's Literature* (2012). Translation library, vol. 103, Amsterdam, Philadelphia: J. Benjamins; Mazi-Leskovar, 'Bridging the Gap between Cultures: Slovenian Translations of American Children's Literature' in Pat Pinsent (ed.), *No Child is an Island* (2006); Peter Sis, 'My Life with Censorship' in *Bookbird 3*, 2009.

17. The year Slovenia gained its independence and ceased to be 'a socialist republic of Yugoslavia'.

18. Sis was the 2012 Hans Christian Andersen laureate.

19. Venuti, 'Translation as cultural politics', p.73 in M. Baker (ed.), *Critical Readings in Translation Studies* (2010).

20. See Darja Mazi-Leskovar 'Domestication and Foreignization in Translating American Prose for Slovenian Children' in *Meta, Translation for Children, Traduction pour les enfants*. (2003). Montreal: Les Presses de L'Université de Montréal.

21. See Perry Nodelman and Mavis Reimer (2003), *The Pleasures of Children's Literature*, 'Childhood Reading and Censorship' (101–107) and Harriet Selverstone, 'Censorship: Issues and Solutions, in Zena Sutherland (1997), *Children and Books* (599–602).
22. *Prigode Toma Sawyerja* (the literary translation of the original title) (1979).
23. Even though the principal age groups reading children's literature are children and teenagers, in the framework of the canon, adaptations may target either pre-school children or school-children.
24. In Lawrence Venuti, *The Translation Studies Reader* (2000).
25. O'Sullivan, *Comparative Children's Literature* (2005: 4).
26. The main opposition being between the perception of a child as the essential part of the personality which will always remain there, perhaps as a 'hidden child', and the view of a child as a 'little adult' only waiting to develop those features that are appropriate for adults.
27. Thus the mutual impact between national identity and children's literature.
28. The title of Anne Pellowski's seminal work.
29. Translation: Encyclopedia of children's literature.
30. According to Oittinen, translations of children's literature have a high status in Finnish children's literature (*Translating for Children*, 2000: xiii). Ghesquière similarly claims in her article 'Why Does Children's Literature Need Translations?' that the Dutch and Flemish literature research 'confirms the crucial role played by translations' (Ghesquière, 2006: 20).
31. The title of a book by Ann Lawson Lucas published in 2003.
32. *The Arabian Nights*, the fairytales of Charles Perrault, the brothers Grimm and Hans Andersen, as well as of Carlo Collodi's *Pinocchio*, Johanna Spyri's *Heidi* and Astrid Lindgren's *Pippi Longstocking*.
33. See 'Why Does Children's Literature Need Translations?' by Rita Ghesquière.
34. See Oittinen, *Translating for Children*.
35. Both articles published in Mona Baker (ed.) *Critical Readings in Translation Studies* (2010).
36. Including Danish, Swedish, Italian, Spanish, Polish and Czech (Heilbron in (ed) Baker 2010: 310).
37. The literature encountered first by Darja Mazi-Leskovar, whose mother tongue is Slovenian.
38. Most Slovenian territory was then a part of the Austrian Empire.
39. More about the first translations is to be found in 'Bridging the Gap between Cultures: Slovenian Translations of American Children's Literature', in *No Child Is an Island: The Case for Children's Literature in Translation*.
40. Olga Grahor was the first recognised Slovenian woman translator from the English language.
41. Adapted by Grahor.
42. He translated from a French version of a German-Latin collection which in turn was compiled from a variety of sources, creating a long 'translation trail' from the Greek original (Lathey 2010: 34).
43. In addition to the detailed account given by Lathey (2010), David Blamires discusses the reception of the Grimms' *Tales* in Lathey (ed.) (2006: 163–74).
44. The application of the term 'invisible' to translators was highlighted in Lawrence Venuti. *The Translator's Invisibility: A History of Translation*, London and New York: Routledge (1995).
45. It is also reproduced in Lathey (ed.) (2006: 190–207).
46. Another article which looks at the translation of one of the Harry Potter books into Spanish, together with works by Richard Adams and Roald Dahl, is Belen Gonzalez Cascallana's 'Crossing Over: The Reception of "Kiddult" Fiction in Spain' in Pinsent (ed.) (2004: 165–77).
47. Elena Xeni, 'The Problems of Translating Humour: A Case Study of Adrian Mole' (pp. 62–73); Darja Mazi-Leskovar, 'Bridging the gap between cultures: Slovenian translations of American children's literature' (pp.155–69); and Margharita Ippolito, 'Translation of culture-specific items in children's literature: the case of Beatrix Potter', (pp.107–18), all in Pinsent (ed.) (2006).

48. See also Andrea McKenzie's discussion of book covers in B. Lefebvre (ed.) (2013).
49. See http://www.ncrcl.ac.uk/epbc/EN/index.asp, accessed 7th June 2014.
50. See http://www.bookchilde.org, accessed 7th June 2014.

10   RECOGNISING THE CULTURALLY INVISIBLE

1. In Rudd (ed.), 2010.
2. Graham Huggan, *Australian Literature: Postcolonialism, Racism, Transnationalism*, Oxford: University Press (2007: 40).
3. See Pinsent (1997: 6–9) for a summary of some of these guidelines.
4. See below for discussion of Ashcroft et al., *The Empire Writes Back* (1989).
5. Peter Barry traces the ancestry of post-colonialism to Franz Fanon's *The Wretched of the Earth* (1961) which voices 'cultural resistance' to France's African empire (1995: 192).
6. Another important theorist who discusses colonial and post-colonial English writing, again that with an adult audience, is Homi Bhabha (1984; 1990).
7. In a chapter whose title, 'Children from Families of Overseas Origin', reflects the period when it was written.
8. Leeson's book is [accurately] described on the book jacket as 'comprehensive and polemical'.
9. Collected in *Art, Narrative and Childhood* (2003) Styles and Bearne (eds). It is worth note that here and elsewhere, Bradford uses the sometimes disputed term, 'Aboriginal' rather than the blander 'indigenous Australian'. Although the latter has sometimes been seen as more 'politically correct', some of those once designated as 'Aboriginal' have regarded it as too broad.
10. In a collection published in 1896, see Bradford in Styles and Bearne (eds) (2003: 66).
11. Information about this almost forgotten text can be found in the proceedings of the Irish Society for Study of Children's Literature (ISSCL) in a synopsis of a conference paper given in 2005 by Ciara Ni Bhroin, 'Division and Union in Maria Edgeworth's *Orlandino*', www.isscl.com/content/uploads/2005/isscl-conference.doc (accessed 26th July 2015).
12. Criticism of *Gulliver's Travels* abounds and is too extensive to be cited here; a useful collection of critical material is to be found in Claude Rawson(ed.), *The Essential Writings of Jonathan Swift* (New York: Norton, 2009) which also includes Swift's *A Modest Proposal* (1729), a strongly worded satire related to the situation of the Irish peasantry, but in no way intended for young readers.
13. The canon of English literature would be immeasurably poorer without the works of Oliver Goldsmith, R.B. Sheridan, W.B. Yeats, Oscar Wilde, J.M. Synge and George Bernard Shaw, to name only a few of those who in the light of subsequent events could be said to have dual national identities.
14. Disability in this book is, however, made interesting in the attractive but ambiguous character of one-legged Long John Silver.
15. In the context of 'silenced' groups, it is of interest that the contributors to Aveling's volume, and several other writers noted here, have acquired their knowledge about disability from personal experience, as indeed is the case of the authors of many of the children's books on the topic.
16. Her article is due to appear in a future issue of *Children's Literature in Education*. It can also be accessed at http://link.springer.com/article/10.1007/s10583-015-9264-0.
17. See Pinsent (2001) for a brief consideration of this aspect.

11   THE LIMITS OF CHILDHOOD: YOUNG ADULT AND CROSSOVER FICTION

1. G. Stanley Hall (1905) *Adolescence: Its Psychology and Its Relations to Anthropology, Sociology, Sex Crime, Religion and Education*. 2 vols.
2. See, for instance, Geraldine de Luca (1978: 89), Rebecca Lukens and Ruth Cline (1995: 171), and Maria Nikolajeva (1996: 66).

3. Raychel Haugrud Reiff (2008) *J.D. Salinger: The Catcher in the Rye and Other Works*, Tarrytown: NY: Marshal Cavendish Corporation, p.80.
4. Cormier admitted that Salinger's novel had 'a definite influence on me'; quoted in Jennifer Keeley (2001: 28) *Understanding I Am the Cheese*, San Diego, CA: Lucent.
5. See especially Robert Le Blanc's *Postmodernist Elements in the Work of Robert Cormier*, Saarsbrucken: VDM Verlag (2009).
6. See Foucault's *History of Sexuality* (1978/1990: 36–49); *Discipline and Punish* (1979: 195–22). A highly accessible account of Foucault's work is the book by Sara Mills in the Routledge Critical Thinkers series (2004).
7. See Chapter Eight for a discussion of queer theory.
8. For instance, the term used to refer to this phenomenon in Norwegian is *allalderslitteratur*, which translates as 'literature for all ages' (Beckett 1999: xiv).
9. Different critics delimit young adulthood in different ways. For instance, Trites (2000) regards YA readers as between eleven and fifteen. Stephens (1999: 183; 184), on the other hand, distinguishes between preteen readers, who are between eleven and fourteen, and adolescent readers who are over fourteen. It is rare for any rationale to be provided for these somewhat arbitrary age boundaries.
10. See, for instance, Haddon, cited in D. Welch (2003) 'The curiously irresistible literary debut of Mark Haddon'. URL: www.powells.com/authors/haddon.html.
11. Julia Kristeva, in an essay titled 'Approaching Abjection', defines the 'abject' as that which 'disturbs identity, system, order' (2004: 232). Adolescence, by virtue of the fact that it is a liminal stage between childhood and adulthood, is a period marked by abjection.

12 OTHER AREAS OF CHILDREN'S LITERATURE CRITICISM

1. In Mallan and Bradford (eds) (2011).
2. This corresponds with the argument put forward concerning translation and adaptation by Darja Mazi-Leskovar in Chapter Nine.
3. Similar issues to those raised by Burn in this article also relate to the adaptation for other media of such authors as J.R.R. Tolkien (*The Lord of the Rings* and *The Hobbit*), Philip Pullman (*His Dark Materials*), and Michael Morpurgo (*War Horse* etc.).
4. In Collins and Ridgman (eds) (2006: 227–50).
5. Although Gupta's study was published before the completion of either the Harry Potter saga itself or the adaptation of the novels for the screen, his observations are very apposite to the whole series.
6. In Briggs et al. (eds) (2008: 301–15).
7. See Chapter Four for an account of Zipes's views in relation to fairytale.
8. See chapters by Anthea Bell and Fiona Collins respectively in Collins and Ridgman (eds) (2006).
9. In Collins and Ridgman (eds) (2006: 185–206).
10. Like the subsequent National Theatre adaptation of Michael Morpurgo's *War Horse*, this was notable for its use of puppets, another well-established performance medium.
11. 'The Disappearing Childhood of Children's Literature Studies' (2013: 156).
12. See for instance, Sally Maynard et al., *Young People's Reading in 2005: The Second Study of Young People's Reading Habits*, London: Roehampton University (2007: 62).
13. Occasional articles appear, such as a very short section on autobiography, largely focusing on diaries, in a chapter by Evelyn Arizpe, Morag Styles and Abigail Rokison, entitled 'Sidelines: Some neglected dimensions of children's literature and its scholarship', in *The Routledge Companion to Children's Literature* Rudd (ed.) (2010: 126–7).
14. A reference to Comenius's classic text of 1657.
15. Subtitled *Capturing the Past*, Collins and Graham (eds).
16. In Mallan and Bradford (eds) (2011: 147–167).

17. *Radical Change: Books for Youth in a Digital Age*, New York: H. Wilson (1999).
18. See 'The Varieties of British Protestant Children's Fiction, Severe Moralising versus Flights of Fancy' in De Maeyer et al. (eds) (2005: 125–144) for an account of this literature.
19. See Chapter Five for a discussion of the religious (or anti-religious) aspects of the fantasy of Tolkien, Lewis and Pullman. Additionally, as Hunt (2005: 302) indicates, there is a 'sustained and persuasive attack 'on Lewis's version of Christianity in Goldthwaite (1996: 220–244).
20. He cites David Jasper (*The Study of Literature and Religion*, 1989/1992) and Graham Ward (*Theology and Contemporary Critical Theory*, 1996/2000). Since both of these are contributors to another volume, *English Literature, Theology and the Curriculum* (ed. Liam Gearon, 1999), it is probable that Gupta would have similar difficulties in relation to the material in this more pedagogically oriented text.
21. 'The Loss of the Father and the Loss of God in English-Language Children's Literature (1800–2000)' (2005: 295–303).
22. See for instance the Palgrave 'New Casebook' series volumes on Pullman (ed. Butler, 2014), Cormier (ed. Gavin, 2012), together with (ed.) Stuart Lee's *Companion* to Tolkien Studies.
23. For instance, a children's book about the Holocaust which has both been popular with readers and led to a well-attended film, and at the same time attracted much unfavourable comment, is John Boyne's *The Boy in the Striped Pyjamas* (2006). For a discussion of the complexity of Boyne's standpoint, see Kirsten Bartels, 'Protecting and Educating: Three kinds of censorship in John Boyne's *The Boy in the Striped Pyjamas*', in *The Journal of Children's Literature Studies*, 6(1), March 2009, pp.98–120.
24. http://www.theje.com/comment-and-debate/comment/111621/the-uk-needs-truly-authentic-children's-book-now, accessed November 2014.
25. An interesting fantasy parallel to this situation can be found in David McKee's *Tusk Tusk* (1978) in which warring groups of white and black elephants give rise ultimately to grey descendants, but even in this uniformly coloured society there are tensions between those with different shaped ears. Despite what might appear at first to be a capitulation to the ideology that everyone ought to be the same, McKee's epigraph 'Vive la différence' indicates his belief in the welcoming of difference, as is also borne out by his later book, *Elmer The Patchwork Elephant* (1990).
26. The full text of this can be found at http://www.rukhsanakhan.com/articles/Freedom%208soeech.pdf(accessed 9th December 2014); a shorter version, 'It's how you say it', was published in *The Horn Book Magazine*, Sept/Oct 2009.
27. Source as for note 26, page 14 of online version of her presentation.
28. *Topographies of the Sacred: The Poetics of Place in European Romanticism*, 2004.

Bibliography

Abate, Michelle and Kidd, Kenneth (2011) *Over the Rainbow: Queer Children's and Young Adult Literature*, Ann Arbor: University of Michigan Press.

Abate, Michelle Ann and Weldy, Lance (eds) (2012) *C.S. Lewis: The Chronicles of Narnia* ('New Casebooks' series), Basingstoke: Palgrave Macmillan.

Allan, Cherie (2012) *Playing with Picturebooks: Postmodernism and the Postmodernesque*, Basingstoke: Palgrave Macmillan.

Andrews, Richard (1991) *The Problem with Poetry*, Milton Keynes: Open University Press.

Applebee, Arthur N. (1978) *The Child's Concept of Story*, London and Chicago: University of Chicago Press.

Appleyard, J.A. (1990) *Becoming a Reader: The Experience of Fiction from Childhood to Adulthood*, Cambridge: Cambridge University Press.

Ariès, Philippe (1962) *Centuries of Childhood*, New York: Vintage.

Arizpe, Evelyn and Styles, Morag (2003) *Children Reading Pictures: Interpreting Visual Texts*, London: Routledge Falmer.

Arizpe, Evelyn and Morag Styles with Abigail Rokison (2010) 'Sidelines: Some Neglected Dimensions of Children's Literature and its Scholarship' in David Rudd (ed.), *The Routledge Companion to Children's Literature*, London: Routledge, pp.125–138.

Ashcroft, Bill, Griffiths, Gareth and Tiffin, Helen (2002; first published 1989) *The Empire Writes Back: Theory and Practice in Post-Colonial Literatures*, London and New York: Routledge.

Auchmuty, Rosemary (1992) *A World of Girls: the Appeal of the Girls' School Story*, London: Women's Press.

Auerbach, Nina (1986; first published 1978) *Communities of Women: An Idea in Fiction*, Cambridge, MA: Harvard University Press.

Aveling, Helen (2009) *Unseen Childhoods: Disabled Characters in 20th-Century Books for Girls*, London: Bettany Press.

Baker, Mona (2010) 'Reframing Conflict in Translation' in Mona Baker (ed.), *Critical Readings in Translation Studies*, London, New York: Routledge, 113–29.

Barker, Martin (1989) *Comics: Ideology, Power and the Critics*, Manchester: Manchester University Press.

Barry, Peter (1995) *Beginning Theory: An Introduction to Literary and Cultural Theory*, Manchester and New York: Manchester University Press.

Bassnett, Susan (1993) *Comparative Literature: A Critical Introduction*, Oxford: Blackwell.

Beckett, Sandra (ed.) (1999) *Transcending Boundaries: Writing for a Dual Audience of Children and Adults*. New York: Garland.

Beckman, Wendy H. (2008) *Robert Cormier: Banned, Challenged and Censored*. NJ: Enslow Publishers Inc..

Bettelheim, Bruno (1976) *The Uses of Enchantment: The Meaning and Importance of Fairy Tales*, London: Thames and Hudson.

Bhabha, Homi K. (1984) 'Of mimicry and men: the ambivalence of colonial discourse' in Philip Rice and Patricia Waugh (eds), *Modern Literary Theory: A Reader*, (1989: 1992), London: Edward Arnold.

Bhabha, Homi K. (1990) *Nation and Narration*, New York: Routledge.

Blount, Margaret (1974) *Animal Land: The Creatures of Children's Fiction*, London: Hutchinson.

Bolton, Gavin N. and Heathcote, Dorothy (1995) *Drama for Learning: Dorothy Heathcote's Mantle of the Expert Approach to Education*, Portsmouth, NH: Heinemann.

Booth, David (2011) 'Censorship' in Philip Nell and Lissa Paul (eds), *Keywords for Children's Literature*, New York and London: New York University Press, pp.26–30.

Boston, Lucy (1973) *Memory in a House*, London: Bodley Head.

Bradford, Clare (2003) 'Aboriginal Visual Narratives for Children: A Politics of Place' in Morag Styles and Eve Bearne (eds), *Art, Narrative and Childhood*, Stoke-on-Trent: Trentham Books, pp.65–77.

Bradford, Clare (2007) *Unsettling Narratives: Postcolonial Readings of Children's Literature*, Waterloo, ON: Wilfred Laurier University Press.

Bradford, Clare (2010) 'Race, Ethnicity and Colonialism' in David Rudd (ed.) (2010). pp. 39–50.

Brennan, Geraldine (2001) 'The Game called Death' in Kimberley Reynolds et al. (eds), *Frightening Fiction*, London and New York: Continuum, pp.92–117.

Briggs, Julia, Butts, Dennis and Grenby, M.O. (eds) (2008) *Popular Children's Literature in Britain*, Aldershot: Ashgate.

Bristow, Joseph (ed.) (1991) *Empire Boys: Adventures in a Man's World*, HarperCollins: London.

Brownjohn, Sandy (1980) *Does it Have to Rhyme?*, London: Hodder and Stoughton.

Bullock, Alan et al. (1975) *A Language for Life*, London: HMSO.

Butler, Charles (2006) *Four British Fantasists: Place and Culture in the Children's Fantasies of Penelope Lively, Alan Garner, Dianna Wynne Jones and Susan Cooper*, Maryland, Toronto and Oxford: The Scarecrow Press, 2006.

Butler, Catherine and Hallsdorf, Tommy (2014) *Philip Pullman's His Dark Materials*, ('New Casebooks' series), Basingstoke: Palgrave Macmillan.

Butler, Catherine and Reynolds, Kimberley (eds) (2014) *Modern Children's Literature: An Introduction* (2nd edn), London: Palgrave Macmillan.

Butler, Judith (1990) *Gender Trouble*. London: Routledge.

Butts, Dennis and Hunt, Peter (2013) *How Did Long John Silver Lose his Leg? And Twenty-Six Other Mysteries of Children's Literature*, Cambridge: Lutterworth, 2013.

Cadogan, Mary and Craig, Patricia (1976) *You're a Brick, Angela! The Girls' Story 1879–1975*, London: Gollancz.

Carpenter, Humphrey (1985) *Secret Gardens: A Study of the Golden Age of Children's Literature*, London: Allen and Unwin.

Carrington, Bridget I. and Harding, Jennifer J. (2012) *It Doesn't Have to Rhyme*, Lichfield: Pied Piper Publishing.

Chambers, Aidan (1985) *Booktalk: Occasional Writing on Literature and Children*, London: Bodley Head.

Cherland, Meredith Rogers (1994) *Private Practices: Girls Reading Fiction and Constructing Identity*, London: Taylor and Francis.

Children's Literature Research Centre (1996) *Young People's Reading at the End of the Century*, London: Roehampton Institute.

Clark, Nicholas (2011) 'Alan Garner's "vehicle of vision": poetic, artistic and musical sources of inspiration for Elidor', *Journal of Children's Literature Studies*, issue 8:2, July 2011, pp.60–80.

Cleary, Joe (2002) *Literature, Partition and the Nation State*, Cambridge: Cambridge University Press.

Coats, Karen (2010) 'Fantasy' in David Rudd (ed.), *The Routledge Companion to Children's Literature*, Abingdon: Routledge, pp.75–86.

Coghlan, Valerie and O'Sullivan, Keith (eds) (2011) *Irish Children's Literature and Culture: New Perspectives on Contemporary Writing*, New York and London: Routledge.

Collins, Fiona M. & Ridgman, Jeremy (eds.) (2004) *Turning the Page: Children's Literature in Performance and the Media*, Oxford: Peter Lang.

Cosslett, Tess (2006) *Talking Animals in British Fiction, 1786 – 1914*, Aldershot: Ashgate.

Cotton, Penni (2000) *Picture Books sans Frontières*, Stoke-on-Trent: Trentham Books.

Cotton, Penni (2004) 'Adult Challenges from the European Picture Book' in (ed.) Pinsent, Pat (2004) *Books and Boundaries: Writers and their Audiences*, pp.53–67, Lichfield: Pied Piper Publishing.

Cotton, Penni (2008) 'Visualising Europe through Picture Books: Where Are We Now?' in (eds) Jennifer Harding and Pat Pinsent, *What Do You See?: International Perspectives on Children's Book Illustration*, Newcastle upon Tyne: Cambridge Scholars Publishing.

Coveney, Peter (revised edn 1967) *The Image of Childhood*, Harmondsworth: Penguin.

Darton, J. Harvey (1st edn 1932; 2nd edn, revised by Kathleen Lines 1958; 3rd edn, revised by Brian Alderson, 1982) *Children's Books in England: Five Centuries of Social Life*, Cambridge: Cambridge University Press.

Davis, David (ed.) (2005) *Edward Bond and the Dramatic Child: Edward Bond's Plays for Young People*, Stoke on Trent: Trentham Books.

De Maeyer, Jan; Ewers, Hans-Heino; Ghesquèire, Rita; Manson, Michel; Pinsent, Pat; and Quaghebeur, Patricia (eds) (2005) *Religion, Children's Literature and Modernity in Western Europe 1750–2000*, Leuven: Leuven University Press.

Deszcz-Tryhubczak, Justyna and Oziewicz, Marek (eds) (2006) *Towards or Back to Human Values? Spiritual and Moral Dimensions of Contemporary Fantasy*, Newcastle: Cambridge Scholars Press.

Di Giovanni, E., Elefante, C. and Pederzoli, R. (2010) (eds) *Writing and Translation for Children: Voices, Images and Texts*, Bern: Peter Lang.

Dixon, Bob (1978a) *Catching them Young I: Sex, Race and Class in Children's Fiction*, London: Pluto.

Dixon, Bob (1978b) *Catching them Young II: Political Ideas in Children's Fiction*, London: Pluto.

Dixon, Bob (1982) *Now Read On: Recommended Fiction for Young People*, London: Pluto.

Doonan, Jane (1993) *Looking at Pictures in Picture Books*, Stroud: Thimble Press.

Dudek, Debra in Philip Nel and Lissa Paul (eds) (2011) *Keywords for Children's Literature*, New York and London: New York University Press, pp.155–60.

Egoff, Sheila, G.T. Stubbs and L.F. Ashley (eds), *Only Connect: Readings on Children's Literature* (1980; 1st edn 1969), Toronto and New York: Oxford University Press.

Eisner, Will (1978) *A Contract with God: A Graphic Novel*, Princeton: Kitchen Sink Press.

Evans, Janet (1998) (ed.) *What's in the Picture: Responding to Illustrations in Picture Books*, London: Paul Chapman Publishing.

Evans, Janet (2009) (ed.) *Talking Beyond the Page: Reading and Responding to Picture Books*. London: Routledge.

Eyre, Frank (2nd edn 1971) *British Children's Books in the Twentieth Century*, London: Longman.

Falconer, Rachel (2008; first published 2009) *The Crossover Novel: Contemporary Children's Literature and its Adult Readership*, New York: Routledge.

Fish, Stanley (1980) *Is There a Text in This Class? The Authority of Interpretive Communities*, London and Cambridge, MA: Harvard University Press.

Fisher, Margery (1986) *The Bright Face of Danger*, London: Hodder and Stoughton.

Flanagan, Victoria (2011, first published 2008) *Into the Closet: Cross-Dressing and the Gendered Body in Children's Literature and Film*, New York: Routledge.

Flanagan, Victoria (2010) 'Gender Studies' in David Rudd (ed.), *The Routledge Companion to Children's Literature*, London: Routledge.

Foucault, Michel (1978/1990) *The History of Sexuality: The Care of the Self, volume 3*, Harmondsworth: Penguin.

Foucault, Michel (1979) *Discipline and Punish: The Birth of the Prison*, Harmondsworth: Penguin.

Fox, Geoff, Hammond, Graham, Jones, Terry, Smith, Frederic, Sterck, Kenneth (1976) *Writers, Critics, and Children*, London: Heinemann.

Freeman, Rosemary (1970) *English Emblem Books*, London: Chatto and Windus.

Fremantle, Susan (1993) 'The Power of the Picture Book' in Pat Pinsent (ed.), *The Power of the Page*, London: David Fulton, pp.6–14.

Garner, Alan (1997) *The Voice that Thunders*, London: The Harvill Press.

Gavin, Adrienne E. (2012) *Robert Cormier*. Basingstoke: Palgrave Macmillan, New Casebook series.

Gibson, Mel (2003) '"What became of Bunty?" The Emergence, Evolution and Disappearance of the Girls' Comic in Post-War Britain' in Styles, Morag and Bearne, Eve (eds), *Art, Narrative and Childhood*, Stoke-on-Trent: Trentham Books, pp.87–100.

Gibson, Mel (2010) 'Picturebooks, Comics and Graphic Novels' in David Rudd (ed.), *The Routledge Companion to Children's Literature*, London: Routledge, pp.100–111.

Godek, Sarah (2005) 'Fantasy – Postwar, Postmodern, Postcolonial: Houses in Postwar Fantasy' in Kimberley Reynolds (ed.), *Modern Children's Literature: An Introduction* (pp. 89–107).

Goldthwaite, John (1996) *The Natural History of Make-Believe*, Oxford: Oxford University Press.

Gooderham, David (1995) 'Children's Fantasy Literature: Towards an Anatomy', *Children's Literature in Education* 23(6), pp.171–83.

Graham, Judith (1990) *Pictures on the Page*, Sheffield: National Association for the Teaching of English.

Graham, Judith (2005) 'Reading Contemporary Picturebooks' in Kimberley Reynolds (ed.), *Modern Children's Literature: An Introduction*, Basingstoke: Palgrave Macmillan, pp.209–26.

Gray, William (2009) *Fantasy, Myth and the Measure of Truth: Tales of Pullman, Lewis, Tolkien, MacDonald and Hoffman*, Basingstoke: Palgrave Macmillan.

Grenby, Matthew O. (2008) *Children's Literature*, Edinburgh: Edinburgh University Press.

Grenby, Matthew O. and Immel, Andrea (eds) (2009) *The Cambridge Companion to Children's Literature*, Cambridge: Cambridge University Press.

Grenby, Matthew O. and Reynolds, Kimberley (2011) *Children's Literature Studies: A Research Handbook*, Basingstoke: Palgrave Macmillan.

Gupta, Suman (2003) *Re-Reading Harry Potter*, Basingstoke: Palgrave Macmillan.

Green, Roger Lancelyn, (1946) *Tellers of Tales*, Leicester: Edmund Ward.

Hallett, Cynthia and Huey, Peggy (2012) *J.K. Rowling: Harry Potter*, 'New Casebook' series, Basingstoke: Palgrave Macmillan.

Hancock, Susan (2005) 'Fantasy, Psychology and Feminism: Jungian Readings of Classic British Fantasy Fiction' in Kimberley Reynolds (ed.), pp.42–57.

Hancock, Susan (2009) *The Child that Haunts Us: Symbols and Images in Fairytale and Miniature Literature*, London: Routledge.

Haviland, Virginia (1973) *Children and Literature*, New York: Scott Foresman.

Heaney, S. (2005) 'Hinton, S.E. (Susan Eloise)' in Bernice E Cullinan, Bonnie L Kunzel, Deborah A Wooten (eds), *The Continuum Encyclopedia of Young Adult Literature*, New York and London: Continuum International Publishing Group Inc., pp.338–40.

Heeks, Peggy (1981) *Choosing and Using Books in the First School*, London: Macmillan Education.

Heer, Jeet and Worcester, Kent (eds) (2009) *A Comic Studies Reader*, Oxford, MS: University of Mississippi Press.

Heilman, Elizabeth (ed.) (2003, 2009) *Critical Perspectives on Harry Potter*, Abingdon: Taylor and Francis.

Hilton, Mary, Styles, Morag, Watson, Victor (1997) *Opening the Nursery Door: Reading, Writing and Childhood 1600–1900*.

Holland, Norman (1968) *The Dynamics of Literary Response*, New York: Oxford University Press.

Hollindale, Peter (1988) *Ideology and the Children's Book*, Stroud: Thimble Press.

Hollindale, Peter (1996) 'Drama' in Peter Hunt (ed.) *International Companion Encyclopedia of Children's Literature*, London: Routledge, pp.206–19.

Hollindale, Peter (1997) *Signs of Childness in Children's Books*, Stroud: Thimble Press.

Hollindale, Peter (2011) *The Hidden Teacher: Ideology and Children's Reading*, Stroud: Thimble Press.

Hornbrook, D. (1998, 2nd edn.) *Education and Dramatic Art*, London: Routledge.

Hourihan, Margery (1997) *Deconstructing the Hero: Literary Theory and Children's Literature*, London: Routledge.

Humm, Maggie (1994) *A Reader's Guide to Contemporary Feminist Literary Criticism*, Hemel Hempstead: Harvester Wheatsheaf.

Hughes, Ted (1967) *Poetry in the Making*, London: Faber.

Hughes, Ted (1976) 'Myth and Education' in G. Fox et al.(eds), *Writers, Critics and Children*, London: Heinemann.

Hume, Kathryn (1984) *Fantasy and Mimesis*, London: Methuen.

Hunt, Peter (ed.) (1990) *Children's Literature: The Development of Criticism*, London: Routledge.

Hunt, Peter (1991) *Criticism, Theory and Children's Literature*, Oxford: Blackwell.

Hunt, Peter (ed.) (1992) *Literature for Children: Contemporary Criticism*, London: Routledge.

Hunt, Peter (1995) *Children's Literature: An Illustrated History*. Oxford, New York: Oxford University Press.

Hunt, Peter (2001a) *Children's Literature*, Oxford: Blackwell.

Hunt, Peter (ed.) (2004) *International Companion Encyclopedia of Children's Literature* London, New York: Routledge.

Hürlimann, B. (1967) *Three Centuries of Children's Books in Europe*, (trans. and ed.) Brian W. Alderson, Oxford: Oxford University Press.

Inglis, Fred (1981) *The Promise of Happiness: Value and Meaning in Children's Literature*, Cambridge: Cambridge University Press.

Isaacs, Neil and Zimbardo, Rose (eds) (1968) *Tolkien and the Critics: Essays on J.R.R. Tolkien's The Lord of the Rings*, IN: Notre Dame University Press.

Isaacs, Neil and Zimbardo, Rose (eds) (1981) *Tolkien: New Critical Perspectives*, Lexington: Kentucky University Press.

Iser, Wolfgang (1974) *The Implied Reader: Patterns of Communication in Prose Fiction from Bunyan to Beckett*, Baltimore: Johns Hopkins University Press.

Jackson, Mary (1989) *Engines of Instruction, Mischief, and Magic: Children's Literature in England from its Beginnings to 1839*, Lincoln, NE: University of Nebraska Press.

Jackson, Rosemary (1981) *Fantasy: the Literature of Subversion*. London: Methuen.

Jentsch, Nancy (2002) 'Harry Potter and the Tower of Babel: Translating the Magic' in Lana A Whited (ed.), *The Ivory Tower and Harry Potter*, Columbia and London: University of Missouri Press, pp.285–301.

Jobe, Ronald (2004) 'Translating for Children: Practice' in Peter Hunt (ed.), *International Companion Encyclopedia of Children's Literature*, London, New York: Routledge. pp.912–26.

The Journal of Children's Literature Studies (vol. 7, issue 1, March 2010) on Pullman.

Keith, Lois (2001) *Take Up Thy Bed and Walk: Death, Disability and Cure in Classic Fiction for Girls*, London: The Women's Press Ltd.

Kendall, Alex (2008) 'Playing and resisting: rethinking young people's reading cultures', *Literacy*, 42(3), November 2008, 123–30.

Kent, David (ed.) (1987) *The Achievement of Christina Rossetti*, Ithaca and London: Cornell University Press.

Klein, Gillian (1985) *Reading into Racism: Bias in Children's Literature and Learning Materials*, London: Routledge.

Klingberg, G. and Ørvig, M. (1978) *Children's Books in Translation*, Stockholm: Almqvist and Wiksell.

Klingberg, G. (1986) *Children's Fiction in the Hands of the Translators*, Lund, Sweden: CWK Gleerup.

Knoepflmacher, Ulrich C. and Myers, Mitzi (eds) (1997) 'From the Editors: "Cross-Writing" and the Reconceptualizing of Children's Literary Studies', *Children's Literature*, 25: special issue, vii–xvii.

Knowles, Murray and Malmkjaer, Kirsten (1996) *Language and Control in Children's Literature*, London and New York: Routledge.

Kocher, Paul (1973) *Master of Middle-Earth: The Achievement of J.R.R. Tolkien*, London: Thames and Hudson.

Kristeva, Julia (1997) 'Approaching Abjection' in Kelly Oliver (ed.), *The Portable Kristeva*, New York: Columbia University Press, pp.229–63.

Kutzer, Daphne (2000) *Empire's Children: Empire and Imperialism in Classic British Children's Books*, New York and London: Garland.

Kuznets, Lois (1994) *When Toys Come Alive: Narratives of Animation, Metamorphosis and Development*, New Haven and London: Yale University Press.

Landsberg, Michelle (1988) *Reading for the Love of It*. London: Simon and Schuster.

Lathey, Gillian (ed.) (2006) *The Translation of Children's Literature: A Reader*, Clevedon: Multilingual Matters.

Lathey, Gillian (2010) *The Role of Translators in Children's Literature: Invisible Storytellers*, London and New York: Routledge.

Leader, Zachary (1981) *Reading Blake's Songs*, London: Routledge.

Lee, Stuart (2014) (ed.) *A Companion to J.R.R. Tolkien*, Oxford: Wiley.

Leeson, Robert (1985) *Reading and Righting: The Past, Present and Future of Fiction for the Young*, London: Collins.

Lefevere, André (1992) *Translation/History/Culture: A Sourcebook*. London and New York: Routledge.

Lenz, Millicent with Scott, Carole (2005) *His Dark Materials Illuminated: Critical Essays on Philip Pullman's Trilogy*, Detroit: Wayne University Press.

Lepman, Jella (2nd edn 2002) *A Bridge of Children's Books*, Dublin: O'Brien Press.

Lerer, Seth (2008) *Children's Literature: A Reader's History from Aesop to Harry Potter*, Chicago and London: University of Chicago Press.

Lesnik-Oberstein, Karin (1994) *Children's Literature: Criticism and the Fictional Child*, Oxford: Clarendon Press.

Lewis, Clive Staples (1952), 'On three ways of writing for children' in Sheila Egoff, G.T. Stubbs and L.F. Ashley (eds) (1980), *Only Connect*, Toronto and New York: Oxford University Press.

Lewis, David (1992) 'What do picture book makers know about reading that we don't?: The postmodern picture book and critical literacy' in Henrietta Dombey, Muriel Robinson(eds), *Literacy for the 21st Century*, Falmer: Brighton Polytechnic, pp.79–86.

Lewis, David (2001) *Reading Contemporary Picturebooks: Picturing Text*, London: Routledge Falmer.

Lewis, David (2009) 'Postmodern Picturebooks: Play, Parody and Self-Referentiality (Review)', *Children's Literature Quarterly*, 34 (1) spring 2009, 91–3.

Lowe, Virginia (2007) *Stories, Pictures and Reality: Two Children Tell*, London: Routledge.

McCallum, Robyn (1999) *Ideologies of Identity in Adolescent Fiction: The Dialogic Construction of Subjectivity*, New York: Garland.

McCloud, Scott (1993) *Understanding Comics: the Invisible Art*, New York: HarperCollins.

McGillis, Roderick (2009) 'Humour and the body in children's literature' in M. Grenby and A. Immel (eds), *The Cambridge Companion to Children's Literature*, Cambridge: Cambridge University Press.

McGillis, Roderick (1987) 'Simple Surfaces: Christina Rossetti's work for children' in David A. Kent (ed.) *The Achievement of Christina Rossetti*, pp.208–30.

McGillis, Roderick (1996) *The Nimble Reader: Literary Theory and Children's Literature*, New York: Twayne.

McGillis, Roderick (ed.) (2000) *Voices of the Other: Children's Literature and the Postcolonial Context*, London and New York: Garland.

McGillis, Roderick (2003) (ed.) *Children's Literature and the Fin de Siècle*, Westport Connecticut: Praeger, International Research Society for Children's Literature.

Malcolm, Noel (1997) *The Origins of English Nonsense*, London: HarperCollins.

Manlove, Colin N. (1975) *Modern Fantasy: Five Studies*, Cambridge: Cambridge University Press.

Manlove, Colin N. (1987) *C.S. Lewis: His Literary Achievement*, London: Macmillan.

Marriott, Stuart (1991) *Picture Books in the Primary Classroom*, London: Paul Chapman.

Marsh, Jan (1994) *Christina Rossetti: A Literary Biography*, London: Cape.

Maynard, Sally; MacKay, Sophie; Smyth, Fiona; and Reynolds, Kimberley (2007) *Young People's Reading in 2005*, Roehampton University and Loughborough University.

Meek, Margaret, Warlow, Adrian and Barton, Griselda (1977) *The Cool Web: The Pattern of Children's Reading*, London: Bodley Head.

Meek, Margaret (1988) *How Texts Teach What Readers Learn*, Stroud: Thimble Press.

Meek, Margaret (ed.) (2000) *Children's Literature and National Identity*, Stoke on Trent: Trentham Books.

Meek, Margaret, and Watson, Victor (2003) *Coming of Age in Children's Literature: Growth and Maturity in the Work of Philippa Pearce, Cynthia Voigt and Jan Mark*, London: Continuum.

Mendlesohn, Farah (2005) *Diana Wynne Jones: Children's Literature and the Fantastic Tradition*, Abingdon: Taylor and Francis.

Mickenberg, Julia and Vallone, Lynne (eds) (2011) *The Oxford Handbook of Children's Literature*, Oxford and New York: Oxford University Press.

Mills, Sara (2004) *Michel Foucault*, London: Routledge Critical Thinkers series.

Milner, David (1983) *Children and Race: Ten Years On*, London: Ward Lock.

Moebius, William (1986) 'Introduction to Picturebook Codes' in Peter Hunt (ed.) (1990), *Children's Literature: The Development of Criticism*, London: Routledge, pp.131–47.

Musgrave, Peter W. (1985) *From Brown to Bunter: The Life and Death of the School Story*, London: Routledge and Kegan Paul.

Naidoo, Beverley (1992) *Through Whose Eyes? Exploring Racism: Reader, Text and Context*, Stoke-on-Trent: Trentham Books.

Neelands, Jonothan (2008) 'Drama: the subject that dare not speak its name', http://www.ite.org.uk/ite_reading/drama_180108.pdf (accessed 4th November 2014)

Ne, Philip and Lissa, Paul (eds) (2011) *Keywords for Children's Literature*, New York: New York University Press.

Nikolajeva, Maria (1996) *Children's Literature Comes of Age: Towards a New Aesthetic*, New York and London: Garland.

Nikolajeva, Maria (1997) *Introduction to the Theory of Children's Literature*, Taillin: Pedagogical University.

Nikolajeva, Maria and Scott, Carole (2001) *How Picturebooks Work*, New York: Garland.

Nikolajeva, Maria (2014) 'Voicing Identity: the Dilemma of Narrative Perspective in Twenty-first Century Young Adult Fiction' in Catherine Butler and Kimberley Reynolds (eds), *Modern Children's Literature: An Introduction* (2nd edn), Basingstoke: Palgrave

Nilson, Alleen Pace (1971) 'Women in Children's Literature', *College English* 32: 918–26.

Nodelman, Perry (1988) *Words About Pictures: the Narrative Art of Children's Picture Books*, Athens, GA: University of Georgia Press.

Nodelman, Perry (1992a) 'The Other: Orientalism, Colonialism and Children's Literature', *Children's Literature Association Quarterly*, 17, 29–35.

Nodelman, Perry (1992b) 'Robert Cormier's *The Chocolate War*: Paranoia and Paradox' in Dennis Butts (ed.), *Stories and Society: Children's Literature in its Social Context*. Basingstoke: Macmillan, pp.22–36.

Nodelman, Perry and Reimer, Mavis (3rd edn 2003) *The Pleasures of Children's Literature*, Boston: Allyn and Bacon.

Nodelman, Perry (2013) 'The Disappearing Childhood of Children's Literature Studies', *Jeunesse: Young People, Texts, Culture*, 5(1) pp.149–63.

Nord, Christiane (1991; 2nd edn 2005) *Text Analysis in Translation: Theory, Methodology and Didactic Application of a Model for Translation-Oriented Text Analysis*. Amsterdam-Atlanta: Rodopi.

Oittinen, Riitta (2000) *Translating for Children*, New York: Garland.

Oittinen, Riitta (2006) 'No Innocent Act: on the Ethics of Translating for Children' in *Children's Literature in Translation, Challenges and Strategies*. Manchester, UK and Kinderhook, USA: St. Jerome Publishing.

O'Sullivan, Emer (2005) *Comparative Children's Literature* (trans.) Anthea Bell, London and New York: Routledge.

Ong, Walter (1982; first published 2002) *Orality and Literacy: The Technologizing of the Word*, London: Methuen.

Opie, Iona and Peter (1951) *The Oxford Dictionary of Nursery Rhymes*, Oxford: University Press.

Opie, Iona and Peter (1959) *The Lore and Language of Schoolchildren*, London: Granada.

Opie, Iona and Peter (1973) *The Oxford Book of Children's Verse*, Oxford: Oxford University Press.

Opie, Iona (1993) *The People in the Playground*, Oxford: Oxford University Press.

Pantaleo, Sylvia (2005) '"Reading" Young Children's Visual Texts' in *Early Childhood Research and Practice (ECRP)* 7(1), pp. 1–13.

Paul, Lissa (1987) 'Enigma Variations: What Feminist Theory Knows About Children's Literature', *Signal*, 54, September 1987: 186–201, reprinted in Peter Hunt (ed.) (1990), *Children's Literature: The Development of Criticism*, London and New York: Routledge, pp.148–64.

Paul, Lissa (1998) *Reading Otherways*, Stroud: Thimble Press.

Philip, Neil (1981) *A Fine Anger: A Critical Introduction to the Work of Alan Garner*, London: Collins.

Philip, Neil (1996) 'Introduction', *The New Oxford Book of Children's Verse*, Oxford: University Press, pp.xxv–xxxvii.

Pinsent, Pat (1997) *Children's Literature and the Politics of Equality*, London: David Fulton.

Pinsent, Pat (2001), 'The Depiction of Elderly Characters in Recent Children's Fiction' in Pat Pinsent and Sue Mansfield (eds), *The Big Issues: Representations of socially marginalised groups and individuals in children's literature, past and present*, Roehampton: National Centre for Research in Children's Literature.

Pinsent, Pat (ed.) (2004) *Books and Boundaries: Writers and their Audiences*, Lichfield: Pied Piper Publishing.

Pinsent, Pat (ed.) (2006) *No Child is an Island: The Case for Children's Literature in Translation*, NCRCL Papers 12, Lichfield: Pied Piper Publishing.

Pinsent, Pat (2007) (ed.) *Time Everlasting: Representations of Past, Present and Future in Children's Literature*, Lichfield: Pied Piper Publishing.

Pokorn, Nike K. (2012). *Post-Socialist Translation Practices, Ideological Struggle in Children's Literature*, Amsterdam, Philadelphia: Benjamins.

Postman, Neil (1994, first published 1982) *The Disappearance of Childhood*, New York: Vintage Books.

Powell, Janet; Gillespie, Carol; Swearingen, Becky; and Clements, Nancy (1993) 'Gender roles in the Newbery Medal Winners', *Yearbook of the American Forum*, http://americanreadingforum.org/yearbook/yearbooks/93_yearbook/pdf/11_powell.pdf

Quicke, John (1985) *Disability in Modern Children's Fiction*, London: Croom Helm.

Pullman, Philip (1998) 'Picture Stories and Graphic Novels' in (eds) Reynolds, Kimberley and Tucker, Nicholas (1998), *Children's Book Publishing in Britain since 1945*, Aldershot: Ashgate, pp.110–32.

Pullman, Philip (2001) 'The Republic of Heaven' in *The Horn Book Magazine*, Nov/Dec 2001, pp. 655–67, available at http://archive.hbook.com/magazine/article/2001/nov01/_pullman.asp

Quigly, Isabel (1982) *The Heirs of Tom Brown*, London: Chatto and Windus.

Reynolds, Kimberley (1990) *Girls Only: Gender and Popular Children's Fiction in Britain, 1880–1910*, Hemel Hempstead: Harvester Wheatsheaf.

Reynolds, Kimberley (1994) *Children's Literature in the 1890s and the 1990s*, Plymouth: Northcote House.

Reynolds, Kimberley and Nicholas Tucker (eds) (1998) *Children's Book Publishing in Britain since 1945*, Aldershot: Scolar Press.

Reynolds, Kimberley; Brennan, Geraldine; and McCarron, Kevin (eds) (2001) *Frightening Fiction*, London and New York: Continuum.

Reynolds, Kimberley (2005) *Modern Children's Literature: An Introduction*, Basingstoke: Palgrave Macmillan.

Reynolds, Kimberley (2007) *Radical Children's Literature: Future Visions and Aesthetic Transformations in Juvenile Fiction*, Basingstoke: Palgrave Macmillan.

Richards, Jeffrey (1988) *Happiest Days*, Manchester: Manchester University Press.

Rose, Jacqueline (1984) *The Case of Peter Pan or The Impossibility of Children's Fiction*, London and Basingstoke: Macmillan.

Rosebury, Brian (1992; 2004) *Tolkien: A Cultural Phenomenon*, Basingstoke: Palgrave Macmillan.

Rosenblatt, Louise (1978) *The Reader, the Text, the Poem: The Transactional Theory of the Literary Work* Carbondale, IL: Southern Illinois University Press.

Rudd, David (2000) *Enid Blyton and the Mystery of Children's Literature*, Basingstoke; New York: Palgrave Macmillan.

Rudd, David (2003) 'Reading Contemporary Picture Books (Review) in *The Lion and the Unicorn*, 27(1), January 2003, pp.147–52.

Rudd, David (ed.) (2010) *The Routledge Companion to Children's Literature*, London and New York: Routledge.

Rustin, Margaret and Michael (1987) *Narratives of Love and Loss: Studies in Modern Children's Fiction*, London and New York: Verso.

Sabin, Roger (2001) *Comics, Comix and Graphic Novels: A History of Comic Art*, London: Phaidon Press Ltd.

Said, Edward (1978) *Orientalism*, New York: Pantheon.

Said, Edward (1993) *Culture and Imperialism*, London: Chatto and Windus.

Sainsbury, Lisa (2005) 'Chronotopes and Heritage: Time and Memory in Contemporary Children's Literature' in Kimberley Reynolds (ed.) (2005), pp.156–72.

Salstad, Louise (2003) 'Narratee and Implied Readers in the Manolito Gafotas Series: A Case of Triple Address' in *Children's Literature Association Quarterly*,28(4), pp.219–29.

Saunders, Kathy (2004) 'What Disability Studies Can Do for Children's Literature' in *Disability Studies Quarterly*, Winter 2004 24(1), www.dsq-sds.org

Schakel, P.J. (1979) *Reading with the Heart: The Way into Narnia*, Grand Rapids, Michigan: W.B. Eerdmans.

Shavit, Zohar (1981). 'Translation of Children's Literature as a Function of Its Position in the Literary Polysystem', *Poetics Today*, 2(4), 171–9.

Shavit, Zohar (1986) *Poetics of Children's Literature*, Athens, GA: University of Georgia Press.

Shippey, Thomas (1982) *The Road to Middle-Earth* London: Allen and Unwin.

Signal 100 (2003) Volume 34, January, May and September issues.

Sims, Sue and Clare, Hilary (2000) *The Encyclopedia of Girls' School Stories*, Aldershot: Ashgate.

Sipe, Laurence and Pantaleo, Sylvia (2008) *Postmodern Picturebooks: Play, Parody and Self-Referentiality*, London: Routledge.

Sis, Peter (2009) 'My Life with Censorship' (*Bookbird*, 2009, no. 3).

Slade, Peter (1954) *The Child at Play: Child Drama*, London: University of London Press.

Smith, Janet Adam (1953) Introduction to *The Faber Book of Children's Verse*, London: Faber.

Spufford, Francis (2002) *The Child that Books Built*, London: Faber.

Steiner, George (1995) *What is Comparative Literature?*, Oxford: Clarendon Press.

Stephens, John (1992) *Language and Ideology in Children's Fiction*, London: Longman.

Stephens, John (ed.) (2002) *Ways of Being Male: Representing Masculinity in Children's Literature and Film*, New York: Routledge.

Stephens, John (2010) 'Multiculturalism' in David Rudd (ed.), *The Routledge Companion to Children's Literature*, London: Routledge, pp.212–13.

Stinton, Judith (1979) (ed.) *Racism and Sexism in Children's Books*, London: Writers and Readers Publishing Cooperative.

Styles, Morag, Bearne, Eve, and Watson, Victor (1992) *After Alice: Exploring Children's Literature*, London and New York: Cassell.

Styles, Morag (1998) *From the Garden to the Street: Three Hundred Years of Poetry for Children*, London: Cassell.

Styles, Morag and Bearne, Eve (eds) (2003) *Art, Narrative and Childhood*, Stoke-on-Trent: Trentham Books.

Styles, Morag (2007) 'Pearce Everlasting: The Past, the Present and the Future in Fiction by Philippa Pearce' in (ed.) Pat Pinsent, *Time Everlasting: Representations of Past, Present and Future in Children's Literature*, Lichfield: Pied Piper Publishing.

Styles, Morag, Joy, Louise, and Whitley, David (2010) *Poetry and Childhood*, Stoke on Trent: Trentham Books.

Swinfen, Ann (1984) *In Defence of Fantasy*, London: Routledge.

Tatar, Maria (1987) *The Hard Facts of the Grimms' Fairy Tales*, Princeton: Princeton University Press.

Tatar, Maria (1993) *Off With Their Heads: Fairy Tales and the Culture of Childhood*, Princeton: Princeton University Press.

Tatar, Maria (1999) *The Classic Fairy Tales*, New York and London: Norton.

Tolkien, J.R.R (1975; first published 1964). 'On Fairy-Stories' in *Tree and Leaf*, London: Allen and Unwin.

Thomson-Wohlgemuth, Gaby (2009) *Translation under State Control: Books for Young People in the German Democratic Republic*, London and New York: Routledge.

Thwaite, Ann (1990) *A.A. Milne: The Man behind Winnie-the-Pooh*, New York: Random House.

Townsend, John Rowe (1st edn 1965; 2nd edn 1974; 25th anniversary edn 1990) *Written for Children*, London: Penguin.

Trease, Geoffrey (1st edn 1949; 2nd edn 1964) *Tales out of School*, London: Heinemann.

Trites, Roberta Seelinger (1997) *Waking Sleeping Beauty: Feminist Voices in Children's Novels*, Iowa City: University of Iowa Press.

Trites, Roberta Seelinger (2000) *Disturbing the Universe: Power and Repression in Adolescent Fiction*, Iowa City: University of Iowa Press.

Tucker, Nicholas (1982; first published 1981) *The Child and the Book: A Psychological and Literary Exploration*, Cambridge: Cambridge University Press.

Tucker, Nicholas (1994) 'My Affair with Judy' in C. Powling (ed.), *The Best of Books for Keeps*. London: Bodley Head, pp.177–81.

Tucker, Nicholas (2003) *Darkness Visible: Inside the World of Philip Pullman*, Cambridge: Wizard Books.

Van Coillie, Jan and Verschueren, Walter P. (2006, first published: 2006) *Children's Literature in Translation, Challenges and Strategies*. Manchester, UK and Kinderhook, USA: St. Jerome Publishing.

Venuti, Lawrence (1995) *The Translator's Invisibility: A History of Translation*, London and New York: Routledge.

Venuti, Lawrence (2000) *The Translation Studies Reader*, London and New York: Routledge.

Venuti, Lawrence (2010) 'Translation as Cultural Politics' in M. Baker (ed.), *Critical Readings in Translation Studies*, London and New York: Routledge. 65–79.

Von Franz, Marie-Louise (1982; first published 1970) *Interpretation of Fairy Tales*, Dallas: Spring Publications.

Wall, Barbara (1991) *The Narrator's Voice: The Dilemma of Children's Fiction*, London: Macmillan.

Waller, Alison (2009) *Constructing Adolescence in Fantastic Realism*, Oxford: Routledge.

Waller, Alison (ed.) (2013) *Melvin Burgess*, Basingstoke: Palgrave Macmillan, New Casebook series.

Walsh, Clare (2004) 'Troubling the Boundary between Fiction for Adults and Fiction for Children: A Study of Melvin Burgess' in Pat Pinsent (ed.), *Books and Boundaries: Writers and their Audiences*, Lichfield: Pied Piper Publishing, pp.142–53.

Walsh, Sharon (1993) 'The Multi-Layered Picture Book' in Pat Pinsent (ed.), *The Power of the Page*, London: David Fulton, pp.15–22.

Warner, Marina (1994) *From the Beast to the Blonde: On Fairy Tales and Their Tellers*, London: Chatto and Windus.

Watson, Victor and Styles, Morag (1996) *Talking Pictures: Pictorial Texts and Young Readers,* London: Hodder and Stoughton.

Webb, Jean (2006) 'Beyond the Knowing: The Frontier of the Real and the Imaginary in David Almond's *Skellig* and *The Fire-Eaters*' in Deszcz-Tryhubczal, Justyna and Oziewicz, Marek (eds), *Towards or Back to Human Values? Spiritual and Moral Dimensions of Contemporary Fantasy,* Newcastle: Cambridge Scholars Press, pp.242–51.

West, M. (1996) 'Censorship' in P. Hunt (ed.) *International Companion Encyclopedia of Children's Literature,* London: Routledge, pp.498–507.

Whited, Lana A, (ed.) (2002) *The Ivory Tower and Harry Potter,* Columbia: University of Missouri Press.

Whitehead, Frank, A.C. Capey and Wendy Maddren (1975) *Children's Reading Interests.* London: Evans Bros. and Methuen.

Whyte, Pádraic (2011) *Irish Childhood: Children's Fiction and Irish History,* Newcastle: Cambridge Scholars Press.

Wilkie-Stibbs, Christine (2002) *The Feminine Subject in Children's Literature,* New York: Routledge.

Wolf, Shelley, Karen Coats, Patricia Enciso and Christine A. Jenkins (eds) (2011) *Handbook of Research on Children's and Young Adult Literature,* New York: Routledge.

Zipes, Jack (1979) *Breaking the Magic Spell: Radical Theories of Folk and Fairy Tales,* London: Heinemann.

Zipes, Jack (1991; first published 1983) *Fairy Tales and the Art of Subversion: The Classical Genre for Children and the Process of Civilization,* New York: Routledge.

Zipes, Jack (ed.) (1993; first published 1983) *The Trials and Tribulations of Little Red Riding Hood,* New York and London: Routledge.

Zipes, Jack (1986) *Don't Bet on the Prince: Contemporary Feminist Fairy Tales in North America and England,* Aldershot: Gower.

Zipes, Jack (1988) *The Brothers Grimm: From Enchanted Forests to the Modern World,* New York and London: Routledge.

Zipes, Jack (1997) *Happily Ever After: Fairy Tales, Children, and the Culture Industry,* New York and London: Routledge.

Zipes, Jack (ed.) (2000) *The Oxford Companion to Fairy Tales: The Western Fairy Tale Tradition from Medieval to Modern,* Oxford: Oxford University Press.

Zipes, Jack (2009) *Relentless Progress: The Reconfiguration of Children's Literature, Fairy Tales and Storytelling,* New York and London: Routledge.

Index

CRITICAL WRITERS

TOPICS